HARD-BOILED

D1571025

HARD-BOILED

WORKING-CLASS

READERS AND

PULP MAGAZINES

Erin A. Smith

Temple University Press
PHILADELPHIA

Temple University Press, Philadelphia 19122
Copyright © 2000 by Temple University
All rights reserved
Published 2000
Printed in the United States of America

∞ The paper used in this publication meets the requirements of the American
National Standard for Information Sciences—Permanence of Paper for Printed
Library Materials, ANSI Z39.48-1984

Library of Congress Cataloging-in-Publication Data

Smith, Erin A. (Erin Ann), 1970–
    Hard-boiled: working-class readers and pulp magazines / Erin A. Smith.
        p. cm.
    Includes bibliographic references and index.
    ISBN 1-56639-768-5 (alk. paper) — ISBN 1-56639-769-3 (pbk. : alk. paper)
    1. Detective and mystery stories, American—History and criticism.
    2. American fiction—20th century—History and criticism.   3. Popular
    literature—United States—History and criticism.   4. Literature and
    society—United States—History—20th century.   5. Periodicals—
    Publishing—United States—History—20th century.   6. Working
    class—United States—Books and reading—History—20th century.
    7. Detectives in literature.   8. Crime in literature.   I. Title.

PS374.D4 S65 2000
813'.087209052—dc21   00-023424

For my mother

Contents

Acknowledgments

have incurred a great many material, intellectual, and emotional debts over the course of this project. A Mellon Fellowship in the Humanities paid for most of my graduate education and let me take a year off from teaching in order to write. The 1996–97 Simone de Beauvoir Named Instructorship in Literature from the Duke University Graduate School provided an additional semester's leave, and gave me the opportunity to teach a seminar on popular books and popular reading to ten of the brightest students a teacher could ever hope to have. George Fair, dean of the School of General Studies at the University of Texas at Dallas, provided funds for travel to archives and conferences and for the preparation of this manuscript.

A number of intellectual communities shaped this project. The Literature Program at Duke University supported the kind of interdisciplinary work I wanted to do and provided me with a great many bright colleagues with whom to do it. Jan Radway's generosity, care, and friendship made this project possible. Cathy Davidson, Tom Ferraro, Karla Holloway, and Barbara Herrnstein Smith were supportive, critical readers. Nancy Hewitt provided sources, encouragement, and a seemingly inexhaustible list of readers' names. The writing life was a good deal less lonely than it might have been because of my writing group: Jennifer Parchesky, Alden Bumstead, Lisa Radinovsky, and Lily Philips, whose careful reading, fellowship, and encouragement made the early stages of this project go more smoothly. The North Carolina chapter of Sisters in Crime taught me a great deal not only about reading as a social practice but also about writing a book and surviving a graduate education. The humor, care, and warm collegiality of Jean O'Barr and Nancy Rosebaugh at Women's Studies made my years at Duke a great deal richer than they otherwise would have been.

A 1997 American Antiquarian Society Summer Seminar in the History of the Book, led by Joan Shelley Rubin and Meredith McGill, provided a vibrant intellectual community and a wealth of generous colleagues and friends who shared their work and offered feedback on mine. The Dallas Area Social History Circle provided the intellectual life, scholarly community, and friendships that have sustained me. The Gender Studies Working Group at the School of Arts and Humanities at UT-Dallas offered an interdisciplinary setting in which to share this work. I have benefited from the thoughtful comments of audience members at meetings of the American Studies Association; the Society for the History of Authorship, Reading, and Publishing; the American Literature Association; and the Center for Working-Class Studies. Finally, my students at Duke University and the University of Texas at Dallas continually remind me of why I care so passionately about popular culture and the links between material and cultural life. I owe special thanks to the students in my spring 1999 graduate seminar on "Trashy Books" for the intellectual community and fellowship they provided.

A great many of these colleagues have generously read and commented on chapters of this book. Jennifer Parchesky, Ellen Gruber Garvey, Alexis McCrossen, Trysh Travis, Jaime Harker, Sean McCann, and Pam Brandwein offered careful readings at critical points. Sean McCann's own work on hard-boiled detective fiction provided the type of intellectual conversation most scholars only dream about. Michael Wilson shared his material on gay and lesbian detective fiction. Dan Wickberg offered provocative conversation about consumer culture and the links between cultural, intellectual, and social history. I would like to thank Janet Francendese, who was busy imagining this as a book long before it was even a completed dissertation. She is a generous and supportive editor. The anonymous reader for Temple University Press provided helpful feedback about reimagining the project.

I have spent a great deal of time immersed in pulp magazines, publishing-business records, and the papers of hard-boiled writers at libraries across the country. Special thanks to Cathy Turner, who introduced me to the collections at the Harry Ransom Humanities Research

Center at the University of Texas at Austin, and who housed and fed me while I worked there. Clifford Fearrington tirelessly hunted down everything related to hard-boiled writing at the HRC. The staff in Special Collections at the Syracuse University library were generous with their expertise about the Street & Smith Collection. Jeff Rankin at Special Collections at UCLA made my work with *Black Mask* a pleasure. The advertisements reproduced from *Black Mask* are courtesy of UCLA Special Collections.

Friends and family have supported and sustained me during this project. Patricia Wood shared her historian's skill and temperament and taught me a great deal about the process of writing a book. Her friendship, faith, and insistence that we celebrate even my smallest victories made this project possible. Natalie Houston made sure I took care of myself. My mother has listened to me talk about this book for years, and she celebrated every step. The pride and support of my extended family sustained me. Djuna Barnes's life with me spans the duration of this project. Her single-minded pursuit of belly rubs, walks in the woods, and games of tug-of-war mitigated my obsessive work habits.

HARD-BOILED

Introduction

After reading "The Maltese Falcon," I went mooning about in
a daze of love (for Sam Spade) such as I had not known for
any character in literature since I encountered Sir Launcelot
when I hit the age of nine.
Dorothy Parker in *The New Yorker* (1931)

And there is Gilbert, the Thin Man's son. You must meet
Gilbert. The book is worth reading for him alone.
Review of Dashiell Hammett's *The Thin Man* (1934)

This speedy tale is more than competently narrated by a cop
with a picturesque line of vernacular and professional lingo.
Review of Dashiell Hammett's *The Dain Curse* (1929)

What's a nice girl like you doing in a genre like this?" In the
five years I have spent researching and writing this book, I
have been asked some version of this question more times
than I can count. The gendering of hard-boiled fiction is
comprehensive, persistent, and on occasion embarrassing.
My favorite moment occurred at a panel on masculinity at
an American Studies Association annual meeting. I
approached one of the panelists, with whom I had carried on
a lengthy e-mail correspondence on the topic of masculinity and magazines, and introduced myself. He was so sur-
prised to find himself talking to a woman that he spilled his
coffee all over his conference paper.

1

The assumption that all serious readers of hard-boiled detective stories are men is widespread. The titles of several critical works are a case in point: *The Black Mask Boys, Tough Guy Writers of the Thirties, The Hardboiled Dicks*.[1] This manly packaging has a long and hallowed tradition. Although some of these texts are now available as Vintage Crime Classics trade paperbacks with arty black-and-white photos on their covers, they were originally published in cheap pulp magazines whose technicolor covers featured tough-looking men with guns and gagged, terrified women falling out of their low-cut dresses.

I discovered these hard-boiled texts through feminist rewritings of the genre from the early 1980s. My acquaintance with Sam Spade, Philip Marlowe, the Continental Op, and countless lesser-known private eyes who walked the mean streets of pulp-magazine fiction during the 1920s, '30s, and '40s was mediated by Sara Paretsky's V. I. Warshawski, Sue Grafton's Kinsey Millhone, and Marcia Muller's Sharon McCone. Although modeled on the hard-drinking, tough-talking investigators of Dashiell Hammett and Raymond Chandler, these private eyes were in part a reaction against the hard-boiled detective stories of the pulp era.

"When I started writing," Sara Paretsky explains, "I wanted to do something very different about the way women are depicted in detective fiction. . . . As a reader of mysteries, I always had trouble with the way women are treated as either tramps or helpless victims who stand around weeping. I wanted to read about a woman who could solve her own problems. . . . I was determined to write a hard-boiled sleuth who was both a woman and a complete professional, someone who could operate successfully in a tough milieu and not lose her femininity."[2]

In the course of talking about this fiction with members of a fan organization dedicated to the reading and advocacy of women's mysteries, I became interested in its literary antecedents—the novels and short stories of Hammett, Chandler, Carroll John Daly, Raoul Whitfield, George Harmon Coxe, Paul Cain, Erle Stanley Gardner, and other writers for pulp magazines such as *Black Mask, Detective Story, Dime Detective,* and *Detective Fiction Weekly* in which this type of story first appeared. Although I began studying this fiction for professional reasons, it rapidly became important to me in ways I had not expected.

Perhaps most significant, these texts are centrally and unambiguously about men and relationships between men. Much of the action takes place in saloons, tobacco shops, and boxing matches, where women are an anomaly. Once inside a hard-boiled text, my senses are filled with what Raymond Chandler called "the smell of a world where men live,"[3] a world I do not know at all well. Having spent most of my academic life reading and writing about women's literature as part of mostly female intellectual communities, I know Carroll Smith-Rosenberg's "female world of love and ritual" far better than I know the mean streets.[4] What are communities of men like? How do they function? What are their codes of conduct? What do they talk about, and what kinds of rhetoric do they use? Reading this fiction has offered me the opportunity to eavesdrop on how one group of mostly white, mostly working-class men made sense of the world through the pulp fiction that circulated widely in their communities between the wars.

I have also fallen in love with hard-boiled humor. Much of this literature is wickedly, dryly, darkly funny, and its creators were masters of sarcasm, understatement, and one-liners, always delivered with a straight face. Raymond Chandler, in particular, had a priceless gift for ridicule and an unerring eye for the foibles of the social and intellectual aristocracy. Much to my surprise, I have increasingly located myself in the camp of the tough-talking men who published their trashy crime fiction in the pulps rather than with Agatha Christie and Dorothy Sayers, whose country-house fiction filled my early adolescence. Chandler's impatience with the pretensions of British mystery writers—literary language; titled aristocrats; allusions to Shakespeare, the ancient Greeks, and Romantic poets—parallel my own impatience with certain academic discourses. The dense, theoretical prose of some academic texts has its perfect opposite in the terse, stripped-down dialogue of hard-boiled crime stories. I see in hard-boiled fiction, then, some of my own desires for a less exclusionary rhetoric and a more democratic academic world.

I share the obsessive interest of hard-boiled fiction in the details of everyday life—clothing, furniture, food, and patterns of speech. Such c(l)ues about relationships of gender, class, education, and power, on which the solutions to hard-boiled mysteries often hinge, also are of critical importance for my own detective work: decoding the unwritten rules of my particular academic space, rules often bewildering because they are socioeconomically and culturally distinct from the rules with which I grew up. Hard-boiled fiction offers me lessons in reading dress and demeanor, and space to consider the substantial consequences of (mis)reading these subtle social texts.

I am in love, as well, with the vaguely inappropriate language of these stories, their tendency to introduce colloquial speech in formal situations and to spin intricate similes about adamantly earthy things. While being formally interrogated by the district attorney in *The Maltese Falcon*, Sam Spade refuses to divulge his suspicions. "My guess might be excellent, or it might be crummy," he says, "but Mrs. Spade didn't raise any children dippy enough to make guesses in front of a district attorney, an assistant district attorney, and a stenographer."[5] I am delighted by his flippancy, the informality of his lingo in the face of a formal interrogation, his smart-ass, flat-out refusal to cooperate.

This rejection of linguistic decorum is no doubt linked to my other fascination: what I have come to call the "attitude problem" of the hard-boiled hero. What must it be like to be moody, difficult, insubordinate, and prone to hostile confrontation? As I made my way through graduate school—painfully earnest and pathologically prone to smiling politely and taking notes—I had a secret life. Inside my perky self was a hard-boiled hero whose detached and sometimes funny commentary was my constant companion. With ruthless thoroughness, my own private film-noir sound track provided cynical summaries of the sound and fury that constitute certain parts of academic life. What would Raymond Chandler have said about this oral exam? What would he have said *at* it? How would he have handled showing up at a little-black-dress gathering in a pastel, floral print skirt? This dutiful daughter has had countless imagined conversations with the bad boys of the mean streets about autonomy, authority, and social life in hierarchical institutions.

Moreover, in an atmosphere characterized by a great deal of angst about the status of intellectuals—organic or traditional—it was refreshing to claim as mentors in my own project men who churned out prose for a penny or two a word, maintaining that the production of sentences, paragraphs, and plots was no different from any other kind of work. No muse. No magnum opus. No ethically fraught discussions about the role of the public intellectual. Just prose production, day after day.

My point here is simply that reading—even that undertaken for academic reasons—is a good deal more complex, contradictory, and deeply enmeshed with personal history than literary models of reading have generally recognized. Reading is a process of multiple and often conflicting identifications, determined as much by our personal and institutional histories as by the structures of the text. If texts are what Kenneth Burke calls "equipment for living,"[6] then they are not only the linguistic artifacts we study in literature class, but also, in part, ourselves. We construct ourselves from the texts our culture provides (printed and otherwise), but we then remake these texts in ways that meet our psychological and social needs.

I am rethinking what constitutes "literature." Rather than studying texts as linguistic artifacts, I am concerned with texts as social processes—economic, political, and psychic transactions among writers, editors, publishers, distributors, and the readers who encounter printed materials, either individually or as part of reading communities.[7] The cultural work of this body of fiction, then, depends not only on the language of the text, but also on the ways of reading specific to given interpretive communities and the contours of the institutions that readers, writers, and publishers inhabit.

This project is informed by my reading of more recent rewritings of the hard-boiled genre by African-American, female, gay, and lesbian authors. Such writers are some of the most sophisticated theorists of hard-boiled fiction around, and their innovative appropriations of a genre historically marked by sexism, racism, and homophobia made me see that the relationships of readers to texts were far more complicated than more traditional forms of textual exegesis would have led me to believe. In addition, my participation in an organization dedicated to the reading and advocacy of women's mysteries has had a great effect on my view of reading as a social practice. The highly personal, "idiosyncratic" ways these readers read—selecting out details of plot, character, or setting with particular resonance for them, and narrating their own concerns through these sites—made me see reading as a profoundly complex psychic and social process. The cultural work of contemporary detective fiction in the lives of female fans made me look again at the cultural work of hard-boiled texts of the 1920s, '30s and '40s in the lives of *their* readers. This fiction must have provided many white, working-class men with a complex idiom through which to make sense of their early–twentieth-century workplaces and the larger world they inhabited.

Reading as a Social Practice

Most of the existing scholarship on detective fiction comes out of a formalist or structuralist tradition that attends to texts as sign systems without attending to the social and economic worlds in which they are written and read. Literary critics have focused their attention particularly on the denouements of detective novels, where the mystery is solved, the various clues woven together into a seamless and coherent narrative, and social order restored. Fredric Jameson argues that mystery readers "read for the ending," so that the rest of the work is degraded to a means to that end.[8] Such exclusive focus on the form of detective fiction has a number of troubling consequences. First, the emphasis on structural continuity overlooks differences in subgenre, setting, and protagonist that are of great importance to fans. Second, such formalist accounts ascribe a monolithic, reactionary politics to detective fiction, claiming that it inevitably recommends an ideology of competitive individualism, or that it affirms existing power structures by locating crime in evil individuals rather than corrupt social institutions.[9] Third, formalist scholarship ignores differences in the conditions of production and primary readership over time and in different media. For example, the 1920s and '30s readers of Dashiell Hammett in the cheap pulp magazine *Black Mask* are not the same readers, demographically, who buy his novels in expensive Vintage Crime Classics paperbacks today. Reading these texts as classics is not at all the same as reading them as trash. The different reading protocols these labels invite in effect rewrite the text.[10]

These notions of popular texts as manipulation of the masses by those in control of the means of cultural production also overlook the role of audiences in shaping mass culture. Although these texts were produced by a small group of writers, publishers, and editors, they had to appeal to popular needs and desires to be profitable. Jameson argues that mass culture succeeds as propaganda for capitalist societies precisely because it does address popular needs and desires—what he calls the "Utopian" longings of readers.[11] Although Jameson is certain that popular narratives smooth over the ideological contradictions in the social order, that they "manage" the Utopian longings that readers bring to them, I am unconvinced. As Alison Light wrote in a study of women's popular fiction, "Reading is never simply a linear con-job but a process of interaction, . . . a process which helps to query as well as endorse social meanings and one which therefore remains dynamic and open to change."[12] The Utopian or transcendent aspects of hard-boiled detective fiction have been overlooked largely because so little work has been done on how audiences made use of this fiction.[13]

In contrast with the scholarly commonplaces about detective fiction as a thoroughly commodified form, the reports of people who read mysteries for entertainment reveal a variety of ways of reading, only some of which have anything to do with the structural imperative to restore narrative coherence and social order at the close.[14] The 1930s reviews of Dashiell Hammett's novels, quoted as epigraphs to this chapter, are a case in point. Although critics uniformly agreed that these were very badly plotted novels, they nonetheless found the colorful vernacular, the suave hero, and the quirky minor characters compelling reasons to read and recommend these stories. These reviewers were "poachers," to use Michel de Certeau's term—readers whose own concerns and preoccupations determined which aspects of the text were most salient.[15] Such idiosyncratic reading practices—identification with minor characters, attention to details of locale or a character's hobbies, ignoring what happens at the end of a story if other moments are more compelling—are common in contemporary audience studies.[16] Such multiple and highly personal ways of reading resonate with Roger Chartier's redefinition of "popular" to refer not to texts themselves but to "a kind of relation, a way of using cultural products."[17] This popular way of reading or appropriating cultural artifacts is like Certeau's poaching in that cultural consumption becomes an active production of meaning that is useful given one's situation, goals, and personal history. Readers do not necessarily find in their mysteries reassurance that the status quo is satisfactory. In the best such texts they find "equipment for living"—structures, characters, scenes, and an idiom through which to make sense of their own experience.

Moreover, social and institutional structures related to literacy, education, and cultural production affect the kinds of equipment for living that readers find. Describing how these structures enable and constrain reading practices, Elizabeth Long distinguishes between "social infrastructure" and "social framing."[18] Social infrastructure is composed of the institutions in which reading is taught and carried out—families, schools, libraries, bookstores, book clubs, and so on. Social framing refers to "collective and institutional processes [that] shape reading practices by authoritatively defining what is worth reading and how to read it."[19] Social framing thus dictates what gets published, reviewed, circulated in libraries, and taught in schools, and also which *ways* of reading are privileged in which contexts. Long argues that the "ideology of the solitary reader," the model of a lone, silent, often scholarly reader that predominates in our culture, has blinded us to the multiple ways books are used, particularly collectively and in ways not endorsed by the academy. Literary theorists have largely overlooked the kind of reading I am proposing here—reading where the boundaries between readers' lives and their texts are fluid and fluctuating and where an advanced level of literacy cannot be taken for granted.

Although it is probably impossible to reconstruct the complexities of even a single individual's reading, however well documented,[20] we can use evidence about the social infrastructure and social framing of certain kinds of reading to reconstruct the codes and institutions through which individual readers made sense of texts. Roger Chartier argues along these lines, suggesting that our reconstructive task is not only literary or linguistic, but also sociological.[21] Cathy Davidson calls this way of thinking about books a "history-of-texts" approach, distinguished from traditional history of the book (which focuses on the economics of book manufacture and distribution) by its additional focus on the generic, stylistic, and literary expectations through which readers and writers make meaning.[22]

The Intellectual Field

This project is informed by three overlapping fields of scholarship: the history of the book, working-class studies, and feminist cultural studies. As my discussion of reading practices has made clear, this study departs from text-based models of literary criticism to reconstruct historical readers and their interactions with a particular set of texts. That is to say, in addition to examining the literature itself, I will attend to the conditions of cultural production and the institutions that shape ways of reading. Since texts can do their work in the world only if they are taken up by readers, my close readings of hard-boiled detective stories will be filtered through the eyes of the reconstructed readers that emerge from a variety of data about interwar pulp-fiction audiences.

I am concerned specifically with a methodological problem in history-of-the-book scholarship. How do we reconstruct the reading practices of those who were outside the record-keeping classes? African-Americans, recent immigrants, the poor, the working classes—those customarily denied meaningful access to advanced literacy or the means of cultural production—have left few traces in the historical record. Lacking the personal libraries, letters, diaries, or minutes of book-club meetings through which we have access to representations of more privileged readers, what kind of space can we create for these "marginal" readers in the history of reading in America? In the absence of documents meeting traditional historical standards of proof, what would constitute evidence of working-class ways of reading?

The hole in the archival record is here to stay. We can, however, reconstruct working-class reading practices from a variety of related information. If representations of popular reading from various different sources coalesce around some common themes, we have probably learned something about working-class readers, regardless of the limitations of the individual sources.

As Robert Darnton reminds us, information about the production and distribution of texts can compensate for a lack of knowledge about readers and reception.[23] Thus, the memoirs of writers, editors, and publishers of pulp magazines can tell us a great deal about the audience for pulp fiction. Whom did they think their most important consumers were? In what ways did they shape their cultural production to meet the needs of these readers? Further, patterns in the advertising in pulp magazines over the years offer a rough indication of the readers' concerns. Although advertisers were seeking to shape readers into consumers, they nonetheless had to appeal to deeply felt needs and desires in order to manipulate their audience.

In addition, some data about the readers of pulp fiction do exist. Most pulp magazines in the 1920s, '30s, and '40s published letters from readers (though pulp editors freely admit that they manipulated these columns, often writing the letters themselves when the volume of fan mail was too small to create the critically important illusion of a lively and active readership).[24] In addition, the University of Chicago Library School produced a large body of research on the reading habits of factory workers in the 1930s. This research does not meet modern scientific standards; it dealt only with nonfiction; and it was driven by a missionary impulse to uplift the pulp-magazine–reading masses. Nevertheless, these studies suggest the contours of the working-class audience these librarians were seeking to reform. Finally, oral-history interviews of British labor leaders after World War II offer vivid accounts of what encountering hard-boiled fiction in cheap paperbacks after the war meant to one set of proletarian readers—readers who may have in some ways resembled the interwar American readers who interest me.

Adult literacy studies also offer fertile ground for reconstructing historical reading practices. One of the basic tenets of critical or liberation pedagogy is that we read well and with ease those texts that are intimately engaged with the pressing issues of our daily lives. Paulo Friere taught Brazilian peasants to read by beginning not with Dick and Jane but with the names of the plants and tools his pupils dealt with every day.[25] Similarly, the hard-boiled pulp fiction read by so many working-class men between the wars echoes some of the key themes in social- and labor-history studies of the period. Just as working-class life was transformed by scientific management, the rise of consumer culture, and the entrance of women in large numbers into paid employment, the pulp fiction that targeted working-class readers featured embattled artisan-heroes, compulsive catalogs of consumer goods, and obsessive attention to young working women. These texts were popular with workers in part because they dealt with issues of burning importance to the maintenance of their gender, class, and professional identities.

No single source of information about working-class reading practices between the wars is particularly compelling in isolation. It is entirely possible that, lacking sophisticated market research, the corporations that published pulp magazines targeted an audience that was not, in fact, its primary readership. I would not want someone to draw conclusions about my life based exclusively on the ads aired during my favorite television shows. Maybe most of the reader letters in pulp magazines were fakes. Maybe the librarians in Chicago were too horrified by the "trash" their subjects read to hear many of the nuances in their accounts of reading. It is conceivable that postwar British labor leaders are not representative of even their own class and nation, much less American proletarian readers of a generation earlier. Moreover, the issues that social and labor historians of the 1980s and 1990s find compelling about the period between the wars may not have been the most salient issues in workers' experience.

Nonetheless, the way these various representations of popular reading practices coalesce around a common reader is impressive. Overwhelmingly, these sources suggest that pulp fiction was read by white, working-class men who were preoccupied with manliness, finding skilled and remunerative work, and the "impression management" increasingly necessary for social advancement. Whatever the specific limitations of each representation of popular reading, it is highly unlikely that they would all be wrong about pulp-fiction readers in exactly the same ways. The gestalt created by considering a variety of data about pulp-magazine readers can, in part, compensate for the specific limitations of individual sources and the paucity of material in the historical record.

This project also intersects with the field of working-class studies. Popular texts offer us clues to working-class ways of being in the world just as voting records and the personal papers of labor leaders do. These stories are collective fantasies, offering representations of the plots, characters, and idioms through which readers of this class made sense of their world. Although these stories were usually written and distributed by men with more wealth and education than the readers they targeted, they had to perform a sort of class ventriloquism if they wanted to sell these narratives to working men.[26]

The study of pulp magazines illuminates in particular the role of workers as participants in and creators of modern consumer culture.[27] Most studies of consumption analyze advertising professionals and the middle-class, white women whom admen identified as the purchasing agents of families.[28] Pulp ads hailed a different kind of consumer: a working-class man, concerned with getting autonomous, well-paid work, practical education, and products to enhance his embattled manliness. Moreover, pulp detective fiction paid a great deal of attention to the skills needed to navigate commodity culture and the ability to read gender, class, and power relationships from the self-presentations of others. These magazines were engaged in making workers feel at home with commodities, in shaping them into consumers. At the same time, the needs and desires of working-class readers determined the kinds of appeals advertisers could make and the kinds of products they could promote. As a consequence, these texts negotiate an uneasy rapprochement between a residual artisan culture centered on skilled production work and an emergent consumer culture that valued men for the commodities they could (or couldn't) afford to buy.

This project is informed throughout by feminist cultural studies. Part Two of this book is filled with readings of hard-boiled detective stories and explications of the different kinds of pleasure they might have provided for the readers of pulp magazines and paperbacks. These stories were sites of struggle over meaning between the relatively privileged class that wrote and published them and the popular classes that consumed them. Like all popular texts, they simultaneously expressed and manipulated their readers' needs and desires. Hard-boiled detective stories hailed working-class readers as the ideal consumers of a commodity culture—ethnically unmarked, bourgeois individuals interested in protecting their "wages of whiteness."[29] This shaping of working-class men's subjectivities, however, was possible only because of the

Utopian impulses at the core of this fiction—nostalgia for a disappearing artisan culture and visions of a differently gendered world. In this way, hard-boiled detective stories participated in the social construction of a class- and race-specific masculinity that was enmeshed with larger changes in the economy and the structure of work. The rise of consumer capitalism, the erosion of all-male work and leisure spaces, and the disappearance of skilled, autonomous work forced white, working men to renegotiate the sources of their gender, class, and professional identities. Hard-boiled detective stories nostalgically re-created the fading artisanal world and the appropriately subordinate women that went with it, while at the same time they called into question the boundaries between what men and women did and were.

The challenge in studying popular culture is taking seriously and examining carefully narratives that surround us more or less continuously and to which we seldom give much conscious thought. The close, careful reading that advanced training in literary and cultural theory makes possible does not mirror the kinds of attention readers customarily give to texts that our culture labels "trash." Nonetheless, the popular narratives of a culture do shape the plots, characters, and language available to us to give meaning to our experience. These modes of critical reading give us tools to see the ways in which popular narratives shape which questions are imaginable and which plots seem possible. Moreover, popular texts are powerful in part because we customarily attend to them so little. Our failure to engage these texts critically allows them to shape our ways of thinking, to circumscribe our notions of subjectivity and visions of community, without our awareness.

Project Structure

This book has two parts. Part One, "Reconstructing Readers," is concerned with the social framing and infrastructure of hard-boiled fiction. It seeks to reconstruct historical readers through the publishing history of pulp magazines and paperbacks, 1930s research on workers' reading habits, and analysis of the texts with which hard-boiled fiction was bound: editorials, reader letters, and advertisements.

Chapter One, "The Hard-Boiled Writer and the Literary Marketplace," situates hard-boiled detective fiction within the cultural hierarchies that prevailed between World War I and World War II. Hard-boiled writing culture was profoundly shaped by the split between "trashy" pulp magazines and "slick," upscale periodicals; by the unstable boundary work of hard-boiled writers and editors with respect to gender, class, and nation; and by writers' and editors' self-interested invocation of "realism" in defense of the genre.

Chapter Two, "The Adman on the Shop Floor: Workers, Consumer Culture, and the Pulps," establishes ads and detective fiction in the pulp magazine *Black Mask* as continuous discourses, and uses ads to make inferences about who hard-boiled fiction readers were and why they read. *Black Mask* advertisers hailed readers who were preoccupied with autonomy, manliness, and self-presentation. These ads uneasily mapped an emergent commodity-linked model of identity based on appearances over an older model of identity based on skilled, artisanal work.

Part Two, "Reading Hard-Boiled Fiction," is more traditionally literary, offering readings of selected texts in light of the reader concerns identified in Part One. I argue that these texts could be read in a variety of ways: as allegories about work, manliness, and labor/management struggles over Taylorism; as guides to dressing for success; as demystifications of the links among language, class, and culture; as sites for managing anxieties about shifting gender roles. Although not every reader of hard-boiled fiction in pulp magazines or paperbacks read in all of these sometimes contradictory ways, it is nonetheless true that these texts enabled certain kinds of "poaching" while not enabling others. The popularity of widely circulated genres can perhaps best be explained by their capacity for being appropriated to meet a whole array of psychological and social needs. "Instead of seeing how the work expresses a basic psychological dynamic," John G. Cawelti argues of formula fiction, "this approach would lead us to ask how the artistic structure makes possible the unified accomplishment of the largest variety of social and psychological functions relevant to the cultural context."[30]

Chapter Three, "Proletarian Plots," contrasts the narrative structures of hard-boiled fiction and classic English detective novels. Rather than restoring social order and narrative coherence at the close, hard-boiled fiction's incomprehensibly complex plots and speed of action resonate with the structure of scientifically managed work. Nonetheless, hard-boiled fiction often uses this form to voice opposition to the de-skilling of work.

Chapter Four, "Dressed to Kill," discusses the significance of the extended, detailed descriptions of clothing and interiors in hard-boiled texts. In part, these stories functioned for their original readers as object lessons in reading how class, gender, and power are embodied in the details of everyday life. These texts, as noted above, were also involved in an uneasy negotiation, reconciling a model of class, gender, ethnic, and sexual identity based on birth and breeding with one based on appearance and the display of commodities.

Chapter Five, "Talking Tough," examines hard-boiled texts as rhetorical worlds. These stories juxtapose different class codes and demonstrate the various uses to which street lingo and learned language could be put. Hard-boiled writing culture viewed education as a form of cultural capital but was nonetheless profoundly suspicious of its usefulness for getting ahead. The colloquial language of this fiction differed markedly from the literary language of high modernism with which it was contemporary, a difference that profoundly shaped its readership.

Chapter Six, "The Office Wife," explores the representation of working women in hard-boiled fiction. Although these stories are filled with young women being paid for doing what until quite recently had been "men's work," these women are invariably (re)defined as sexual objects, domestic nurturers, or vulnerable figures in need of a chivalrous male rescuer. While these texts adamantly return women to their traditional places, however, they also muddy the boundaries between men and women by reimagining identity as performance or masquerade.

A brief Afterword explores some directions for thinking about hard-boiled fiction after World War II, focusing particularly on the rewritings of this historically racist, homophobic, and misogynist genre by African-American, female, gay, and lesbian writers. Their appropriations foreground the troubling of gender, ethnic, and sexual identity already implicit in the founding texts of the genre. In addition, these rewritings are further evidence of the kinds of poaching that readers do, rereading and transforming texts in ways that address current needs, goals, and situations.

Reconstructing Readers

Far from being writers—founders of their own place, heirs of the peasants of earlier age now working on the soil of language, diggers of wells and builders of houses—readers are travellers, they move across fields they did not write, despoiling the wealth of Egypt to enjoy it themselves. Writing accumulates, stocks up, resists time by the establishment of a place and multiplies its production through the expansion of reproduction. Reading takes no measures against the erosion of time (one forgets oneself *and* also forgets). It does not keep what it acquires, or it does so poorly and each of the places through which it passes is a repetition of the lost paradise.

Michel de Certeau, *The Practice of Everyday Life* (1984)

ow can we re-create something as ephemeral as reading once the readers who interest us are dead? How can we reconstruct the lives and views of those who have left few traces in the historical record? These are the methodological problems at the center of Part One. Wealthy people with access to education and print media leave all sorts of evidence—diaries, letters, autobiographies, annotated personal libraries—of what they read and how they read it. However ephemeral the reading process may be, the writings of such readers give us representations of their reading selves. The social position of less privileged readers—African-Americans, immigrants, the poorly educated, the working classes—made it unlikely that they would leave this kind of evidence. Lacking the education, leisure, and discretionary income necessary to own many books or write at any length about their experiences, such readers left few traces.

What are we to do with these silences, these conspicuous absences in the history of reading in America? Are there other ways to get at the literacy levels, texts, and reading practices that were characteristic of these "marginal" readers? Did others—librarians, social workers, teachers, government agencies, publishers, writers, advertisers—leave accounts? If so, what can we learn from these accounts about the mostly privileged observers and the mostly unprivileged observed? If we surround this gap in the historical record with information from a wide variety of other sources, does that constitute adequate evidence of these marginal readers' ways of reading? Must all these secondary accounts agree in order to be convincing?

This book is a reconstruction of the reading practices of one set of marginal readers—the white, working-class men who encountered hard-boiled detective fiction in pulp magazines between 1923 and the collapse of the pulp-magazine market in the early 1950s. Because these readers were outside the record-keeping classes, and because this type of literature was dismissed as trivial by almost everyone involved, we have no accounts of the ways in which such fiction intersected or failed to intersect with readers' lives on the shop floor and in working-class families and communities. Lacking such records, I approach the question of the cultural work of hard-boiled detective fiction from numerous other directions. What did pulp writers, editors, and publishers have to say about their audience? What can we learn from readers who wrote letters to their favorite publications or won prizes in the contests these magazines periodically sponsored? What kinds of people did the advertisements in pulp magazines target? To what themes did pulp fiction repeatedly return? What did librarians of the period think the proletariat spent its time reading? What does interwar labor history tell us about the concerns of workers?

These sources coalesce around a primary readership that was white, male, often immigrant, and working-class. These readers were preoccupied with obtaining and keeping jobs that earned a family wage and ș

with asserting a manliness defined by physical strength, autonomous work, and the subordination of women. They were interested in social advancement, and they recognized that this required an understanding of how owners and managers dressed, spoke, and carried themselves. Readers preoccupied with these issues, those predisposed to make sense of their world in these terms, would have viewed hard-boiled detective stories quite differently from critics trained in Western philosophy. Pulp fiction for working-class readers was less about crime and the process of detection than about the hard-boiled private eye's struggles for autonomy at work, his skill at reading class and social position from details of dress and decor, his manly physical and rhetorical prowess, and his tortured relations with women.

Constructing a scenario, however speculative, about how these and other marginal readers made sense of their texts is necessary if we wish to construct a history of reading in America that looks a little less like the *Social Register* and a little more like the American reading public. Robert Darnton argues that "Worldviews ... are bound to be fuzzy around the edges, and they will slip through the fingers if one grabs at them as if they were pages from the *Congressional Record.*"[1] Ways of reading are like worldviews, and may, in fact, be indistinguishable from them. Better to engage in a scholarly way with evidence that is sometimes maddeningly vague and incomplete than to dismiss the study of reading outside the record-keeping classes as not worth doing because it does not offer historians the kind of proof to which our training accustoms us.

1

The Hard-Boiled Writer and the Literary Marketplace

Into this underworld of literature most of us never dive unless, like Mr. Hoover's Committee on Recent Social Trends, we are curious about the literary preferences of those who move their lips when they read.

Vanity Fair, June 1933

It is not pleasant to think of the immature minds and mature appetites that feed on such stuff as their staple fodder, but there is no ducking the fact that sensationalism is the age-old need of the uneducated. The steady reader of this kind of fiction is interested in and stirred by the same things that would interest and stir a savage.

Harper's, June 1937

The June 1931 issue of *Black Mask*, the most important publishing outlet for hard-boiled detective fiction between the wars, printed the following letter from a new reader:

> I have just read my first copy of *Black Mask* and am writing to ask you why in the world you don't use good paper. If you had been using good paper I would undoubtedly have started reading it years ago, but I never thought of doing so, because I took it to be just another one of "those" magazines that flood the newsstands which I never buy. I never dreamed that it had such wonderful stories in it. I bet there are thousands more like me and that you are losing thousands of sales by not using white paper.[1]

"Those" magazines were pulp magazines. Named for the untrimmed, rough, wood-pulp paper on which they were printed, pulp magazines were unambiguously "trash," cheaply produced escape literature designed to be thrown away once read.[2] During their heyday in the 1920s, '30s and '40s, hundreds of pulp titles crowded newsstands, their garish covers competing for the attention of their 10 million regular readers.[3] Although the covers most often featured stylized, brightly colored paintings of scantily clad women and violent men, these seven-by-ten-inch magazines were remarkably unassuming on the inside. Column after column of uninterrupted, densely packed print greeted the reader, punctuated only by an occasional pen-and-ink line drawing and a few pages of ads clustered at the front and back. Between 1896 and 1953, a reader could expect to pay from five to twenty-five cents for roughly 130 pages of stories, a great deal of fiction for the money.

The pulps were direct descendants of nineteenth-century dime novels, cheaply produced fiction published by Beadle & Adams, Street & Smith, and other companies that targeted the urban working classes between the 1840s and the 1890s. A few of these titles endured until World War I. The first pulp magazine was Frank Munsey's *Argosy*, an all-fiction weekly periodical that competed with dime novels for an adult, male audience. When changes in postal regulations made it prohibitively expensive to distribute dime novels through the mail, many of the largest publishers simply repackaged their cheap fiction as pulp magazines, continuing to feature favorite series characters such as Nick Carter and Buffalo Bill.[4] Street & Smith, the largest dime-novel publisher, switched over to pulp format in 1915. The pulp-magazine business boomed between the wars, driven by falling costs and rising literacy levels. Well into the twentieth century, pulp magazines adhered to nineteenth-century publishing practices, eschewing the heavy use of advertising and relying on cheap production costs and newsstand sales to stay in business.[5]

The magazines that our first-time *Black Mask* reader preferred—those printed on white or "good" paper—were "respectable" magazines such as *The Saturday Evening Post, Ladies Home Journal,* and *Cosmopolitan.* These mass-market magazines, printed on the "slick" paper necessary for high-quality reproduction of images, featured short fiction, articles on a variety of general-interest topics, handsome illustrations, and glossy ads for consumer products. Their high production costs were offset by advertising revenues that made possible relatively modest cover prices.

Until the late nineteenth century, only the wealthiest Americans read magazines. Genteel, well-educated readers kept themselves informed about art, literature, European travel, and manners by reading high-quality monthly magazines, such as *Century*, *Harper's*, and *Scribner's*, whose 25- or 35-cent cover price placed them beyond the means of most Americans. In 1893 Frank Munsey kicked off the "magazine revolution" by cutting the price of *Munsey's Magazine* from twenty-five cents to ten cents and publishing articles of broader interest. The low price attracted a new mass audience with which to lure advertisers, who subsidized the substantial costs of production.[6]

Munsey's new strategy—low price, large circulation, lots of advertising—was taken up by a whole generation of entrepreneurs, including S. S. McClure, John Brisben Walker, George Horace Lorimer, Cyrus H. K. Curtis, and Edward Bok. By slashing prices and aiming editorial content at a general audience, these mass-market magazines achieved unprecedented levels of circulation, most of it through subscription. Although circulations of 100,000 to 200,000 copies had previously been considered respectable, by 1900 *Ladies' Home Journal's* circulation approached 1 million.[7]

The *Black Mask* reader's reference to "'those' magazines" indicates that the low quality of pulp magazines was such a cultural commonplace that he need not explicitly name them or their specific failings. Rather than challenge this stereotype, the editor published letters such as this one that claimed *Black Mask* was exceptional, that it was really an honorary slick. Hard-boiled fiction emerged from this much-maligned world of pulp magazines, originating in *Black Mask* in the early 1920s. It subsequently appeared in countless other pulp publications, including *Dime Detective*, *Detective Fiction Weekly*, *Clues*, and *Detective Story*.

This chapter analyzes the publishing world out of which hard-boiled detective fiction emerged, and the war of words between the pulps and the slicks about what constituted good fiction. By describing the prevailing cultural hierarchy, I hope to re-create what it meant to read or write for the pulps between the wars—acts profoundly marked by gender, class, and national identity.

On Authorship: The Hard-Boiled Writer as Fiction Factory

Pulp fiction earned so little respect largely because the pulps operated with a different notion of authorship from the liberal model prevailing in more "literary" circles. Pulp writers were paid from one to five cents a word for the prose they generated at astonishing rates—an average of 3,000 to 5,000 words per day, although the stars did twice as much.[8] Walter Gibson, writing as Maxwell Grant, churned out two 40,000-word novels a month for Street & Smith's pulp *The Shadow*.[9] "You had to keep them coming all the time . . . otherwise you'd starve," claimed veteran pulp writer Richard Sale.[10] Pulp writers had little to say about the aesthetics of their fiction, but they recounted with pride their long hours, speed, and productivity.

Modernist writers of the time operated on the lone artist/creator model, preoccupied with the place of the individual talent in literary tradition.[11] Pulp writers, however, were less artists than manufacturers, paid for making a product much as factory workers were.[12] "I am a fiction factory," Erle Stanley Gardner wrote to Joseph Thompson Shaw when the latter took over the editorial helm of *Black Mask* in 1926.[13] Gardner was the picture of cooperation with his pulp editors. Explaining that he thought the function of an author was to write fiction that helped sell magazines, he was willing to do endless revisions to get the "merchandise" to his "wholesaler's" specifications.[14] Change an ending? Fine. Need to cut? Don't even bother to consult him. Don't like the "atmosphere"? Send it back with instructions for a rewrite.[15] "Let me know what you want and I'll try to manufacture something right to order," he told an editor at *Argosy*, a *Black Mask* competitor.[16] Gardner's diaries are refreshingly free of the writerly angst one would expect from a more self-consciously literary author, but at the bottom of each day's page he recorded the number of words he'd produced and his total pay.[17]

Most pulp writers also lacked the elite university training of more "literary" writers, though some pulp-magazine editors and a few writers were graduates of prestigious colleges.[18] Editors often saw the pulps as entry-level jobs in the publishing industry—a way to prove themselves before moving on to more lucrative positions with book publishers or mass-market magazines. Those who made their living writing for the pulps, however—a core of several hundred writers responsible for a disproportionately large percentage of the output—did not have this kind

of education. Frank Gruber, a pulp writer, recalled that few of his colleagues had college degrees at all, much less the majors in English or
journalism common among writers for mass-market magazines.[19]

Moreover, the names of authors in the pulps were often owned by
the magazine, with many writers using the same name or a single writer
having several pseudonyms. Steve Fisher's stories appeared in Street &
Smith's *Clues* and *The Shadow* under the names Steve Fisher, Stephen
Gould, Grant Lane, and William Bogart. If several stories by an author
appeared in a single issue, one or more usually appeared under a pen
name. In some cases a lone writer wrote an entire issue, using a different name for each story.[20]

Clearly authorship had a different meaning in the pulps than it did
in the slicks or in book publishing. Whereas "respectable" authors were
paid for writing a story—a literary work—pulp authors were paid for
the quantity of words they produced. Whereas more self-consciously
literary writers thought of their work as creative self-expression, pulp
writers often did not get or take credit for their work at all. Writing
"serious" fiction required broad reading in Western classics; writing
pulp fiction required no more education than that of the average man
on the street. While slick-paper fiction was framed as unique, creative
utterance, pulp fiction was merely a commodity. Recognizing that their
notion of authorship was distinct, pulp writers had their own professional organization—the American Fiction Guild—which offered a
newsletter with marketing tips and bi-weekly networking lunches in
New York to anyone who had sold five stories to pulp magazines.[21]

Pulp writers focused on the labor of writing rather than on genius or
inspiration when asked to discuss their work in *Black Mask*'s writers' column. "I wonder how many writers have reached the conclusion that
authorship is made up of 90% desire and tenacity, 10% imagination and
0% genius?" wrote one. Another confessed: "I've long ago lost the twin
foolish ideas that fiction is done by inspiration and that it isn't work." [22]
The authors' columns were full of the painful labor that had produced
the text: nail chewing, anxious pacing, endless redrafting, talking to oneself.[23] Stories were not aesthetic objects in hard-boiled writing culture,
but craft work whose links to human labor remained in the forefront.
H. E. Stover summed it up: "Frankly the whole thing is hard work."[24]

Even the advertisements in *Black Mask* stressed this view of literary and
artistic creation. Ads offering training in journalism or drawing emphasized that no special "gift," "talent," or "genius" was necessary. Most of

the work in either field, the ads asserted, was done by relative unknowns whose skills were acquired through practice rather than inborn.[25]

Black Mask, then, made no distinction between cultural production and any other kind of production, between the realms of art and life. In other words, hard-boiled writing culture refused the distinction between the aesthetic and the everyday that, Pierre Bourdieu argues, is at the center of the bourgeois worldview.[26] One writer summed up the popular ethos characteristic of hard-boiled writers in the *Black Mask* column, "Our Readers' Private Corner": "How do I work at my fiction generally? Simply go at it every morning like any man at his work."[27]

Pulp Audiences: Those Who Move Their Lips When They Read

Another reason the pulps commanded so little respect was that their readers were widely held to be socially and economically marginal. They were working-class, young, and poorly educated; many were immigrants.[28] Although Harold Hersey, a publisher of pulps, claimed that his readers came from all walks of life, he conceded that the majority were probably office or factory girls, soldiers, sailors, miners, dockworkers, ranchers, and others who worked with their hands. One survey by Popular Publications found that the typical reader of the company's pulps was "a young, married man in a manual job who had limited resources and lived in an industrial town." Hersey reported that the largest volume of sales was in the Midwest.[29]

Research from the University of Chicago library school in the 1930s confirms these reading patterns.[30] William S. Gray and Ruth Munroe found that 55 percent of the pulp-magazine audience had only a grade-school education, 29 percent had a high-school education, 7 percent had some college, and 9 percent had college degrees. According to Douglas Waples's statistics, detective and adventure magazines were read roughly ten times more often by residents of a working-class Chicago neighborhood than by middle-class residents of a St. Louis suburb.[31] In fact, contemporary cultural commentators lamented that workers read little besides pulp magazines.[32]

A number of pulp magazines between the wars formalized their appeal to working men and women by sporting what amounted to union labels.[33] Street & Smith's *The Shadow: A Detective Magazine* prominently featured the statement "This magazine produced entirely by union labor" on its front cover in the early '30s, reassuring workers that their hard-earned cents would not be used to employ scabs. The title page of Clayton's *Clues* went even further, pledging that its stories had been "purchased under conditions approved by the Authors' League of America," that the magazines were "manufactured in Union shops by American workmen," and that "each newsdealer and agent is insured a fair profit."[34] Clayton's bid for consumer goodwill invoked an unstable class alliance—the "producing classes"—that included not only craft workers, laborers, and machine operators but also small-business men, clerks, professionals, and farmers.[35]

Harold Hersey referred to his pulp readership as "juvenile anywhere from sixteen to sixty," and young readers were widely held to be a significant part of the pulps' audience.[36] Moreover, the workers, immigrants, and poorly educated grown-ups who read the pulps were easily made into metaphoric children by the librarians and journalists who passed judgment on their reading tastes. Pulp publishers repeatedly used such words as "clean" and "wholesome" to describe their fiction, a defense against the ubiquitous charge that the pulps were violent, sensational, and immoral. Editors reported feeling a great deal of moral responsibility for their young readers, and one went so far as to ask Erle Stanley Gardner to change the ending of a story so as not to corrupt *Black Mask*'s adolescent readers.[37]

Pulp magazines did, in fact, attract readers from other social strata. *Black Mask*, eager to prove that not all of its readers were socially and economically marginal, published letters from doctors, lawyers, professors, and businessmen. Joseph Thompson Shaw, the editor of *Black Mask*, distinguished his "regular letter writing readers" from what he called some "darned big men around town"—bankers, professionals, important businessmen—whose approval of *Black Mask*'s stories meant a great deal more to him. Erle Stanley Gardner wrote Shaw about every upscale reader he ran across—a doctor who gave *Black Mask* to patients who needed cheering up, a "big New York businessman" and his cronies at the golf club.[38] *Black Mask* was much more preoccupied with "class" readers than its competitors ever were, probably because of its position as the "aristocrat of the detective field,"[39] the most selective of the mystery pulps.

The stigma attached to reading pulp magazines in educated circles could be formidable, however.[40] Harold Hersey thought that college men and women did not read pulp magazines, although they might have enjoyed reading them in childhood. "Sophistication" had set in by the college years, and most "would not be caught dead" with anything as "lowbrow" as a pulp.[41] Many of the high-class readers of pulp magazines whom Erle Stanley Gardner occasionally ran across were ashamed of their tastes. They "confessed" to being readers of *Black Mask*, and admitted that they were often so embarrassed about asking for it at the newsstand that they whispered their request.[42]

The other format in which hard-boiled detective stories sold well was the paperback, which appeared on the scene in 1939 with the launching of Pocket Books.[43] The paperback cost twenty-five cents, little more than a pulp magazine; targeted many of the same readers; and largely replaced the pulps when their market folded in the years after World War II. A 1941 survey of 40,000 readers by Pocket Books confirmed that buyers of paperbacks sounded remarkably like the buyers of pulp magazines. "Locomotive engineers, musicians, mechanics, salesmen, clerks, waitresses, writers, editors, schoolteachers, ranchers, and farmers" were buying two to twenty times more books than they had formerly bought, because Pocket's cheap editions made them affordable.[44]

Paperbacks closely resembled pulp magazines in other ways. Most readers purchased paperbacks where they purchased their pulp magazines—at newsstands, drugstores, train stations, and bus depots—rather than in bookstores, where regular book-trade customers preferred to shop. Most paperbacks were distributed by periodical distributors, bypassing traditional book-distribution channels entirely.[45] Like fiction magazines, paperbacks did not get reviewed in newspapers. Moreover, paperbacks were scandalous for the same reasons pulp magazines were. One historian describes paperbacks as "little more than second-rate trash. Literary flotsam. Schlock turned out to appease a gluttonous mass appetite for sex and sensationalism."[46]

The pulp-publishing business and the early world of paperbacks overlapped considerably. Many paperback-publishing houses, particularly those specializing in mysteries (Dell, Avon, Popular Library), were started by men who had learned how to sell cheap fiction in the pulp-magazine business.[47] Street & Smith owned Chelsea House, a publisher of twenty-five–cent paperback originals. Chelsea House advertised heavily in all the Street & Smith pulps, informing readers that their favorite authors from *Detective Story*, *Love Story*, and *Western Story* wrote paperbacks, too.

Sometimes the hard-boiled detective fiction in pulp magazines and the hard-boiled fiction in paperbacks were the same fiction. Many hard-boiled detective novels were minimally edited reprints of serials from pulp magazines. Fans of Raymond Chandler's novels will have a disturbing sense of déjà vu when they read his pulp fiction, since the characters, the plots, and whole pages of dialogue in the novels were cannibalized from the pulp fiction he had published in *Black Mask* and *Detective Fiction Weekly*. After publishing his first novels, he republished unedited collections of his magazine fiction in book form.

Readers of hard-boiled detective stories in pulp magazines or paperbacks included those who were not regular book-trade customers. Perhaps the best argument for an economically and socially marginal audience is the dearth of data available. Mass-market magazines during this period did a great deal of market research about middle-class consumers. That these widely practiced techniques were not applied to pulp magazine audiences suggests that publishers did not believe their incomes were large enough to make them attractive targets for national brand advertising.

Hard-boiled fiction, written by hack writers paid piece rates, may have had particular appeal for working-class readers, whose own worldviews were determined in part by the daily grind of production work. The social situation and personal history of an author profoundly shapes his or her writing, and hard-boiled writers were no exception. The pride in hard work, speed, and productivity that is called for by a life pounding the typewriter for a few cents a word leaves traces in hard-boiled detective stories—traces that readers with comparable experiences and values would have found deeply resonant.[48] Because writers' lives and readers' lives were in some ways homologous, there was a good symbolic fit between the attitudes and values of the white working men who read the pulps and the pulp-fiction forms they appropriated to express and reinforce their worldviews.

A Literature for He-Men

Not only was pulp fiction given what Michael Denning calls "mechanic accents" by its hack writers and marginalized audience, it was aimed emphatically at men. Because of the close collaboration between mass-market magazine publishers and national-brand advertisers, most slicks targeted white, middle-class women as purchasing agents for their families.[49] Frank Gruber explained why he disliked slick magazines' stories: "Most of them were terribly effeminate . . . and I was more at home with the virile, masculine type of story.[50] Similarly, Raymond Chandler recalled his discovery of pulp fiction: "Wandering up and down the Pacific Coast in an automobile, I began to read pulp magazines, because they were cheap enough to throw away and because I never had any taste at any time for the kind of thing which is known as women's magazines."[51]

This characterization of pulps for men and slicks for women is not quite accurate. Some mass-market magazines, most notably *The Saturday Evening Post*, did target male readers. Moreover, though the vast majority of pulp titles were action and adventure magazines aimed at men, every major pulp publisher had at least one romance pulp for women. The circulations of women's pulps usually topped all the others, so male readers of pulp fiction probably did not outnumber female readers.[52]

Specialization in the pulp market occurred gradually. The first pulp magazines featured all kinds of fiction, but by their heyday in the '20s, '30s, and '40s, there were about 200 highly specialized pulp titles, dedicated to detective fiction, pirates, boxing, war, football, Westerns, aviation, science fiction, and romance, among other subjects. Pulps were niche-marketed by gender, age, and other demographic characteristics. H. L. Mencken and George Jean Nathan toyed with the idea of starting a Negro pulp in the 1920s before founding *Black Mask*, but decided that there was not enough money in the black community to support one.[53] A June 1930 trade bulletin that Street & Smith distributed to its newsdealers explained which pulp magazines went with which audience. *Detective Story* was intended for "men in all walks of life"; *Top-Notch* targeted "the up-and-coming young man"; *Wild West Weekly* was "a young chap's magazine."[54] Gender was clearly the most important demographic category: Romances were for women; the countless adventure pulps were for men. Even the catholically named *Argosy All-Story* assumed a male audience. In the late 1920s it welcomed "stories of nearly any type" as long as they had "strong masculine appeal." "Slushy romances" were, of course, out of the question.[55]

By the late 1930s, more than fifty detective magazines figured in the mix of the roughly 200 pulps in general circulation. Warner Publications' *Black Mask*, with a peak circulation of 103,000 in 1930, was the elite of the tough-guy fiction pulps.[56] *Black Mask* mirrored the product specialization taking place in the pulps.[57] In the early years, it did not publish detective fiction exclusively, much less only tough-guy detective fiction. Although it began in 1920 with the subtitle "An Illustrated Magazine of Detective, Mystery, Adventure, Romance and Spiritualism," it rapidly focused on more masculine genres. By 1926 it featured Westerns, detective stories, and general adventure, and by 1927 it was subtitled "The He-Man's Magazine." Westerns figured prominently throughout the 1920s, with cowboy covers outnumbering detective covers in some years. In 1932 *Black Mask* became a detective magazine.

Editorial statements during this period echoed the increasing masculinization of the subtitles. Phil Cody, the second editor of *Black Mask*, presided over the shift from genteel mysteries to tougher stuff, most notably the work of Dashiell Hammett. In a 1926 editorial, Cody told his readers why circulation was continuing to climb—because "*Black Mask* gives its readers more real, honest-to-jasper, he-man stuff . . . than any other magazine."[58] "He-man" is an important term, notable for its redundancy. First, the need for a modifier suggests that "man" no longer signified unambiguous masculinity on its own. Second, it implies the existence of a troublesome category of male people—"she-men"— whose biological sex and performed gender were fundamentally at odds. This troublesome figure—the male homosexual—litters the pages of hard-boiled fiction between the wars. In addition, Cody's redundant emphasis on the authenticity of this masculine fare—it is both "real" and "honest"—suggests an undercurrent of anxiety about the integrity of manliness during this period.

Joseph Thompson Shaw, the editor at the helm while *Black Mask* consolidated its reputation for featuring the best tough-guy mysteries around, published an editorial in 1933 in which he described the ideal *Black Mask* reader: "He is vigorous-minded, hard . . . responsive to the thrill of danger, the stirring exhilaration of clean, swift, hard action. . . [He] knows the song of a bullet. The soft, slithering hiss of a swift-thrown knife, the feel of hard fists, the call of courage."[59] The phallic imagery with which this ideal reader is described makes clear that the reading experience is sexualized.

To the modern reader, the copy in *Black Mask* does seem anxiously overdone. *Black Mask* regularly informed readers about the manly exploits of its writers as soldiers, airmen, police officers, and outdoorsmen. Offering further evidence that its writers were not she-men, one "Behind the Mask" column listed all the *Black Mask* writers over six feet tall, a column that greatly irritated the five-foot-eight Erle Stanley Gardner.[60]

Black Mask dressed its female editors in the drag of first initials. The first editor, F. M. Osborne, reportedly used her initials in order "to project a masculine image," because the magazine was targeting men.[61] Fanny Ellsworth, editor of *Ranch Romances*, a more profitable pulp also owned by Warner, used her initials on the *Black Mask* masthead after she replaced Joseph Thompson Shaw as editor in 1936. Ellsworth's editorship was an industry scandal. "A shock ran through the publishing world," Frank Gruber commented. "A woman at the helm of *Black Mask!*"[62] Gruber maintained that Ellsworth did her job well, but commented that "You would have thought she would be more at home with a magazine like *Vogue* or *Harper's.*"[63]

Indeed, Ellsworth felt that the hard-boiled brand of fiction was far too limiting, and she sought to include "a more humanistic" type of story in *Black Mask*. That female editors were a scandal at *Black Mask* is noteworthy, because numerous other major detective pulps, which had less investment in the hard-boiled variant, were edited by women, and nobody in the industry seemed particularly bothered. Street & Smith's *Detective Story* was edited in the 1930s by Daisy Bacon, who also edited *Love Story*. In the 1940s it was edited by Ruth Miller. Both were listed by their full names on the title page.

Women were also writing hard-boiled stories during this period, although their heroes were usually men and they often wrote under male pseudonyms.[64] *Black Mask* published several female writers, notably Erika Zastrow and Katherine Brocklebank, while Shaw was editor (1926–1936). However, women writers were seldom featured in interviews or blurbs for the next month's edition, as their male colleagues were. Even at Street & Smith's less hard-boiled *Detective Story Magazine*, women were more likely to be writing departments such as "What Handwriting Reveals" or filler than to be writing fiction.[65]

The women who read *Black Mask* seem little better accommodated than the women who edited or wrote for it. Roughly a fifth to a quarter of the names listed as *Black Mask* contest winners or runners-up in the 1930s and '40s belonged to women, yet the existence of these readers was always treated as an anomaly. Most letters from women had headlines that identified them: "From the Ladies," or "A mere woman."[66] Moreover, these readers devoted a great many words to apologizing for or explaining their presence in this masculine space. "Is it permissible for a mere woman to express a few comments?" asked one by way of an introduction. "Although I suppose the *Black Mask* is supposed to be more of a man's magazine, I assure you we women like an occasional thrill in our reading matter also."[67] Another female reader was even more hesitant about speaking up in this world of tough-talking men: "Although this is not my first letter to *Black Mask*, being a woman, I hated to express my opinion."[68]

"Feminine" material fared little better. Shaw spent the late 1920s in hot pursuit of someone to write stories about a female detective. After receiving a number of letters from readers praising one of Erle Stanley Gardner's stories, Shaw decided that Gardner was his man—the one with the necessary "feminine touch." The experiment left Shaw sounding decidedly squeamish, however. "I do not want too much femininity," he told Gardner's agent, "rather a masculine treatment of a female character." In Shaw's imagining of the project, Gardner's regular detective Ed Jenkins would be joined by a young female detective who enters the story as his enemy but warms to him as he chivalrously rescues her again and again. Shaw hoped that this would provide "a touch of feminine interest that would not let down our he-man readers and would at the same time bring in a swarm of new ones of both genders." A female detective, then, could penetrate the covers of *Black Mask*, but only as an incompetent, nearly indistinguishable from the other vulnerable women in need of rescue by a hard-boiled hero. (Gardner declined the assignment, but he did suggest that *Black Mask* contact Nell Martin, a female pulp writer who might be willing to take on the job.)[69]

In 1934, Shaw's editorial strategy for getting the perennially unprofitable *Black Mask* into the black was to add likable characters, "glamour," and "a touch of romantic appeal" to the he-manly regular offerings. An exchange of letters on the topic between Shaw and Gardner ended with Shaw's defensive statement that "This magazine is by no manner going to be feminine," and a promise to review his own letters to see what had given Gardner this impression.[70]

Black Mask's all-male character was a key part of its appeal. The pulp publisher Harold Hersey explained it this way: "One is not afflicted in the fiction magazines with an infinite variety of copy relating to female complaints and perplexities."[71] Detective, Western, and adventure pulps were woman-free zones, zones rapidly disappearing from everyday life. As all-male work and leisure spaces dwindled in working-class communities, imagined communities of working-class male readers emerged in part as psychic compensation.[72] Women became voters in 1920, transforming the once all-male world of partisan politics.[73] Between 1880 and 1930, the female wage-labor force increased twice as fast as the adult female population. By 1930, half of all single women and a quarter of all female adults were in the paid workforce. Moreover, these working women were increasingly working side by side with men. The number of women employed in domestic service in private homes ("invisible" working women) declined, while the number of those employed in offices, stores, and other public places increased.[74]

Not only were all-male workplaces disappearing, but working-class men and women increasingly spent their leisure time in mixed-sex activities. Between 1880 and 1920 there was a transition in working-class life from the homosocial cultures of the Victorian era to the heterosocial cultures of the modern world. The center of working-class communities moved from the men-only saloon, where leisure, mutual aid, and male bonding were of a piece, to an increasingly mixed-sex world of commercial leisure—the movies, amusement parks, dance halls—where young men and women met and socialized.[75]

The loss of formerly all-male sites for work and leisure required a variety of material and ideological compensations. Hard-boiled writing culture functioned as a homosocial imagined community that addressed some of the needs once met on the shop floor, in the voting booth, or in the saloon. The male writers of the pulps saw themselves not as artists but as workmen who produced piecework prose for people like themselves. Furthermore, the imagined worlds of hard-boiled fiction are filled with men's spaces—the mean streets (where women, as in turn-of-the-century saloons, do not go unescorted), boxing matches, tobacco shops, bars.

The "*Black Mask* boys," as those in the industry called them, were just such a homosocial community. Male camaraderie runs deep through their letters. Erle Stanley Gardner invited most of the *Black Mask* crowd to visit his ranch in California, and many of them came to engage in such manly pursuits as hunting, camping, fishing, horseback riding, golf, and staying up late to argue by the fire. They exchanged gifts at Christmas, sent one another souvenirs from their travels, and mailed dirty limericks back and forth. Shaw set Gardner up with new writers to mentor through correspondence; asked him to visit Hammett when Hammett's health (and productivity) were failing; and asked him for news and his impressions of others in the circle of writers. The annual reunion lunch in New York was well attended, and those who had to miss it asked for a report of it in their letters.

Gardner's characterizations of the *Black Mask* crowd usually invoked team sports. "I've always regarded the Black Mask bunch as part of a family or a baseball team in which each one had his work to do, and I've tried my darndest to do my share," he told Shaw as they approached a professional parting of the ways in 1929–30. Gardner mourned losing not only the reading public he had so profitably cultivated over the years, but also the fellowship of being part of the magazine's team of regular writers. "Naturally I hate to leave a magazine I've been with so long," he wrote, "I like the personal set-up, and probably won't come to New York again since the personal visits with the Black Mask gang meant a hell of a lot to me."[76]

Hard-boiled writing culture created an all-male imagined community that included writers, readers, and the he-manly heroes of this fiction. For some, reading pulp fiction was also a refusal to read slick magazines, which trafficked in genteel, feminine fare and placed consuming women at the center of American life, where producing men had once reigned.

The Pulps and the Slicks: Negotiating Cultural Hierarchy

Throughout the period between the wars, artisanal, masculine pulp magazines and genteel, feminine slick-paper magazines engaged in a war of words about which publications would represent average Americans— that mass audience left untapped by elite publications such as *Atlantic Monthly*. The slicks dripped with disdain for their sensational brethren. For example, a 1933 *Vanity Fair* article entitled "The Pulps: day dreams for the masses" maligned pulp writers as ignorant hacks, denigrated pulp readers as marginal literates, and deemed these magazines "gaudy, blatant, banal," representative of "the incursion of the Machine Age into the art of tale-telling."[77] The article was so critical that Shaw took up his pen to defend his pulp in a subsequent editorial column. Although his primary concern was the quality of *Black Mask* fiction and the professionalism of its writers, he got in a few digs at what he viewed as the average *Vanity Fair* reader—"the society matron who considers it smart to have on her table the so-called class magazine with its illustrations regardless of its text."[78] Pulp fiction, so the story went, was good enough to sell itself without the pretty pictures and expensive advertisements necessary to make slick-paper fiction appealing to its status-seeking, effeminate audience.

Most of the "respectable" classes shared *Vanity Fair*'s view of the pulps, assuming that "we" never read such things, although the lower classes might. A 1935 study of reading habits of residents of a Queens,

New York, neighborhood elicited all sorts of scorn for the pulps from the patrons of the public library. Very few reported reading pulp magazines, but many took the opportunity to write comments in the margin of their survey: "This trash has no place in the public library" and "God forbid."[79] Researchers in library schools of the period inevitably lamented the preponderance of pulp magazines in the reading their research subjects did, and identified the improvement of their literary tastes as a major policy goal.[80]

Black Mask's positioning vis-à-vis slick-paper magazines was actually a lot more complex than Shaw's editorial implied. Although full of sneering disdain for handsomely illustrated "class" magazines read by society women, *Black Mask* endlessly rehearsed the successes of its writers who had been discovered by the slicks. According to this model of cultural value, texts can be ranked according to a single measure of aesthetic value. There were good stories and there were bad stories. The authorities who decided questions of cultural value occupied the most privileged positions in the publishing industry with slick magazines and major newspapers. As a consequence, proving the excellence of *Black Mask* fiction involved arguing that it was indistinguishable from slick-paper fiction. This was Shaw's strategy. When *The Saturday Evening Post* accepted a story by Frederick Nebel, a *Black Mask* regular, an entire "Behind the Mask" writers' column commemorated the event: "This accomplishment puts upon Fred Nebel the hallmark of approval and acceptability of the smooth paper brethren and 'sistern' and further confirms what we have always maintained, that he is among the very best in the field."[81] Another column marked the storming of the slick-paper gates by Erle Stanley Gardner, Frederick Nebel, and Dashiell Hammett, who had been published in *Liberty*, *Collier's*, and *Redbook*, respectively.[82] "Behind the Mask" continued to feature highbrow praise for *Black Mask* writers throughout the '30s and '40s. Many columns were little more than catalogs of the slick-magazine, book, film, stage, screen, and radio credits accumulated by its writers.[83]

Shaw accepted the slicks/pulps hierarchy that shaped the social infrastructure of publishing. The existence of a pulp magazine that featured high-quality fiction did not challenge the cultural devaluation of the pulps; it merely gave *Black Mask* honorary slick-paper status. The publishing world largely followed Shaw's lead on this. Even some of the slicks' indictments of the worthless fiction in which pulp magazines trafficked deigned to cite *Black Mask* as the exception.

Still, *Black Mask*'s self-congratulation did not conceal its ambivalence about having its writers taken up by the "respectable" publishing establishment, which paid them a good deal better. "Take a Laugh" was the title of an editor's column that detailed how critics were just now "discovering" the type of detective story that *Black Mask* had been publishing for years: "For all the 'new type' stories, which on their appearance in book form, the critics are becoming so enthusiastic about, you read first in *Black Mask*—Hammett's *Red Harvest, The Dain Curse, The Maltese Falcon,* and *The Glass Key,* Raoul Whitfield's *Green Ice* and *Death in a Bowl.* Pick up any of the Sunday literary reviews and read about the 'discovery' of a 'new type of detective fiction writing,' and have a laugh."[84]

This column was fairly typical in its contradictory mix of disdain and desire for cultural legitimacy. Although one was supposed to sneer at the slick-paper magazines for their tardy discovery of tough detective fiction, one was also supposed to take their attentions as evidence of *Black Mask*'s worth. In this radically democratic vision, it does not matter where fiction comes from. Worthy work, even if it starts out in the trashy underworld of literature, will rise on its merits to an appropriate position in the hierarchy of cultural value. Moreover, whether we are rich or poor, highly educated or barely schooled, we are all capable of recognizing aesthetic quality—quality on which we will inevitably agree.

Some writers and readers did not accept the implicit hierarchy of value that held slick-paper stories in higher esteem than pulp fiction. Erle Stanley Gardner exchanged a great many heated words with Shaw in the early 1930s over Shaw's "arty" tastes, his slavish attention to who got published in the slicks, and the privileged treatment he accorded Dashiell Hammett, the slick-paper golden child. "I have said before, and I am going to keep yelling it until somebody stops me, that if a man wants to get *Saturday Evening Post* type of fiction or *Liberty* type of fiction, he buys the *Post* or *Liberty* at five cents and saves exactly fifteen cents on the transaction," Gardner berated Shaw in one particularly heated exchange. "If he wants to buy *Black Mask* type of fiction he has got to pay fifteen cents more to get it. Therefore, at least as far as that man is concerned, the *Black Mask* type of fiction is superior to the *Saturday Evening Post-Liberty* type of fiction.[85] As a consequence, the exasperated Gardner continued, the editor of *Black Mask* ought to use his writers' columns to talk about *Black Mask* rather than the slick-paper outlets in which *Black Mask* regulars were beginning to appear.

It's clear from this passage that Gardner's aesthetics were a great deal more pluralistic and conditional than Shaw's.[86] Gardner maintained that slick-paper fiction and pulp fiction were two different and incomparable things. If one wanted "arty" fiction, one bought *The Post* or *Collier's*. If one wanted action, adventure, and escape, one purchased pulp fiction. Neither was better; they were just useful for different purposes. Moreover, Gardner thought that trying to sell "arty" fiction like Hammett's to people who were seeking pulp-fiction pleasures was a recipe for commercial disaster. "You have lost the sales viewpoint and gone arty," Gardner accused the executives at Warner Publications, arguing that *Black Mask's* failure to turn a profit was linked to Shaw's preference for Hammett's more "literary" fiction over his own "plain honest-to-God wood pulp" writing, which ranked higher in reader-preference polls.[87] Some readers of the pulps shared Gardner's disgust with the assumed superiority of the slicks. In a letter appearing in *Clues* in 1938, one reader asked: "Am I supposed to think because a writer appears sometimes in *Collier's*, or *Post*, or the *Bar, Grill, and Tavern Weekly* that he is any better than my old friends who have been writing for me for years, and whom I enjoy? To heck with that. Don't go highbrow. Give us lots of shooting duels and other peril."[88]

The vast majority of hard-boiled fiction in the '20s, '30s, and '40s never did go highbrow. As a consequence, few modern readers have heard of Carroll John Daly, Paul Cain, Dwight W. Babcock, Norbert Davis, Lester Dent, William Brandon, Roger Torrey, Theodore Tinsley, or other writers who remained hacks, paid by the word.

A few writers did achieve tenuous highbrow respectability. Dashiell Hammett, Raymond Chandler, Frederick Nebel, and George Harmon Coxe were published in expensive hardback editions in Alfred Knopf's Borzoi line of mysteries.[89] Hammett's *The Maltese Falcon* was published in a 1934 Modern Library edition, the first detective novel to be featured in the prestigious series of modern literary classics.[90] But even Hammett and Chandler were unable to transcend their pulp origins completely. Hard-boiled fiction remained uneasily situated in the cultural hierarchy.[91] As a result, many reviewers in the '30s and '40s took up the problem of hard-boiled fiction's "respectability" in their reviews. Some critics merely recognized the dual or triple positioning of the books: One called Hammett the "darling of brows both high and low."[92] Other reviewers felt the need to reassure the highbrows about the appropriateness of this fiction: "To be caught with a Raymond Chandler whodunit in hand is a fate no highbrow reader need dread."[93] Some critics, however, seem to have preferred that their reading of this fiction be a little disreputable: "Now that Dashiell Hammett is beginning to be taken seriously by the highbrows, my first enthusiasm for him is beginning to cool a little."[94] Part of the appeal for highbrows was clearly slumming—being a tourist on the wrong side of the cultural tracks, with all the forbidden pleasures such transgression promised. Even the few pulp writers who were accorded some measure of literary legitimacy were granted it because of their lowbrow origins. The appeal of this fiction for educated readers was, in part, that it came out of worlds that did not include people like them.

Hard-boiled detective fiction navigated the hierarchy of cultural value in complex and contradictory ways. It emerged from the trashy literary underworld of pulp magazines, but *Black Mask*, which put hard-boiled stories on the map, was a pulp with pretensions. Although most of its writers languished in relative anonymity, cultural authorities subsequently claimed a few of them for highly reputable publishing houses and mass-market magazines. Although the majority of readers who encountered it in pulp magazines and cheap paperbacks were probably from the producing classes, significant numbers of scholars subsequently became enthusiastic readers. Hard-boiled fiction took on different meanings as the structures that its writers, readers, and publishers inhabited shifted. Changes in the conditions of production and the class of targeted readers remade these texts, whose language often remained unchanged as it moved from format to format. Hard-boiled detective stories can reward both self-consciously literary readings of highly educated scholars and the modes of popular reading that interest me. For this reason, the genre itself is alternately dismissed as trash and celebrated as an overlooked wing of modernism.[95]

Chandler's Vindication of Hard-Boiled Writing Culture

Perhaps the richest document in the war of words between the pulps and the slicks was Raymond Chandler's self-serving historiography of the detective story, "The Simple Art of Murder," published in *Atlantic Monthly* in 1944.[96] In it, he argued for greater realism in detective fiction, differentiated his own brand of "realistic" detective fiction from the classical English mystery that preceded it, and canonized Dashiell Hammett as the key figure of the hard-boiled school. This was Chandler's attempt to claim a share of the market from the genteel British ladies whose books and slick-magazine stories had dominated the detective-fiction marketplace. In the process, however, he radically undermined his own claims about gender, national, and class identities by acknowledging their basis in performance or masquerade.

The first section of Chandler's essay raised the specter of novels of lasting merit being left to grow dusty on the shelf while "old ladies" push and shove to get at mysteries entitled *"The Triple Petunia Murder Case* or *Inspector Pinchbottle to the Rescue"* (3). Most such novels were written by members of the London Detection Club, the organization of English mystery writers that set the rules for writing detective fiction in the years after World War I. They just kept churning out the same ridiculous stuff year after year: nosy spinsters, fusty old aristocrats bumping one another off in eminently civilized and grossly improbable ways, doddering dolts from Scotland Yard who take 300 pages to solve a case that the Los Angeles police would have wrapped up in half an hour.[97]

Chandler had nothing but disdain for silly novels of this sort. He saved much of his best invective for Agatha Christie's *Murder on the Orient Express*, in which, it turns out, all the people in a sleeper car took turns stabbing the victim. "This is the type that is guaranteed to knock the keenest mind for a loop," Chandler wrote. "Only a halfwit could guess it" (9). He indicted Dorothy Sayers not only for her grossly improbable novels but for her critical writings on mystery. Chandler called Sayers' introduction to the first *Omnibus of Crime* anthology an "essay in critical futility" because it failed to acknowledge that classical detective fiction of the kind she wrote was an "arid formula" that no longer contained much interest or originality (12).

Although he spent most of the essay heaping ridicule on the best-selling giants of the British golden age (1920–1937), Chandler insisted that the English had no monopoly on outrageous plots; he chose British examples because critics still favored English mysteries and because "the Americans, even the creator of Philo Vance, only make the Junior Varsity" (10). The differences between dreary British fiction and dreary American fiction were largely cosmetic for Chandler: The silliness took place in Miami hotels rather than Elizabethan gardens, and the characters drank frozen daiquiris rather than port (10).

This bad fiction was everywhere. Chandler estimated that two-thirds to three-quarters of all mystery fiction sold was based on the same old arid Detection Club formula. It appeared in "the big shiny magazines, handsomely illustrated, and paying due deference to virginal love and the right kind of luxury goods" every week of the year (10). He was correct; classical detective fiction achieved its popular success in the United States in the pages of slicks such as *Collier's, McClure's, Cosmopolitan,* and *The Saturday Evening Post.* The immense popularity of serialized Sherlock Holmes stories in *Collier's* from 1903 to 1905 motivated other slick-paper magazines to run similar stories.[98]

Having dismissed slick-magazine fiction, Chandler turned to the world of pulp magazines, where hard-boiled fiction had first appeared. As Chandler put it in the most quoted passage of the essay, Dashiell Hammett "gave murder back to the kind of people that commit it for reasons, not just to provide a corpse; and with the means at hand, not hand-wrought dueling pistols, curare and tropical fish" (14). What's more, Hammett did all this with "style." This style, Chandler maintained, putting Hammett in the distinguished company of Walt Whitman, Theodore Dreiser, and Ernest Hemingway, was "the American language" (15). Good detective fiction, then—the realistic type—was "American." Chandler did concede that the "American language" in which good detective fiction was written was not exclusively American anymore. Tough-talking Australians, for example, might have qualified for citizenship on Chandler's terms.

The canonization of Hammett was not the end of the story. The old ladies from the opening of the essay reared their graying heads again when Chandler tried to defend Hammett from those who claimed that he did not write detective stories at all—merely tough novels with a little mystery thrown in for interest.[99] Chandler characterized such critics as "the flustered old ladies—of both sexes (or no sex) and almost all ages—who like their murders scented with magnolia blossoms. . . " (16). Like the remarkably fluid national categories, the gender categories show a lot of flux. The enemies (of either sex) were women—perhaps best embodied by Dorothy Sayers, the theorist of the bunch. The bad "British" fiction of ridiculous plots and impossible gentility was feminine (whether women wrote it or not), and the good "American" fiction was masculine by virtue of being set in the streets of an inherently corrupt world.

At the conclusion of his essay, Chandler argued that Hammett, "realistic" as he might have been, had neglected another important aspect of art—a quality that Chandler called "redemption." It is worth quoting at length: "But down these mean streets a man must go who is not himself mean, who is neither tarnished nor afraid. The detective in this kind of story must be such a man. He is the hero; he is everything. He must be a complete man and a common man and yet an unusual man. He must be, to use a rather weathered phrase, a man of honor. . . . He must be the best man in his world and a good enough man for any world" (18). Chandler's detective-hero is a lot of things, but above all he is a man. By sheer force of repetition, Chandler hammered home that "art," at least of the detective-fiction sort, was not about silly British ladies or folks who read the slick, shiny women's magazines, but about heroic American men like those who read or wrote for the pulps.

Chandler wrote about hard-boiled fiction in the same heavily gendered terms as *Black Mask*'s editors. He repeated the pulps/slicks dichotomy that was a critical part of publishing's infrastructure. He implicitly referred to social class in his ridicule of ancestral estates and his celebration of the mean streets. But he linked the otherwise familiar gender- and class-boundary work with issues of nationalism.[100] This harnessing of Americanness, maleness, and literary quality characterized many of Chandler's contemporaries, who were engaged in founding the discipline of American Studies in the 1940s and 1950s. The "Americanness" that, these critics claimed, constituted literary excellence was inevitably embodied in a man, a rugged individual who struggled to maintain his autonomy in the face of an entrapping society and a wilderness to be conquered, both cast in unmistakably feminine terms.[101] The cynical loners of hard-boiled fiction—perpetually beset by one or more femmes fatales—are cut from the same cloth as the more canonical literary heroes of American literature.

Although Chandler framed this as an essay about the aesthetics of crime fiction, his primary concern was professional rivalry with the real women of the London Detection Club. The best-selling and most critically acclaimed British mystery authors of the 1920s and '30s were disproportionately women—Agatha Christie, Dorothy Sayers, Josephine Tey, Margery Allingham, Ngaio Marsh, Patricia Wentworth, and Gladys Mitchell, to name a few. Though there were some successful male authors of classical detective fiction between the wars, women were so prominent that the occupation of mystery writing could seem as "feminine" as teaching or nursing. Moreover, classical English detective fiction, murders aside, trafficked in remarkably feminine currencies— emotion, private life, domestic spaces. Hard-boiled texts defined themselves against feminized, classical English fiction and addressed themselves to the shifts in gender roles occurring with the entrance of women into all-male work and leisure spaces. What the hard-boiled writers of the '20s and '30s were doing was attempting to wrest control of a specific section of the literary marketplace for men and manly fiction from the women who had dominated the field.[102]

The London Detection Club's quaint name belied its influential role as a professional organization. Founded in 1928, it claimed as members most of the significant British mystery writers. The club formulated rules about what should and should not be done in the mystery genre. Club members and their American disciples shared the view that it was probably bad form to rely on coincidence, intuition, or hunches rather than reason; that one should never withhold clues from a reader; and that moderation should be practiced in the use of gangs, conspiracies, ghosts, hypnosis, Chinamen, lunatics, and evil twins.[103] Taking the Detection Club oath, members also swore to respect "the King's English."

Hard-boiled writers broke these rules with adolescent abandon. Even a cursory cataloging of instances from Hammett and Chandler alone is impressive. Hammett's *Red Harvest* and *The Glass Key* present American cities overrun by rival gangs; Sam Spade relies heavily on his secretary's feminine intuition in *The Maltese Falcon*; the Continental Op wrestles a ghost at the headquarters of a California cult in *The Dain Curse* before catching the lunatic/murderer; and Chandler's Marlowe visits a psychic in *Farewell, My Lovely*. Their books revel in underworld slang and other butcherings of the King's English, and they wickedly ridicule classical detective stories. In *The Lady in the Lake*, Marlowe playfully introduces himself to an inquisitive landlady as Philo Vance, S. S. Van Dine's dreary junior-varsity detective. In *Farewell, My Lovely* the nosy spinster next door, a stock figure of classical detective fiction, is an unreliable witness, thus undermining the feminine source of authority of classical texts. Near the end of *The High Window*, Marlowe parodies the rational detective of classical fiction, pretending to deduce a murderer's identity from the characteristics of his cigarette ash.

But while he dismissed British women as lousy writers of detective fiction and installed American men at the apex of writerly achievement, Chandler radically undermined his own claims. Ousting Agatha Christie for Dashiell Hammett seems a simple enough rhetorical move, but Chandler muddied these categories to such an extent that we are no longer sure whether Christie is, in fact, the British woman and Hammett the American man. If old ladies can be of either sex, their gender being determined not by nature but by a propensity to write grossly improbable fiction featuring insufferably silly detectives, then some men (S. S. Van Dine) are clearly "women" and (theoretically at least) some women are really "men."[104] What Chandler did in this essay was to redefine gender and national identities in terms of performance. Identity had less to do with biology than with performing certain behaviors and costuming oneself in certain ways.

Raymond Chandler's "The Simple Art of Murder" makes what Judith Butler calls "gender trouble."[105] What good is a binary model of gender if some of the men are women, some of the women are men, and switching from one gender to the other is as easy as moving one's murders from ancestral estates to the wrong side of the tracks? The virulence of Chandler's attack on the "old ladies" of the London Detection Club is a measure of his anxiety about the slipperiness of the boundary he draws between men and women.[106] This gender dynamic—emphatically returning women to their appropriate, traditional place while simultaneously calling into question the categories on which such a nostalgic politics is based—is characteristic of hard-boiled fiction between the wars, a point to which I return in Chapter 6.

Chandler's essay suggests that the war of words between the pulps and the slicks over which would represent ordinary Americans was both economic and psychic. Chandler wanted his books to sell as well as Dorothy Sayers's and Agatha Christie's. The residual world of pulp publishing was locked in a struggle for readers with the emergent world of mass-market magazines that were much more attractive and affordable, thanks to national-brand advertising. Chandler's emphasis on "realism," however, suggests that this debate was also about competing visions of the real. Amy Kaplan identifies realism as a site of struggle over how to represent a world grown increasingly unrepresentable because of rapid social change, increasing class differences, and the emergence of competing forms of mass culture.[107] If this is the case, then slick-paper magazines and the classical detective fiction they printed offered a version of reality that placed women, women's ways of knowing, and the consumption in which middle-class women engaged at the center. Pulp magazines and the hard-boiled fiction they marketed placed the disappearing artisanal world of men in the position of privilege. The war of words between the pulps and the slicks was part of a larger debate over the ways in which mass consumption would change how ordinary people experienced the world. This debate was carried out through the overlapping and mutually constitutive idioms of gender, class, and nation. Moreover, the heat of the rhetoric—the pains to which the pulps and the slicks went to distinguish themselves from each other—is evidence of just how difficult it was to tell artisanal, American men from genteel, Anglophile women in a consumer culture where identities were increasingly constructed through performance.

The Adman on the Shop Floor

Workers, Consumer Culture, and the Pulps

Pulpwood magazines offer two methods of escape from
reality: one, by their fiction—that magic carpet that carries the
reader off to parts unknown; the other, by their advertising
of comparatively inexpensive means to keep the reader
physically and mentally fit so that he can take the hero's part
in any romantic adventure he reads about, or dreams of
having himself.

Advertising pages are as much a part of the magazine as
those devoted to stories: parallel lines spoken by two sets of
people with but a single thought....

Harold Hersey, *Pulpwood Editor* (1937)

"Crack! His fist landed squarely behind the bully's ear and down
he fell in a heap. Quick as a flash, he turned to face the other
hold-up man who, with a fist closed, was right on top of him.
Another thud and another limp form lay on the ground.
Quivering with tense excitement, he stood over the two prostrate figures waiting for them to get up, but they did not
move. Both were knocked cold."[1] A fight scene from one of
the many hard-boiled crime stories printed in *Black Mask* in
the 1920s and 1930s? It certainly sounds like it. But this
pugilistic passage comes not from *Black Mask*'s fiction but
from its ad pages. It was offered as proof not of the hard-

boiled hero's physical prowess and unquestionable manhood, but of the effectiveness of Earle E. Liederman's bodybuilding program, which was heavily promoted in *Black Mask* during this period.

The ads and the fiction that appeared in *Black Mask* sound remarkably similar. Both concerned themselves with work, manliness, and the embodiment of class and social position in dress, speech, and manners. Both were sparsely illustrated and relied heavily on dialogue and first-person narrative. Together they articulated a working-class variant of consumer culture that has been mostly overlooked in studies of American magazines and advertising.

Pulp advertising and pulp detective fiction were engaged in a complex relationship of reciprocal influence that engaged both the everyday concerns of white, working-class men and the products of the new consumer economy. With their monomaniacal dedication to work, anxiously overdone manliness, obsessive interest in clothing and interiors, and tough-talking machismo, hard-boiled private eyes were the perfect salesmen for the products advertised in *Black Mask*—job training by correspondence, bodybuilding programs, conduct manuals, and elocution lessons. After hard-boiled fiction had sold readers on the benefits of skilled, autonomous work, physical prowess, and the importance of reading how class and power are embodied in dress, speech, and manners, it remained only for advertisers to step in with the necessary products.

But hard-boiled detective stories also articulated the day-to-day concerns of working-class men, beset increasingly by de-skilled work, the incursion of women into their all-male spaces, and the astronomical growth in education and literacy that made their relative lack of formal schooling an increasing hindrance. Advertisements, most of which were bound in separate sections at the front and back of the magazine, offered material solutions to the psychic needs articulated by the fiction. These ads offer a wealth of clues to the readers whom pulp publishers targeted, the kinds of appeals they found effective, and the reader concerns they could profitably exploit.

Reading Ads, Reconstructing Readers

Roland Marchand, a historian of advertising, points to several significant methodological limitations of using advertisements as clues to popular worldviews: "We do not know exactly why they were popular or successful; we do not know if audiences shared or adopted the ideas presented; and we have reasons to suspect that the authors had motives or biases that did not completely coincide with those of the audience."[2] Although I agree that we do not know why any single advertisement was popular, I believe that examining a large body of successful ads for resemblances in the appeals they make does tell us something about what was important to readers of that magazine. Further, although we do not know whether audiences shared or adopted the attitudes put forth in advertisements, we do know that it was in the financial interest of advertisers to make appeals that culminated in a purchase. If the same kinds of appeals endured over a period of twenty or thirty years, we can reasonably conclude that whether or not readers agreed with the ideas, they found the ads compelling enough to buy the product. Finally, although the men who wrote and placed ad copy in pulp magazines were educated members of an emergent professional-managerial class, they had to perform a class ventriloquism of sorts in order to entice working-class shoppers to buy.[3]

Admen could easily measure the effectiveness of the ads placed in pulp magazines, because most were mail-order ads.[4] Mail-in coupons included a tracking number to identify the magazine or group of magazines from which the reader had clipped the ad, giving the advertiser an accurate count of consumers reached through a specific periodical. Pulp advertisers often paid according to the quantity of orders received rather than paying a fixed amount for the advertising space.[5] This kind of consumer-feedback loop allowed advertisers to pinpoint the most effective appeals for a particular reading public.

Most important, indirect sources such as advertisements are among the few material remains we have with which to construct a plausible scenario of how the readers of pulp magazines read their lives into these texts and these texts into their lives. Constructing such an account, however speculative, is necessary if we wish to write a representative history of reading in America.

Advertising and the Working Class

Examining pulp magazines complicates the history of American magazines and advertising in the early twentieth century. It is a scholarly commonplace that the working classes were invisible in advertising between the wars, that advertising's public consisted of the upper and upper-middle classes—those with large enough disposable incomes to be consumers on a significant scale.[6] "One has to search diligently in the ads of the 1920s and 1930s to find even fleeting glimpses of such common scenes as religious services, factory workers on the job, sports fans enjoying a boxing match or baseball game, or working class families at home," Roland Marchand writes.[7] To be sure, such scenes were largely missing from mass-circulation magazines between the wars, but depictions of working-class families at home, factory workers on the job, and books that promised to teach one to box littered the ads in pulp magazines.

For example, ads for the International Correspondence School (I.C.S.) were ubiquitous in pulp magazines. Harold Hersey, the publisher of dozens of pulps, claimed that I.C.S. ad copy was "as familiar as the fiction sheets themselves."[8] He thought that had he known more about I.C.S. students— how old they were; where they lived; their race, class, and religious beliefs; which jobs they chose to train for; whether they finished their courses or got discouraged—he might have been able to sell more magazines by matching his editorial content more closely to their concerns.

These ads addressed working life from a variety of perspectives. Some included long testimonials from owners and managers about the value of I.C.S. training—how few I.C.S. men were out of a job in spite of the Depression, how a man who spent his lunch break learning more about his job was bound to rise into the executive ranks.[9] Others focused on working-class households: "Was *this* part of your marriage contract?" asked one ad. (See Illustration 1.) "Did you tell her that she would have to do the washing? That she would have to wear last year's clothes?"[10] Many of the ads were first-person narratives of an I.C.S. student's rise (or intended rise) through the ranks. One man explained how awkward it was to accept the congratulations of his foreman, over whose head he had been promoted because of his I.C.S. training.[11] Another man, who had noticed that all the recent promotions at his company were I.C.S. students, told his wife: "I've thought it out, Grace. I'm as good a man as any one of them. All I need is special training—and *I'm going to get it*. If the I.C.S. can raise other men's salaries, it can raise *mine*. If it can bring a better home with more comforts to Jim and his family, it can do it for *us*. See this coupon? It means *my* start toward a better job."[12] Citing the large and growing numbers of I.C.S. students fitting themselves for better jobs through independent study, the ad urged the reader to follow suit. The mail-in coupon at the bottom of the page listed occupations for which I.C.S. could train you—electricity, railways, wiring, machine-shop practice, builder, draftsman, sheet-metal worker, and a variety of other unambiguously working-class fields. Workers were almost completely absent from the national-brand advertising in slick-paper magazines and on the radio, but the ads in pulp magazines were clearly for and about them.

Pulp Magazines as Consumer Culture

Scholarship on advertising and consumer culture focuses almost exclusively on the middle class and the "respectable" media that targeted such people—slick-paper magazines, newspapers, and radio.[13] The history of mass-circulation (slick) magazines is so enmeshed with the history of American advertising as to be almost indistinguishable. Richard Ohmann goes so far as to suggest that these magazines "were an outgrowth of advertising which, in turn, was a strategy of big capitalists to deal with the historical conditions in which they found themselves"— persistent overproduction and the resulting need to sell more goods. Christopher Wilson calls slick monthlies "the crucible of modern consumer culture" because they originated national-brand advertising and market research on a large scale and because they were the primary institution through which consumer rhetoric penetrated almost all other aspects of American life.[14]

There was hardly an aspect of slick-paper publication not transformed by this collaboration with national-brand advertisers. Here is a partial list of the changes:

> It transformed the publisher from dealer in editorial wares to dealer in consumer groups as well. It helped to expand the role of magazines, and it significantly altered the publisher's attitude toward circulation. It stimulated the publisher to research, especially in the characteristics of the market he served and in the effectiveness of his publication in reaching that market. It affected the format of magazines and their presentation of editorial copy. It raised the threat of influence by advertisers on editorial policy.[15]

Moreover, recent scholars have convincingly argued that fiction and advertising were mutually reinforcing discourses in slick-paper magazines between 1880 and 1920. Advertising-supported magazine fiction prepared the way for advertisers of specific brands by featuring certain product categories in a favorable light and by encouraging readers to conceive of themselves as consumers. The professional-managerial class emergent around the turn of the century was constituted, at least in part, by the ads and fiction in these mass-circulation magazines.[16]

Was *this* part of your marriage contract?

DID you tell her that she would have to do the washing? That she would have to wear last year's clothes? That she would have to skimp and save to buy even the necessities of life?

For her sake—for the sake of the children who are growing up—*for your own sake*—don't let the precious hours of spare time go to waste.

Make up your mind right now that not another day shall pass until you make your start toward success. Simply say "*I will,*" and the International Correspondence Schools will come to you with the help you need. Do it to-day!

*Mail the Coupon for
Free Booklet!*

- -

INTERNATIONAL CORRESPONDENCE SCHOOLS
Box 2129, Scranton, Penna.

Without cost or obligation, please tell me how I can qualify for the position or in the subject *before* which I have marked an X:

BUSINESS TRAINING COURSES

☐ Business Management
☐ Industrial Management
☐ Personnel Organization
☐ Traffic Management
☐ Business Law
☐ Banking and Banking Law
☐ Accountancy (including C.P.A.)
☐ Nicholson Cost Accounting
☐ Bookkeeping
☐ Private Secretary
☐ Spanish   ☐ French

☐ Salesmanship
☐ Advertising
☐ Better Letters
☐ Show Card Lettering
☐ Stenography and Typing
☐ Business English
☐ Civil Service
☐ Railway Mail Clerk
☐ Common School Subjects
☐ High School Subjects
☐ Illustrating   ☐ Cartooning

TECHNICAL AND INDUSTRIAL COURSES

☐ Electrical Engineering
☐ Electric Lighting
☐ Mechanical Engineer
☐ Mechanical Draftsman
☐ Machine Shop Practice
☐ Railroad Positions
☐ Gas Engine Operating
☐ Civil Engineer
☐ Surveying and Mapping
☐ Metallurgy
☐ Steam Engineering
☐ Radio

☐ Architect
☐ Architects' Blue Prints
☐ Contractor and Builder
☐ Architectural Draftsman
☐ Concrete Builder
☐ Structural Engineer
☐ Chemistry   ☐ Pharmacy
☐ Automobile Work
☐ Airplane Engines
☐ Navigation
☐ Agriculture and Poultry
☐ Mathematics

Name..

Street
Address..   3-6-24

City.....................State.........................

Occupation...
Persons residing in Canada should send this coupon to the International Correspondence Schools Canadian, Limited, Montreal, Canada.

1. Ads for I.C.S.—International Correspondence Schools—were ubiquitous in pulp magazines between the wars. (*Black Mask* VII, No. 8, October 1924, p. 7, courtesy of the International Correspondence Schools)

Those magazine historians who have addressed pulp magazines agree that the pulps were untouched by the "magazine revolution" of the 1890s, which allowed slick-paper publishers to achieve huge circulations by selling magazines cheaply and relying on advertising to pay the substantial production costs.[17] Pulps were essentially repackaged dime novels—leftovers from the nineteenth century. They were comparatively ad-free, and unlike the subscription-driven slicks, they relied overwhelmingly on newsstand sales.[18] Their history is, at best, a footnote to the central story of American magazines in the twentieth century—the collaboration of mass-market magazine editors and advertisers in the consolidation of consumer culture.

Sean McCann offers the best articulation of this position:

> While pulp magazines ... undoubtedly play an important part in the making of a national commercial leisure culture, they were not really the step in the advance of the Culture Industry for which they are often taken. In fact, it was the slick magazines that displayed so many of the culture critics' most lamented side effects of commodification—from pure mass appeal and shallow lifestyle mongering through market surveying. Pulp magazines, by contrast, remained small-scale, under-capitalized, nearly preindustrial "dealers in reading matter."[19]

In McCann's view, the pulps were "almost passive conduits of fiction," conceived of by their publishers as "essentially low-cost distributors of reading material." This residual publishing world provided a half-century window of protest against the rise of commodity culture as embodied in the pages of their slick competitors, and offered a living to a group of writers who lacked the education and cultural capital required for employment in more respectable publishing outlets.[20]

This is essentially the tale told by pulp writers and publishers of the time. *Black Mask* and others claimed that since pulp fiction was able to sell itself without the assistance of glossy illustrations and shiny ads, pulp fiction was clearly superior to the stories found in slick-paper magazines. Pulp publisher Harold Hersey discussed the structure of the publishing industry in a 1937 memoir: "There is a great show made about the independence of the editorial from the advertising department in a smooth-paper sheet. It is freedom in name only. . . . The pulp, on the contrary, has little or nothing to worry about in this regard."[21]

This account of pulp magazines and advertising is a misleading one. It is true that the pulps were not as dependent on national advertisers to cover their costs of production and that they ran, proportionately, many fewer ads than most slicks of the time. For example, *Black Mask* carried from eight to twenty-five pages of advertising in the 128-page magazine between the wars, whereas the average slick-paper magazine was more than half ads by 1907 and more than 65 percent ads by 1947.[22] Nevertheless, pulp magazines did engage consumer culture meaningfully, although in a different way from their slick cousins. Moreover, the focus of consumer-culture scholarship on white, middle-class women has left a huge area—the consumption of leisure and recreational goods by men—largely unexplored.[23]

Pulp magazines' significant participation in consumer culture is easy to overlook because of the distinction between the pulps and the advertising-supported slicks—a distinction that commentators of the period eagerly reinforced. However, the line between pulp publishing and slick-paper publishing was not really all that sharp. The magazine industry in the early twentieth century was not neatly divided into a few corporate slick-paper publishers on one hand and many small, independent pulp publishers in a competitive free market on the other. There were a few giants, but most magazine publishers of both pulps and slicks were relatively small businesses engaged in fierce competition for readers and advertisers. Both types of magazine saw large numbers of start-ups and failures.[24] Failures, replacements, sales, and name changes were so common that even industry insiders had difficulty keeping track of who published what. Street & Smith's internal business records from the 1930s contain a "Supplementary Index for Group Magazines" listing the company's competitors and the pulps they published. The list is rife with handwritten additions, deletions, and notes of name changes.[25]

Moreover, the slick-paper publishers and the pulp publishers were often one and the same. Frank Munsey owned both *Argosy*, the first pulp, and *Munsey's*, whose price reduction had kicked off the slick-paper "magazine revolution." It made no difference to Munsey whether his money came from pulps or slicks, just as long as it came. Street & Smith killed off its remaining pulps after World War II, when production costs got too high, and concentrated on the more profitable slicks.[26]

The pulp market looked more competitive than it actually was. Although there were many pulp magazines with relatively small circulations, few companies published only one title. Most owned a line of magazines and quickly replaced any titles that became unprofitable. Pulp titles had a lower profit per issue than slick titles, so a long list of titles was necessary for a respectable income.[27] Street & Smith, the largest company, had approximately thirty-five pulp titles at any given time; Popular Publications had twenty to twenty-five. Other major houses were Munsey's, Dell, Fiction House, Standard, Warner, Culture Publications, and Clayton Magazines.[28] Publishers that owned strings of publications frequently sold advertising space in the whole group as a unit, reporting combined circulation when the figures were required. *Black Mask* belonged to such a group.[29] Many editors edited more than one pulp—sometimes as many as eight or ten—and the companies often shifted editors from magazine to magazine.[30] In addition, there was a great deal of traffic in fiction between the various magazines owned by a single company. A story purchased for one pulp quite often ended up in another in the weekly or monthly last-minute scramble to fill the pages of every magazine. Street & Smith, for example, regularly moved stories among *Clues, Detective Story, Crime Busters,* and *The Shadow.*[31]

Fiction also traveled between pulps and slicks. Dashiell Hammett was probably sent to *Black Mask* after initially publishing in *Smart Set,* the upscale periodical that H. L. Mencken and George Jean Nathan had hoped to subsidize with the profits from *Black Mask* and two other pulps. H. C. North, an early editor of *Black Mask,* apologized for the long delay in rejecting one of Erle Stanley Gardner's stories, for he had sent it along to *Smart Set*'s editors to see whether they wanted it. It was no secret that stories rejected from the pulps often later found homes in slick-paper magazines. North told Gardner that he fully expected to see the rejected story appear unrevised in *The Saturday Evening Post* or *Cosmopolitan,* since this had happened many times in the past.[32]

Finally, many magazine publishers did a lot more than put out magazines. They also published books and newspapers, owned radio stations, and made educational and industrial films. Some of the larger companies were vertically integrated, involving themselves not only in publishing but in paper milling, marketing, subscription, and distribution.[33]

Clearly, pulp publishing was as intimately enmeshed with corporate capitalism as was slick-paper magazine publishing, and the boundaries between pulps and slicks were a good deal more porous than the rhetoric from either side would suggest. Frederick Clayton, the editor of the pulp magazine *Argosy,* made this point in an irate letter to the *New York Times* after the *Times* had published an essay defaming the pulps. Offering a substantial list of writers who published simultaneously in the pulps and the slicks, Clayton concluded: "No! Slick-paper magazines and pulp-paper magazines are not the worlds apart that you imagine them to be...."[34]

Pulp editors were also masters of market research, a practice at the center of discussions of consumer culture and slick-paper magazines.[35] They were forever surveying their readership about their likes and dislikes in order to create a more marketable product. Almost every pulp had columns of reader letters, ran periodic surveys of readers, or included mail-in coupons on which a reader could rank his or her favorite stories and authors in each issue. To encourage readers to take part, such inducements as free issues of the company's other pulps were offered. Street & Smith's *Crime Busters* offers the best example of market research at work in the pulps. Absolutely everything in *Crime Busters* was regulated by reader feedback. Each month two or three pages of text were given over to analyzing the numbers from reader rankings of stories in the previous month's issue. Using text and graphics, *Crime Busters'* editors demonstrated how they had learned from reader feedback to increase the number of satisfied readers with each successive issue.

Moreover, *Crime Busters* encouraged its writers to tailor their fiction to reader desires: "We give each of our authors complete returns on the ballots, and every one gets all remarks and comments on his own story in detail, as well as a general summary of all other remarks and suggestions. We have created a keen rivalry among the authors, all seeking to land on the top when the ballots are counted. That all means that they strive to give you the very best they've got."[36] *Crime Busters* even surveyed readers on the advertising that best met their needs, promising them a free magazine for the return of the ballot. Readers were asked their age, occupation, sex, marital status, weekly salary, the ages of family members, and a variety of consumer data. Did they own or rent their home? Did they have a car? What about life insurance? What brands of toothpaste, shaving cream, razor blades, and hair tonic did they use? Which brands of cigars, cigarettes, beer, or whiskey did they usually buy?[37]

Erle Stanley Gardner, the *Black Mask* writer most interested in getting reader feedback in order to help him tailor his fiction, employed a disabled veteran in a VA hospital to keep an ear out for comments from fellow residents about stories in the pulp magazines they regularly read.[38] Gardner repeatedly asked Joseph Thompson Shaw, *Black Mask*'s editor, to run mail-in ballots for readers to vote on favorite authors and stories.[39] The lack of reliable data on reader desires was an endless source of frustration for him: "Sitting out here in the sticks all I can do is get hunches, and sometimes put two and two together and make six. . . . And it irritates me, for the thing that I love above all things is getting data and analyzing sales possibilities. I wish I could get more of a slant on the situation."[40]

Gardner's letters are full of speculation about the best way to measure reader satisfaction.[41] He considered letters from readers "about the best opportunity, both an editor and an author have, of checking up on the popularity of a story."[42] Industry opinions were divided on this issue. *Detective Fiction Weekly*, for instance, used letters to shape the magazine in meaningful ways, but publishers at Fawcett simply ignored letters, regarding those fans who would bother to write as not representative.[43] What the pulp industry did agree on, whether or not letters were viewed as a useful tool, was that one should tailor fiction to meet reader desires—that stories were market-researched products.

Black Mask's market research during the '20s and '30s was typical. In 1922, *Black Mask*'s editor twice included a note to readers requesting feedback on that month's issue,[44] and periodic requests for reader input continued throughout the '20s and into the Depression. In the early years, *Black Mask* printed letters from readers, some of which meticulously critiqued every story in the previous issue.[45]

In one 1923 issue, the editor clothed his market research in the familiar rhetoric of family and community. Under the title "We and Our Readers," he invited the reader to become a personal correspondent of the editor: "A bond of cordial good feeling exists between our readers and us. They guide us in everything we do in *Black Mask*. You are cheerfully invited to join this big, growing family and to get into the habit of writing to the editor. Send him your criticisms, your suggestions. He'll always answer you personally and maybe print your letter in 'Our Readers' Private Corner.'"[46] The relationship between buyer and seller in this formulation was constituted not by the exchange of currency but by "a bond of cordial good feeling." Although *Black Mask* had tens of thousands of subscribers in the early 1920s, the editor represented them not as a mass, but as "family." Moreover, writing to the editor was imagined as personal communication rather than commercial correspondence. In this way, *Black Mask* engaged modernity in the same way advertisers did. "Through consumer response, through trial and error, and through close observation of the other media of popular culture," Roland Marchand writes, "advertisers gradually observed and responded to a popular demand that modern products be introduced to them in ways that gave the appearance and feel of a personal relationship."[47] In this way, advertisers (and pulp editors) could adopt profitable but faceless modern business practices while soothing the concerns of individuals about the growing impersonality of the marketplace.

Black Mask's packaging of market research changed over time. Around 1926, the advertisements for makeup, lessons in dressmaking, and bust enhancers disappeared, along with fiction aimed at women. He-man rhetoric replaced editorial lip service to family. In 1929, Shaw inaugurated another round of market research with a personal appeal to readers, headlined "HELP!" At a recent meeting, Shaw explained, he had insisted to the admen at *Black Mask* that he knew what *Black Mask* readers really liked to read. The admen had laughed at him. Angered, Shaw said, he had made a sizable wager that he could pick out the reader favorites from the stories in the two most recent issues. He called on readers to help him win this bet by mailing in the names of their favorites.[48]

Once again, market research was imagined in terms of small communities characterized by personal exchanges. You, as the reader, were not helping a corporation market its product better, you were helping out your old friend Cap Shaw, who had engaged in some pretty heavy wagering with the corporate types. That the bad guys in this scenario were admen is a wonderful bit of irony. Shaw got his market research done by begging readers to come to his defense against professional market researchers.

The wager was important. Wagering was one of many all-male rituals through which communities of working-class men were constituted and consolidated early in the century.[49] To invoke this ritual in the context of corporate marketing did the same kind of ideological work that the rhetoric of family had once done: It made the enormous, impersonal scale of national markets knowable to individual readers. This example worked somewhat differently, however, because it evoked all-male communities, reconstituting the disappearing homosocial spaces of working men. If mass-produced consumer culture was being rhetorically integrated into the fabric of working-class life, it was nonetheless being made attractive and familiar to working men only, a departure from the middle-class variant, which targeted the wife as the family's purchasing agent.

The appearance of a new column or department in *Black Mask* was inevitably followed by an invitation for readers to make their opinions known. Did they like it? Dislike it? What would make it better? Should it continue? In 1930, Shaw began a column in which readers and writers could exchange ideas, a department that grew out of reader demands made in letters over the years. At the end of the first column, Shaw asked, "Does she get the gas or does she get the brake? ... It's up to you. ... Just say what you want. ... We want only to please."[50] Shaw's metaphors put the male reader in the driver's seat, in control of a feminized automobile whose exclusive purpose was to bring him pleasure.

This is not to say that pulp-magazine editors and admen always behaved in identical ways. If the slick-paper advertisers assumed that they were rational men writing to appeal to a body of irrational, flighty, female consumers,[51] *Black Mask* often asserted that its readers were welcome on the production and marketing end as well.[52] One example is a campaign that *Black Mask* ran to increase circulation in the mid-1920s. "Are you with us?" the title of one column asked. "You fellows who read the *Black Mask* every month and think it's just about the best magazine of its kind—will you lend us a hand? We know there are a lot of you who do think so, because we get your letters and our sales are increasing. The question is, will you tell your friend Bill about it—and maybe Hank and Pete also?"[53] The desire for increased market share here was articulated not in percentages or aggregates, but as getting Hank, Pete, and Bill to read *Black Mask*. More important, *Black Mask* was in effect hiring its readers to be marketing agents and distributors. They were offered the imaginative equivalent of corporate bonuses (cash, prizes, free subscriptions) based on the number of new readers they brought in. Campaigns such as this had been used by *Ladies' Home Journal* and other women's magazines since the turn of the century, the idea being to harness women's social networks to sales, while framing the activity as one of sociability rather than commerce. *Black Mask* masculinized this common practice.

This rhetoric, which effaced the real, material boundaries between producers and consumers, manifested itself in other ways. In 1924, Phil Cody, *Black Mask*'s editor, published a "Notice to Our Readers" (yet another market-research scheme) in which he made all of *Black Mask*'s readers associate editors. Telling them they had approximately 125 pages to dispose of as they saw fit, he urged them to mail in proposals for their ideal edition of *Black Mask*—favorite authors, stories, types of stories, departments, ideal length of features, favorite magazines they would like *Black Mask* to resemble, and so on. He ended his invitation with a call to work: "This is your magazine; you are on its editorial staff; get on the job!"[54]

In some ways, imagining consumer research as hiring your readers had the same results as figuring mass publics as family, or as the guys in the neighborhood saloon. Workplaces, like homes and bars, were knowable spaces. To imagine market research as employment was to make it familiar to working-class men. In other ways, however, thinking of readers as employees opposed the ideology of slick-paper ads. Whereas admen in the slicks were convincing/seducing a female public to buy their wares, *Black Mask* admen were inviting readers like themselves to engage in all-male rituals. Whereas consumers hailed as feminine were to think of shopping as choosing a suitor, the masculine consumers hailed by *Black Mask* were to think of their purchases as a ritual adjunct to joining a lodge or men's club. The desired outcome was the same—the reader bought the magazine and its advertised goods—but the rhetoric through which the selling took place drew the lines between "us" (editors and admen) and "them" (consumers) differently. Rather than offering wisdom from on high, *Black Mask* talked to its consumers man-to-man.

As market-researched products of corporate publishing houses, pulp magazines engaged in the promiscuous intermingling of commercial and editorial content that slick-paper magazines had pioneered. The slicks had done away with separate advertising sections by the 1910s and early 1920s, dissolving the physical boundary between promotion and features. The separation persisted longer in the pulps, but by the mid-1930s *Black Mask* had begun to embed one-third–page and half-page ads within the text of the magazine.[55] Further following the practices of slick-magazine publishers, *Black Mask* sometimes positioned ads next to editorial matter that would enhance their powers of persuasion. For example, a new column taking readers' questions about fingerprints appeared next to an ad for a program that would teach you how to become a fingerprint expert.[56]

Strengthening the connection, *Black Mask* made use of what is known as "editorial copy"—ads that blended into the editorial content of the magazine, sometimes mimicking the fiction with which they appeared.[57] Editorial copy revealed that even the noncommercial parts of magazines were, in fact, commercial. "Follow this Man!" urged an ad from the late 1920s. "Secret Service Operator 38 is on the Job." A brief narrative of adventure, danger, and intrigue every bit as overblown as those appearing in the issue's fiction followed, before the ad finally promised that you, too, could live this glamorous life if only you learned the science of fingerprints in your spare time.[58] Another ad urged, "Be a Detective / Make Secret Investigations / Earn big Money, Work home or travel / Fascinating Work. Excellent Opportunity. Experience Unnecessary."[59] It was a small ad, all text, with no elaborate narrative. The advertiser didn't need to convince readers that the occupation was glamorous, exciting, and manly, because the *Black Mask* stories with which his ad was bound already did that. They were, in a sense, part of his ad copy.

The authors were another crucial link between the worlds of advertising and hard-boiled fiction. During the 1920s Dashiell Hammett wrote detective stories for *Black Mask* in the afternoon, having spent his morning writing ad copy for a San Francisco jeweler. He was, by all reports, an extraordinarily successful copywriter.[60] The meticulous descriptions of clothing and interiors that characterize Hammett's fiction and the ability of his private eyes to make judgments based on small details of self-presentation resonate deeply with ads of the period. The hard-boiled hero's capacity to read the class and character of a suspect from his dress, speech, and bearing was not so different from the ever-vigilant eye of the adman, calling attention to poorly cut clothes, out-of-fashion furniture, and poor grammar, which might ruin one's chances in life if not remedied at once.

The influence was reciprocal. Not only did hard-boiled fiction function as advertisements for certain product categories, but during the dark days of the Depression admen appropriated the term "hard-boiled" for themselves. When panicked and poverty-stricken consumers stopped buying, admen were laid off in droves. Those who remained responded by reimagining themselves as "hard-boiled" salesmen, turning their attention back to the bottom line (selling) from their forays into art and pandering to the feminine masses in the 1920s. Through this appropriation of images of blue-collar masculinity (rolled-up sleeves, clenched fists, muscular arms, hard work), white-collar admen allied themselves with producer/artisans rather than with the fickle shoppers whose "consumer constipation" was to blame for the state of the economy.[61]

Pulp ads and slick ads advertised different kinds of goods. Slick-paper ads evoked powerful desires and feelings of inadequacy that could be assuaged only by the purchase of consumer goods. Pulp ads, on the other hand, tried to convince working-class readers that additional work, training, or self-help would lead to a better-paying job.[62] Pulp ads were a kind of remediation for working-class consumers, designed to help them earn enough money to make it worthwhile for advertisers to bother creating or evoking their consumer desires.[63] A slick-paper ad might try to sell you a tie; a pulp ad was more likely to urge you to supplement your income by selling ties to others. The process of pursuing the middle-class income necessary to become a mainstream consumer involved a particular kind of consumption as well—of correspondence courses, etiquette books, elocution lessons, and job training.

The Case of *Black Mask*

From 1920 to 1951, *Black Mask* ran ads that consistently pushed the same products and services—bodybuilding, job training, and guides to self-presentation through proper speech, manners, and dress. The copy constantly circled around the same themes—manhood, skilled and remunerative employment, the perpetually critical appraising eye of others. Mail-order coupons delivered consumer feedback, and consistent response rates proved that these products and pitches maintained their appeal. *Black Mask* readers, in other words, were the kind of people who read for these things, who were predisposed to interpret their texts and their world in terms of these concerns.

The largest group of *Black Mask* ads was concerned with employment and income—getting a job, keeping a job, getting a better job, making extra money (in your spare time! without ever leaving home!). The sparest ads contained little more than headlines giving the job title and a high-end salary: "Be a Railway Traffic Inspector: Earn Up to $250 per month," "Earn $75 to $200 a week: Be an Auto Expert."[64] Others promised that readers could easily supplement their incomes: "You can Make $18 Daily Selling Scissors" or "$25 a day selling shirts."[65]

Black Mask advertisers also engaged in contemporary debates over workplace conditions. Between the Civil War and World War II, the American industrial-labor market underwent "homogenization." Scientific management, Fordism, and production speed-up reduced formerly skilled jobs to unskilled or semiskilled levels, wrested control of the labor process away from skilled workers, and created an ever-larger supervisory corps of engineers, foremen, and managers.[66] Ads such as the I.C.S. series repeatedly urged readers to get the training they needed to obtain skilled work that retained a measure of autonomy.

This ad for Coyne's training program in the new field of electricity (see Illustration 2) is representative: "If you are tired of being a cog in a machine—or tired of working in an uncertain, 2x4-inch job with no future—here is a real opportunity! . . . Stop Gambling With Your Future and LEARN ELECTRICITY where jobs hunt men at $50 a week and up. . . . No Experience or Education Needed! Practically any man can master the "ins-and-outs" of Electricity—as taught in the Great Shops of Coyne. You don't need one bit of previous experience or any more than common-school education. Any number of our highly successful graduates never completed eighth grade."[67]

Note that this ad equates an unskilled worker with "a cog in a machine"—someone performing a dull, repetitive function. Reduced to an easily replaced part, the worker had no job security or hope of mobility. A "man" skilled with electricity, on the other hand, earned a higher wage, and his expertise let him negotiate with employers from a position of power. Note, too, that the lack of formal education was no hindrance to professional success. Countless ads in *Black Mask* made similar reassurances. Targeting readers with limited education, many other ads promised a high-school diploma or its equivalent in a hurry. "Go to school at home!" the American School of Correspondence urged. "High School Course in Two Years!" Even booksellers tried to jump on the bandwagon. "Is a High School Education worth $2.98 to You?" asked one, offering a set of sixty home-study textbooks.[68]

The language used in these *Black Mask* ads echoed the speech of working men addressing one another. One advertised training method was "so simple, thorough, and up-to-date that you can easily understand and apply every line of it—no big words, no useless theory, no higher mathematics—just plain, every-day, straight-from-the-shoulder, man-to-man English—the kind you and I use everyday."[69] This ad not only distinguished useful knowledge from the kind obtained in school; it was full of resentment against the exclusionary rhetoric of the more literate. This ad both flattered a working man's sense of himself and encouraged him to stay in his socially sanctioned place. It reflected his plainspoken, manly way with words back to him as superior to more educated, effete ways of speaking. Of course, the assurance that he need not bother himself with the language of the well-educated also insured that he would never move with ease outside the circles into which he had been born.

Not coincidentally, autonomous work, plain speaking, and manliness meshed in the world of *Black Mask*. In the culture of workers

WHEN?

IF YOU WERE FIRED TOMORROW

If the boss came down with a grouch—or you made a mistake—And You GOT FIRED, could you get another job at the same pay right away? Or would you have to go job-hunting like any ordinary untrained man who gets fired? Think it over! If you are tired of being a cog in a machine—or tired of working in an uncertain, 2x4-inch job with no future—here is a real opportunity! Read about it—it may be the big turning point of your whole career!

Stop Gambling With Your Future and

LEARN ELECTRICITY

WHERE JOBS HUNT MEN AT $50 A WEEK AND UP

LET me make you a real money-maker. Let me take you out of the "hired-help" class—and start you on the road to real success, in 90 days. Make up your mind to say good-bye forever to precarious, tiresome, routine jobs—crabby bosses—and low pay that can never be more than $35 or $40 a week! You don't need to tolerate them any longer!

Amazing Opportunity

Electricity is calling for trained men—and Coyne, 12-week graduates are at the top of the preferred class. Hundreds of them have stepped out of our doors into wonderful jobs paying from $75 to $200 a week! And our free employment bureau regularly secures 40 to 90 positions a week for others.

Learn Without Lessons

Electricity is surprisingly easy to learn this practical way without books or dry lessons. That's the secret of Coyne training. All training consists of ACTUAL and PRACTICAL work on fine big electrical equipment—dynamos, transformers, etc. (Real ones—not models). You learn by doing—and experts work right with you every step of the way.

FREE R. R. FARE
Right now I am making a special offer to pay any man's railroad fare to Chicago from any point in the U. S., upon enrollment. Send coupon for details.

No Experience or Education Needed!

Practically any man can master the "ins-and-outs" of Electricity—as taught in the Great Shops of Coyne. You don't need one bit of previous experience or any more than common-school education. Any number of our highly successful graduates never completed eighth grade.

2 Extra Courses FREE

If you act now—I'll not only pay your railroad fare to Chicago—but I'll give you two big, extra courses absolutely without charge—RADIO and AUTOMOTIVE ELECTRICITY. Furthermore, I'll help you to locate a part-time job while learning! FREE employment service after graduation, too. We place 40-90 men in wonderful jobs every week!

Send for FREE Book

Just give me a chance to tell you about the wonderful things that Electricity has in store for you after 12 happy weeks at COYNE. Send the coupon for my free, illustrated book containing over 150 photographs and details of my special offer. No obligation. Mail it today!

BIG BOOK FREE

COYNE
ELECTRICAL SCHOOL
H. C. Lewis, President, Dept. 27-66
1300-10 W. Harrison St.
CHICAGO, ILL.

Coyne Electrical School,
H. C. Lewis, Pres., Dept. 27-66,
1300-10 W. Harrison St., Chicago, Ill.
Dear Mr. Lewis:
Without obligation, send me your free illustrated catalog and details of your R. R. Fare offer.
Name ....
Address ....
City .... State ....

vi   Please mention NEWSSTAND GROUP—MEN'S LIST, when answering advertisements   Feb.

2. Many *Black Mask* ads urged readers to get the training they needed for jobs that retained a degree of autonomy. (*Black Mask* IX, No. 12, February 1927, p. vi, courtesy of Coyne American Institute)

throughout the nineteenth century and into the twentieth, calling someone a man acknowledged his "dignity, respectability, defiant egalitari-
anism, and patriarchal male supremacy."[70] *Black Mask*'s ad pages were
filled with a variety of goods that could enhance one's manliness: guns,
motorcycles, bodybuilding programs, weight training. Manliness in such
a culture involved not only skilled, autonomous work that earned a family wage, but feats of physical strength and courage.[71] An Earle Liederman ad asked: "How Strong Are You? Can You do These Things?
Lift 200 or more overhead with one arm; Bend and break a horse shoe;
Tear two decks of playing cards; Bend spikes; Chin yourself with one
hand?"[72] Charles Atlas related how he transformed himself from a
skinny, flat-chested weakling to the "World's Most Perfectly Developed
Man" through exercise. His picture offered proof of his prowess.[73]

The authenticity of the manhood created by these programs was
beyond question, the ads insisted. "I don't just give you a veneer of
muscle that looks good to others," stated Earle Liederman in one of his
ads (see Illustration 3). "I work on you both inside and out. I not only
put big, massive arms and legs on you, but I build up those inner muscles that surround your vital organs. The kind that give you real pep
and energy, the kind that fire you with ambition and the courage to
tackle anything set before you. . . . When I'm through with you, you're
a real man. The kind that can prove it."[74]

Pulp ads promised transformed selves and remade bodies, and they
sold the necessary accessories. *Black Mask* advertised a .38-caliber "real
'He-Man' gun," and an automatic described in phallic terms: "a man's
gun built for hard service. .32 calibre, shoots 10 quick shots, hard and
straight."[75] Another indispensable extension of a he-man's body was the
Harley Davidson Twin—"the Mount for a He-Man!"—which put an
awful lot of power between a man's legs.[76] *Black Mask* advertised he-
manly periodicals such as *Real Courage* ("You will like it . . . for every
REAL MAN likes it"), and *Field and Stream*, which tailored an ad to hard-
boiled fiction fans: "It takes a he-man with good, red blood in his veins
to enjoy *Black Mask* (we don't believe there are many couch-cooties
reading it), and it's very seldom that a he-man with red blood in his veins
doesn't thoroughly enjoy days and nights in the open with rod or gun."[77]

Such reassurances about the integrity of a reader's manliness suggest
anxiety about the stability of gender identity. If men were paid a family wage for performing skilled, autonomous work outside the home,
what did the de-skilling of manufacturing jobs and scientific manage-

If You Were Dying To-night

and I offered you something that would give you ten years more to live, would you take it? You'd grab it. Well fellows, I've got it, but don't wait till you're dying or it won't do you a bit of good. It will then be too late. Right now is the time. To-morrow, or any day, some disease will get you and if you have not equipped yourself to fight it off, you're gone. I don't claim to cure disease. I am not a medical doctor, but I'll put you in such condition that the doctor will starve to death waiting for you to take sick. Can you imagine a mosquito trying to bite a brick wall? A fine chance.

A Re-Built Man

I like to get the weak ones. I delight in getting hold of a man who has been turned down as hopeless by others. It's easy enough to finish a task that's more than half done. But give me the weak, sickly chap and watch him grow stronger. That's what I like. It's fun to me because I know I can do it and I like to give the other fellow the laugh. I don't just give you a veneer of muscle that looks good to others, I work on you both inside and out. I not only put big, massive arms and legs on you, but I build up those inner muscles that surround your vital organs. The kind that give you real pep and energy, the kind that fire you with ambition and the courage to tackle anything set before you.

All I Ask Is Ninety Days

Who says it takes years to get in shape? Show me the man who makes any such claims and I'll make him eat his words. I'll put one full inch on your arm in just 30 days. Yes, and two full inches on your chest in the same length of time. Meanwhile, I'm putting life and pep into your old back-bone. And from then on, just watch 'em grow. At the end of thirty days you won't know yourself. Your whole body will take on an entirely different appearance. But you've only started. Now comes the real work. I've only built my foundation. I want just 60 days more (90 in all) and you'll make those friends of yours who think they're strong look like something the cat dragged in.

Earle E. Liederman as he is to-day

A Real Man

When I'm through with you, you're a real man. The kind that can prove it. You will be able to do things that you had thought impossible. And the beauty of it is you keep on going. Your deep full chest breathes in rich pure air, stimulating your blood and making you just bubble over with vim and vitality. Your huge, square shoulders and your massive muscular arms have that craving for the exercise of a regular he man. You have the flash to your eye and the pep to your step that will make you admired and sought after in both the business and social world. This is no idle prattle, fellows. If you doubt me, make me prove it. Go ahead. I like it. I have already done this for thousands of others and my records stand unchallenged. What I have done for them, I will do for you. Come then, for time flies and every day counts. Let this very day be the beginning of new life to you.

Send for my book

"MUSCULAR DEVELOPMENT"

It is chock full of large size photographs of both myself and my numerous pupils. Also contains a treatise on the human body and what can be done with it. This book is bound to interest you and thrill you. It will be an impetus—an inspiration to every red-blooded man. I could easily collect a big price for a book of this kind just as others are now doing, but I want every man and boy who is interested to just send the attached coupon and the book is his absolutely free. All I ask you to cover is the price of wrapping and postage—10 cents. Remember this does not obligate you in any way. I want you to have it. So it's yours to keep. Now don't delay one minute—this may be the turning point in your life to-day. So tear off the coupon and mail at once while it is on your mind.

EARLE E. LIEDERMAN

Dept. 1711, 305 Broadway, New York

EARLE E. LIEDERMAN
Dept. 1711, 305 Broadway, N. Y. City.

Dear Sir:—I enclose herewith 10 cents for which you are to send me, without any obligation on my part whatever, a copy of your latest book, "Muscular Development." (Please write or print plainly.)

Name ....

Address ....

City .... State ....

Please mention NEWSSTAND GROUP when answering advertisements

3. *Black Mask*'s ads placed great emphasis on physical strength and courage, offering readers all sorts of products and programs to enhance their embattled manliness. (*Black Mask* V, No. 7, November 1922, p. 121)

ment make laborers? Boys? Women? Cogs? In addition, the all-male communities through which working-class manhood was (re)produced were disappearing. *Black Mask* ads sought to reconstitute a culture of manly, skilled artisans, celebrating the power and pay of highly trained workers, their distinctive form of plain speaking, and the physical strength they valued. This is not to say that this worldview had unambiguously progressive political consequences. "If you want a steady Government position where strikes, hard times, politics, etc. will not affect you, where you can draw twelve months' pay every year and then when you become old be retired on a pension for the rest of your life, get on Uncle Sam's payroll," stated one ad.[78] This emphasis on earning a high and steady wage, however it may have benefited the worker who landed a government job, did not address the wages of laborers as a class. The ad's construction implied that layoffs and strikes were parallel occurrences, that both were merely interruptions in one's pay over which one had no control. It took no notice of the fact that most strikes during these years had strong grassroots support and that they often resulted in better wages for workers. Layoffs seldom did. Pulp ads, like hard-boiled crime stories, encouraged readers to think of themselves as individuals, not as classes or larger social groups. Hard-boiled heroes might talk back, demand autonomy at work from bosses and clients, and be knowledgeable navigators of the social world, but they do not belong to professional or labor organizations. Similarly, pulp ads prodded individual working men to rise in the world through job training and self-improvement, but did not proffer a vision of a fundamentally restructured class system.

What kind of readers do these ads suggest, and in what ways did ads try to shape readers' concerns and behavior? First, readers emerge as laborers who desired skilled and interesting work (men's work) at a decent wage. Second, these readers were learners, taught first that they needed some kind of training or knowledge and second that the advertised product could provide it. Moreover, they were people who wished to claim practical experience as a valuable (if not the most valuable) form of knowledge. They were believers in the power of skill and expertise, pursuers of individual self-improvement and social mobility. They also believed that such things came not only through job skills but through how one presented oneself.

Like the upscale ads Roland Marchand considers in *Advertising the American Dream*, pulp ads trafficked in the "parable of the first impression," which taught that careers and social reputations were made by one's appearance—clothing, manners, visible consumer choices.[79] In a large, complex, urban world, social exchanges increasingly took place between strangers. These strangers, with no prior knowledge of one another's character or history, had to make judgments based on appearance alone. In such a world, bad breath, poorly cut clothes, or a tacky living room could indeed spell disaster for one's career or social life.

In describing the transformation of American culture around the turn of the century, Warren Susman distinguishes between a nineteenth-century culture of character, tied to the needs of a producer economy of scarcity, and a twentieth-century culture of personality, tied to the needs of a consumer economy of abundance.[80] These were competing worldviews, residual and emergent, that often coexisted in an uneasy tension. Character was essential for maintaining the social order in an economy requiring hard work, thrift, and self-sacrifice, but the economy of abundance called for a personality that desired self-realization—specifically through the purchase of consumer goods—rather than self-denial. The cluster of terms that go with the culture of character have to do with one's moral fiber: duty, work, honor, reputation, integrity, and, most important, manhood. The culture of personality, in contrast, focused on manners, personal grooming, and apparel.[81]

Pulp magazines addressed themselves to the tensions between a residual model of identity based on one's essential character and an emergent one based on personality. What constituted manhood in a world where skilled artisanal work and the family wage that used to accompany it were eroding? If autonomous work and solidarity with shop-floor colleagues constituted a man's gender and class identities, where did a world defined increasingly by consumption and consumer choices leave him? Could a worker reconcile his manly, artisanal depths with the impression management seen as increasingly necessary for success in the modern world? Was manliness anything more than performance or masquerade (feats of physical prowess, ways of speaking), an identity constructed or reiterated from the raw materials of commodity culture?[82]

Like slick-paper magazine ads, pulp ads were forever making a reader aware of his possible failings in self-presentation and the social and professional consequences of these social gaffes. Pulp ads, however, devoted more text to elaborating the worldview that produced such concern for self-presentation. Pierre Bourdieu argues that because bourgeois labor markets reward qualities of appearance in a way that blue-collar work does not, the working class has less interest in self-presentation.[83] Consequently, pulp ads targeting workers had to make a case for the importance of self-fashioning. The long-winded didacticism of pulp ads such as this one is striking:

> In this day and age attention to our appearance is an absolute necessity if you expect to make the most out of life. Not only should you wish to appear as attractive as possible for your own satisfaction, which is alone well worth your efforts, but you will find the world in general judging you greatly, if not wholly, by your "looks." Therefore it pays to "look your best" at all times. Permit no one to see you looking otherwise; it will injure your welfare! Upon the impression you constantly make rests the failure or success of your life.[84]

Promoting a device that promised to straighten and beautify crooked or ugly noses, this ad targeted Jewish and southern Italian immigrants, who made up an increasingly large proportion of the American working class. With a tone of high seriousness about remaking immigrants, who lacked a classical profile, into "real" Americans, the ad insisted that life success depended on assimilation and reshaping bodies to pass for native-born. A slick-paper version of the ad might have asked, "Why didn't you get that promotion? Could it be your nose?" relying on readers to make the connection between appearance and career trajectory. Having been exposed to mass-market advertising since the turn of the century, professional-managerial-class readers of slick magazines were addressed as savvy consumers of ads, capable of making complex connections between succinct ad copy and illustrations, of grasping implied meanings based on their experience with advertising.[85] Because pulp publishers regarded their readers as still new to consumer culture and less at home with the kind of discourses that marked advertising, pulp ads sound verbose to the modern ear. These wordy ads were old-fashioned in style; they were hand-me-downs from the world of "respectable" advertising, which had cast them aside for more minimalist styles thirty or forty years earlier.

Pulp ads were text-heavy. This was partly because publishing photographs was expensive and cheap paper did not reproduce them well, but these text-driven ads may also have had specific appeal to a working-class audience. Turn-of-the-century publishers believed that busy businessmen preferred succinct ads, whereas farmers, housewives, and others with less education and less demanding careers would find long ads informative or entertaining.[86] In addition, these text-heavy ads, being what Judith Williamson calls "hermeneutic ads," addressed consumers specifically as readers or interpreters.[87] Selling education and literacy in addition to the products advertised, they gave back to consumers an image of themselves as serious readers, the kind of people who waded through densely packed prose uninterrupted by images.

Other pulp ads, such as the series for work clothes that Lee ran in *Black Mask* in the late '30s and early '40s, focused on dress, bearing, and manners.[88] Most were comic-strip ads, featuring working-class men who ceased languishing in their dead-end jobs and got promoted once they began dressing for success in Lee overalls. Lee urged these unambiguously blue-collar workmen—the carpenters, bricklayers, plasterers, sheet-metal workers, machinists, and plumbers for whom Lee manufactured overalls, customized for each occupation[89]—to adopt a white-collar way of purchasing and inhabiting clothes—for their appearance as opposed to their function. Early–twentieth-century workers distinguished carefully between work clothes and Sunday (leisure) clothes. One's work clothes were merely what was best for getting the job done. One's leisure clothes, however, were visible displays of self-respect and community standing in social rituals such as churchgoing and Sunday visits.[90] In urging workers to think of their work clothes as Sunday clothes, advertisers were importing a bourgeois way of viewing the world. In some sense, all bourgeois clothes were Sunday clothes in that they advertised the wearer's status by testifying to his independence from labor that might get him dirty. This bourgeois concern with work dress was an ill-fitting one where manual labor was concerned, however.

The uneasy coexistence of an artisanal model of identity and the new model of identity based on purchase and display of commodities is apparent in a 1941 Lee ad. (See Illustration 4.) "Many men think they are 'stalled' when actually they are just sidetracked because their real ability is disguised by ill-fitting, 'ordinary work clothes'," the copy read. "You can have that smart, get-ahead appearance with popular Lee 'promotion clothes'. They draw favorable attention to you and your work at no extra cost. . . ."[91] This ad maps a commodity-based model of identity onto an older model based on character. The ad claims that self-presentation, though it won't get you that promotion in itself, will make it possible for your "real ability" (character) to become visible. "You had the ability all the time!" the wife of a newly promoted worker tells her husband in another Lee ad. "Lee overalls made you look the part!"[92]

Like the admen Marchand discusses, who smoothed the road to modernity by giving new products the voices of old friends, these ads

Do You Want Promotion?... More Pay?

Do You LOOK The Deserving Man You Are?

Many men think they are "stalled" when actually they are just sidetracked because their real ability is disguised by ill-fitting, "ordinary work clothes". The remedy's simple.

You can have that smart, get-ahead appearance with popular Lee "promotion clothes". They draw favorable attention to you and your work at no extra cost per month of wear and with a big plus in both pride and comfort!

Your Lee will fit *you!* It's made on exclusive Lee tailored-size patterns for your build, your size, your weight. It will *wear*—and *keep* its good looks. Lee uses exclusive fabrics—Agan Jeans, Treg Twills, Jelt Denim—each Sanforized-Shrunk*.

Don't wait. Start with Lee now. You can't lose because every Lee is guaranteed to look better, fit better, last longer—or your money back! See your Lee dealer. Mail the coupon.

Lee UNION-MADE · TAILORED SIZES · SANFORIZED-SHRUNK
*Fabric Shrinkage Less Than 1%.

FREE! Mail Coupon Now!

COLOR-MATCHED SHIRTS & PANTS ✓
OVERALLS ✓ . . . *Genuine Jelt Denim*
UNION-ALLS ✓ . . *with the Hinge Back*
DUNGAREES ✓   SHOP COATS ✓

THE H. D. LEE MERC. COMPANY   Dept. P-6
(Address Nearest Factory)
Kansas City, Mo.   Minneapolis, Minn.   Trenton, N. J.
South Bend, Ind.   San Francisco, Calif.   Salina, Kans.
Please mail me free illustrated literature, color swatches, and name of my nearest Lee Dealer. Am interested mostly in
☐ Overalls ☐ Union-All ☐ Whipcords ☐ Shirts & Pants

Name_____

Address_____

City_____ State_____ W4106

4. This ad for Lee work clothes, like many in *Black Mask*, promised that social and professional success would come to those who learned the art of impression management. (*Black Mask* XXIV, No. 2, June 1941, inside back cover, courtesy of the Lee Corporation)

eased the transition from an artisanal depth model of identity to a com-modity-based surface model by maintaining that these two ways of con-ceiving of the world did not actually conflict. At least in this ad, the residual culture of skilled working men coexists easily and effortlessly with consumer culture; commodity capitalism, in fact, helps a working man gain recognition for his skill and expertise.[93] The ad uses a mar-keting trick known as the bait and switch. Working-class men are drawn in by the promise of recognition for their embattled artisanship, but the ad offers them a new outfit instead, assuring them that it amounts to the same thing. Although the availability of ready-made clothes depended on the mass-production techniques that were responsible for de-skilling the clothing trades, this ad nevertheless insisted that con-sumer culture would help an artisan get ahead at work.

Among the most numerous impression-management ads were those promoting self-help guides to perfecting speech and writing. They often began with questions—tests of a reader's failings in self-presentation. "Do You Make these Mistakes in English?"; "Are You Ashamed of Your English?"; "Does YOUR English Betray You?" they demanded.[94] The dire consequences of such failures were made clear by what followed:

> Every time you talk, every time you write, you show what you are. When you use the wrong word, when you mispronounce a word, when you punctuate incorrectly, when you use flat, ordinary words, you handicap yourself enor-mously. A striking command of English enables you to present your ideas clearly, forcefully, convincingly. If your language is incorrect it hurts you more than you will ever know, for people are too polite to tell you about your mistakes.... A command of polished and effective English denotes educa-tion and culture. It wins friends and favorably impresses those with whom you come in contact. In business and in social life correct English gives you added advantages and better opportunities, while poor English handicaps you more than you now realize.[95]

We can draw a number of conclusions from this ad. (See Illustration 5.) First, there are several implied readers. The fact that such ads were more likely to stress the reader's English than his speech or writing suggests an immigrant readership, but the questions could also address a native speaker who desired to distinguish himself from the immigrant masses through cultivated and eloquent speech.

Second, the subjects in this ad are unambiguously the performance-based subjects of Susman's culture of personality. ("Every time you talk, every time you write, you show what you are.") In this paradigm, non-

Do You Make these Mistakes in ENGLISH?

Sherwin Cody

Many persons say "Did you hear from him today?" They should say "Have you heard from him today?" Some spell calendar "calender" or "calander." Still others say "between you and I" instead of "between you and me." It is astonishing how many persons use "who" for "whom," and mispronounce the simplest words. Few know whether to spell certain words with one or two "c's" or "m's" or "r's," or with "ie" or "ei." Most persons use only common words—colorless, flat, ordinary. Their speech and their letters are lifeless, monotonous, humdrum. Every time they talk or write they show themselves lacking in the essential points of English.

Every time you talk, every time you write, you show what you are. When you use the wrong word, when you mispronounce a word, when you punctuate incorrectly, when you use flat, ordinary words, you handicap yourself enormously. A striking command of English enables you to present your ideas clearly, forcefully, convincingly. If your language is incorrect it hurts you more than you will ever know, for people are too polite to tell you about your mistakes.

Wonderful New Invention

For many years Mr. Cody studied the problem of creating instinctive habits of using good English. After countless experiments he finally invented a simple method by which you can acquire a better command of the English language in only 15 minutes a day. Now you can stop making the mistakes which have been hurting you. Mr. Cody's students have secured more improvement in five weeks than had previously been obtained by other pupils in two years!

Learn by Habit—Not by Rules

Under old methods rules are memorized, but correct habits are not formed. Finally the rules themselves are forgotten. The new Sherwin Cody method provides for the formation of correct habits by constantly calling attention only to the mistakes you yourself make—and then showing you the right way, without asking you to memorize any rules.

One of the wonderful things about Mr. Cody's course is the speed with which these habit-forming practice drills can be carried out. You can write the answers to fifty questions in 15 minutes and then correct your work in 5 minutes more. The drudgery and work of copying have been ended by Mr. Cody! You concentrate always on your own mistakes until it becomes "second nature" to speak and write correctly.

FREE—BOOK ON ENGLISH

A command of polished and effective English denotes education and culture. It wins friends and favorably impresses those with whom you come in contact. In business and in social life correct English gives you added advantages and better opportunities, while poor English handicaps you more than you now realize. And now, in only 15 minutes a day—in your own home—you can actually see yourself improve by using the 100% self-correcting method.

A new book explaining Mr. Cody's remarkable method is ready. If you are ever embarrassed by mistakes in grammar, spelling, punctuation, pronunciation, or if you cannot instantly command the exact words with which to express your ideas, this new free book, "How to Speak and Write Masterly English," will prove a revelation to you. Send the coupon or a letter or postcard for it now.

SHERWIN CODY SCHOOL of ENGLISH
179 Searle Building   Rochester, N. Y.

- - - - - - - - - - - - - - - - - - - -

SHERWIN CODY SCHOOL OF ENGLISH
179 Searle Building, Rochester, N. Y.
Please send me your Free Book "How to Speak and Write Masterly English."

Name ....

Address ....

City .... State................

5. *Black Mask* ads promised that social and material success would come to those who learned to write and speak as owners and managers did. (*Black Mask* IX, No. 7, September 1926, p. 6)

standard pronunciation and poor spelling and grammar were not merely an unfortunate veneer that disguised your true talents; they were, in fact, you. The good news was that you could get the "education and culture" associated with proper speech and writing and make yourself indistinguishable from those who had been raised with such advantages. This metamorphosis worked on both the individual and mass levels, since the proliferation of bourgeois speech and manners diluted their power to signify class distinctions. Note, however, that the ad invites readers to conceive of themselves as individuals rather than as part of a class. The polished speaker was not expected to powerfully articulate the needs of the laboring classes, but only to get himself a better job.

Third, the ad breeds insecurity. You were not to trust your own judgment, since you did not even know when you were making the errors in speech and writing that would condemn you to social and professional stagnation. In this ad, colleagues were too polite to tell you of your failings. In others, they didn't know enough to advise you: "Unless you have a perfect guide you may be holding yourself back from whatever business and social advancement you desire."[96] Rather than relying on his father or on friends or coworkers, a man needed a paid expert to guide him through his self-fashioning.[97] These ads did not reconcile new ways of making sense of the world, new ways of constituting subjects, with old ones. They discredited traditional worldviews and folkways in order to replace them with the authority of corporate experts.[98]

Black Mask was full of ads touting successful men who had learned "How to Work Wonders with Words," as the title of one such guide put it. In the world of these ads, this skill gave men more power and pay at work: "It is the power of forceful, convincing speech that causes one man to jump from obscurity to the presidency of a great corporation." It allowed laborers to overcome their lack of formal schooling: "With only a grammar school education, I could never express my ideas in a coherent, self-confident way."[99] Finally, it made workers men, since the metamorphosis from strangled silence to articulate self-assertion was unambiguously gendered. One man described the shock of his colleagues when his fifteen minutes a day of at-home oratory paid off in a powerful speech at work: "They thought I was a Weak Sister—But I took their Breath Away."[100] Moreover, the power of speech in these ads was not so much about convincing others as about talking them into submission. The caption for one ad read: "Afraid of My Own Voice, But I Learned to Dominate Others Almost Overnight." This ad's happily-ever-after was the protagonist's learned ability to "bend others to my will . . . dominate one man or an audience of thousands."[101] The promises of such ads raise a number of troubling issues about authenticity, about how identities are formed and read. If a man's rise in social and professional life was fueled not by character but by clothes, speech, and manners, how did one distinguish the men of true merit from the fakes? Did decking oneself out in the trappings of success make one successful? The persistence of these ads suggests that a significant number of working-class men found these ideas persuasive enough to try to remake their bodies and their words. These impression-management ads were much more common in *Black Mask* than in *Detective Fiction Weekly* or *Dime Detective*, its primary competitors, echoing *Black Mask*'s editors' greater preoccupation with "class" readers.

Another type of ad overtly addressed questions of identity, pushing cheap imitations of commodities associated with wealth, access, and power. The most common ads were for "lachnite gems," which were promoted as virtually indistinguishable from genuine diamonds, even by experts. The ads promised that if anyone questioned the "diamond" ring's authenticity within ten days, the buyer could return it for a complete refund. A later version of the ad boasted that 200,000 people were now wearing these lachnite gems, all presumably passing them off as diamonds.[102] This promotion had subversive potential. Once fake diamond rings became commonplace, the genuine articles would lose their power to signify wealth and privilege. These ads both urged workers to pass for bourgeois and made bourgeois status more difficult to recognize.

Identities were constructed diferently in the ads that focused on class mobility and those that focused on manliness. A man could transcend his working-class upbringing by mastering proper clothing, manners, and speech, but could not achieve manliness through masquerade. *Black Mask* readers, as the ads constructed them, could have their cake and eat it too. Their manliness was beyond question, but their social position could be altered through a little dedication and some wise purchases. To hold such mutually contradictory convictions must have been difficult—a difficulty testified to by the incessant reassurances about the ease and substantial rewards of class ventriloquism and the authenticity of manhood.

The readers who emerge from what presumably were successful advertising appeals in *Black Mask* were overwhelmingly working men. These men had lost a sense of collective gender and class identity because the production in which they were engaged had become less important than the consumer goods they could or couldn't afford to buy and display. For three decades, advertisers in *Black Mask* made use of these anxieties in complex and contradictory ways. They promised job training and bodybuilding to reconstitute the fading culture of autonomous, manly artisans while simultaneously pushing the impression management necessary in the consumer society that had contributed to its decline. Every worker socially and economically enabled by his newfound facility at impression management was one fewer citizen of the disappearing artisanal culture.

If the ads are to be trusted, *Black Mask* readers, into the 1940s, still hoped to demonstrate the physical prowess, patriarchal male supremacy, and free agency of "real men," although this feat required an increasing number of purchases. The world of impression management was still so new as to require all sorts of bolstering and justification. Some admen insisted that attention to one's appearance would help bring a working man recognition for his expertise; others emphasized the need to replace inadequate traditional forms of authority with corporate experts. These strategies testify to what was at best an uneasy rapprochement between consumer culture and working-class life for *Black Mask* readers.

Black Mask ads and fiction were presented as almost seamlessly connected. Ads urged readers to become skilled, well-paid workers; hard-boiled heroes knocked heads with clients and agency owners over their workplace autonomy. Ads urged readers to remake themselves into real men; *Black Mask* fiction gave them role models. Ads focused readers' attention on the wrinkles in their clothes, the errors in their speech, and the vulgarity of their manners; the magazine's heroes offered instruction in reading how class, gender, and power relationships were embodied in dress and bearing.

In some ways, these ads and the products they sold can be seen as empowering to readers, offering individual workers the skills necessary to make sense of bourgeois culture. These texts also urged individual workers to train themselves for work that was still comparatively autonomous. In other ways, however, these ads addressed readers exclusively as individuals, closing off possibilities for considering themselves a class with common interests worth pursuing collectively. At bottom, *Black Mask* cast class position in terms of individual enterprise rather than institutional arrangements that might require political change or redress.

These advertising appeals, because they were refined by years of consumer feedback, can help to reconstruct readers who left little archival evidence. Popular ads that speak consistently to a particular set of concerns strongly support the inference that these issues mattered in readers' lives, that they profoundly shaped their ways of reading the world.

PART II

Reading Hard-Boiled Fiction

The more closely a subject relates to what is familiar to the
given reader, the more interesting it is.
What People Want to Read About (1931)

The expression of the readers' predispositions, and hence
their influence, does not stop once the publication is in the
readers' hands. Other acts of "selection" take place during
the actual reading and affect the readers' interpretations.
What Reading Does to People (1940)

These epigraphs come from a group of studies on the reading
practices of ordinary people, conducted in the 1930s by
scholars affiliated with Douglas Waples at the University of
Chicago Library School.[1] What did people from various different walks of life want to read? What kinds of printed
material were available to them, and at what prices? What
reading skills did they have? What did people actually read?
How were their choices influenced by their gender, age, education, income, and place of residence? How could librarians and adult-literacy workers better serve their needs?

Factory workers were of special concern to these
researchers. What kind of reading would their long days of

labor allow? What could be done to increase the appeal of reading and to decrease the appeal of drink and dissolution? What was to be done about workers' preference for pulp magazines over more "suitable" forms of literature? Though these studies had some limitations—they focused primarily on nonfiction, the categories of analysis were inconsistent, and they often began with the assumption that workers' reading choices needed to be improved—they are nonetheless among our best sources of information about readers who were outside the record-keeping classes, and about the kinds of print they encountered.

Affordable and accessibly written, pulp magazines were the literature of choice for most workers. Librarians, educators, and cultural critics of all kinds lamented that the proletariat, in fact, read little else. Pulp editors, publishers, and advertisers concurred that the targeted readers of detective, Western, and adventure pulps were young, working-class men with little formal education. In a 1931 study, readers of this class reported that they were interested in reading about labor, the labor market, and getting ahead in their jobs, topics that interested better-educated men and women very little.[2] Moreover, if advertisers are to be trusted, these readers' desires to get ahead on the job extended into concerns with manliness, skilled, well-paid work, and the self-fashioning necessary for social mobility. What would such readers have made of the hard-boiled detective stories that filled pulp magazines between the wars? If we bring a reconstructed mechanic's eye to bear on these stories, what aspects stand out?

For these readers, hard-boiled detective stories were centrally concerned with the loss of workplace autonomy, the appropriation of white men's historic privilege by women and uppity ethnics, and the diminished importance of production work compared with consumption—an activity in which women were more likely to engage. These stories were "Americanizing" narratives in that they hailed readers as normatively white, implicitly bourgeois, and male. If one were still enmeshed in the dense networks of kin and culture that defined ethnic enclaves, hard-boiled detective stories addressed one as a man for whom work was all-consuming and family and community ties almost completely absent. Such fiction encouraged a reader to think of himself in unhyphenated "American" ways, ways that defined selves as autonomous, self-serving individuals. Moreover, ethnicity and race in these texts were figured as performances, positions one could take up and inhabit when it served one's interest. In this way, hard-boiled fiction, like much mass culture in the 1930s, urged a rearrangement of the overlapping identities of the ethnic working class, emphasizing the common ground of class experience over the differences of language and culture that had stymied organizing across lines of national origin until the formation of the C.I.O. (Congress of Industrial Organizations) in 1937.[3]

Hard-boiled detective stories also managed some of the psychic fallout from the transformation of work by Taylorism in the 1920s and 1930s. Skilled workers of older, northern-European stock were increasingly being replaced by unskilled and semiskilled workers from southern and eastern Europe, and the expertise that once resided in the mind of the master craftsman increasingly belonged to the white-collar engineers and managers who oversaw the work of the new immigrants. Concern with getting ahead on the job increasingly meant concern about the loss of autonomy (read manhood) on the shop floor and the erosion of the family wage that had accompanied skilled craft work. The disappearance of distinctions between their skilled, white, manly selves and those unskilled, not-so-white, effeminate, or even female others was cause for concern. What did it mean for a labor aristocracy of skilled, white men when the jobs they had done were carried out by blacks, Chinese, the swarthy masses from southern and eastern Europe, and (God forbid) women, who were entering paid work in record numbers between the wars? Further, what did it mean for this labor aristocracy when they were no longer paid the real or virtual wages of whiteness that had come to feel like their birthright since the nineteenth-century consolidation of an American working class? *Black Mask*'s detectives were nostalgic re-creations of the autonomous craftsman, who was increasingly at odds with the modern, bureaucratic world.

The landscape of working-class life was also transformed between the wars by the rise of consumer culture. Department stores appeared in cities and suburbs, mass-marketed magazines ruled the day, and in the 1920s advertising went through its first golden age. Working-class men and women inhabited this consumer society and defined themselves in (or against) its terms. Although marketers initially targeted buyers with larger wallets, by the 1920s the better-paid fraction of the working class could also participate in consumer culture in significant ways. Many had radios, and almost all went to the movies, dance halls, or amusement parks. What was a working man to do when the basis of his class and gender identity—all-male production work—became less important than the skill with which he purchased and displayed commodities?

Hard-boiled detectives paid close attention to the details of self-presentation—speech, dress, manners—demystifying the ways in which
gender, class, and culture were embodied in consumer society. The
hard-boiled hero was a nostalgic re-creation of the artisan, but he was
at the same time a pragmatic manipulator of commodities, a savvy citizen of a consumer's world.

Hard-boiled detective stories were also sites for working out the new
relationships between men and women at work, relationships that often
differed little from the patriarchal marriages characteristic of the generation before. Detective pulps were places where male privilege was
imaginatively reinvented, where women who took up men's work were
nonetheless defined in domestic and subordinate ways. Nevertheless,
there is enough "gender trouble" in these texts to suggest a Utopian,
transgressive space between biological sex and performed gender.

The piecework prose producers who were the first authors of hard-
boiled detective stories created texts that managed working-class men's
anxieties about modern life. These texts shaped readers into consumers
by selling them what they wanted to hear: stories about manly artisan-
heroes who resisted the encroachment of commodity culture and the
consuming women who came with it.

Proletarian Plots

The dingus is still undoubtedly rather complicated.

Dashiell Hammett on his novel *The Dain Curse*

Mr. Chandler's plots ... drift up one picaresque side alley
after another, like a dog looking for a lamp-post.

Ralph Partridge, reviewer

The hard-boiled detective seems an unlikely proletarian hero.[1]
He is not a worker in the traditional sense, or even labor's
ally. Like the operatives of the most famous detective agency,
the Pinkertons, who functioned largely as strikebreakers, the
private detective is usually hired to protect the interests of
those with significant property.[2] Nevertheless, if we take
working-class readers seriously as active makers of meaning,
we can hear the "mechanic accents" of this fiction and recognize its resonance with structures of feeling prominent in
the early–twentieth-century worker's life. The detective
worked in a seedy neighborhood, took flak and interference
from his employers, struggled to make ends meet, spoke a
tough, colloquial slang, and showed a great deal of concern
with his working conditions and his autonomy on the job.
Workers exhausted from long hours of labor and in need of
escape and distraction made hard-boiled fiction their own,
since it was cheap, available, readable, and easily interpreted
in light of their everyday concerns.

Hard-boiled fiction was a profoundly ambivalent proletarian literature, however.[3] It addressed the reader specifi-

cally as an individual, a way of thinking of oneself more characteristic of the bourgeoisie.[4] The early–twentieth-century American working class was overwhelmingly a class of first- and second-generation immigrants, men and women who were part of dense, self-enclosed networks of family and kin bound together by ties of religion, ethnicity, and work. Family connections helped land an individual a first job, and the family's stability and financial well-being determined how his wages would be used. Since industrial work between the wars was increasingly routine, menial, and unsatisfying, many workers valued family and community over their occupation or the products of their labor.[5]

In stark contrast, hard-boiled detectives were individuals completely defined by their work. Dashiell Hammett's Continental Op, who appeared in thirty-six short stories and two serialized novels in *Black Mask* in the 1920s, remains nameless throughout his career, known only by his job title. He has no wife, no children, no parents, no home to speak of, no fraternal organizations, no emotional attachments to anyone. Reading such fiction was an imaginative escape from the ethnic enclave, an invitation to imagine oneself as an individual, an unhyphenated *American* individual. Moreover, this fiction helped habituate new immigrants from southern and eastern Europe to the work routines and work culture of earlier immigrants from Britain, Ireland, and Germany, whose anxieties about the de-skilling of craft work shaped labor's agenda well into the 1930s.[6]

The workaholic private eyes who filled *Black Mask*'s pages between the wars had everything to do with changes in the structure of work in the early decades of the twentieth century.[7] Scientific management pioneered by Frederick Winslow Taylor challenged workers' notions about the links among manhood, skill, and autonomy at work. These challenges were most acutely felt by the skilled workers, who were disproportionately native-born or earlier immigrants from northern and western Europe. Pulp detective fiction was involved in the renegotiation of these men's gender and class identities.

In other words, one of the ways working men appropriated these tales was as allegories about workers' control and autonomy. Although scientific management dates from the 1910s, major conflicts between labor and management over its implementation on a significant scale came in the late '20s and early '30s.[8] This places hard-boiled pulp fiction squarely in a time characterized by intense struggles over who would control the pace and method of production. These struggles informed both the form

and subject matter of hard-boiled fiction in complex and politically contradictory ways. Although the narrative structures of hard-boiled fiction
were continuous with the logic of scientifically managed work, the plots
were used by readers to voice opposition to the de-skilling of work and
to invoke a powerful nostalgia for a culture of artisans.

Taylor-ed Plots

The plots of hard-boiled detective stories were notoriously complex
and convoluted.[9] While working on the 1946 screen adaptation of Raymond Chandler's *The Big Sleep* (1939), Howard Hawks and William
Faulkner, the director and screenwriter, respectively, got into an argument over who had killed the Sternwoods' chauffeur, Owen Taylor.
They wired Chandler, who was working on a screenplay at another studio. Chandler reportedly considered the question for a while and wired
back that he hadn't the faintest idea.[10]

The Big Sleep starts as an investigation by Philip Marlowe into an
attempt to blackmail Carmen Sternwood, the daughter of a wealthy
general, over her gambling debts. Arthur Geiger, the blackmailer, owns
a bookstore that fronts for a pornography ring. He is shot while taking
pornographic pictures of Carmen, who has clearly been given a sizable
dose of illegal drugs. Geiger's body is stolen from the scene of the crime.
Owen Taylor, the Sternwoods' chauffeur (who had once eloped with
Carmen), is found dead the next morning, hit over the head before his
car was sent off the end of a pier. Joe Brody, another blackmailer with
ties to the dirty-book trade, threatens to make public the pornographic
pictures of Carmen (stolen from Geiger, but not by Brody). Carmen's
older sister, Vivian, thinking she will have to pay Brody off, goes to a
gambling tycoon named Eddie Mars for the money. Carmen arrives at
Brody's with a gun, looking for the pictures. Before they can either buy
or forcibly reclaim the pictures, however, Brody is shot by Carol Lundgren, Geiger's male lover, who thinks that Brody was Geiger's killer. (He
wasn't.) Geiger's body reappears. Marlowe rescues Vivian from one of
Mars's armed thugs. Carmen shows up naked in Marlowe's bed.

Agnes, the late Joe Brody's girlfriend, gets a new beau, Harry Jones,
who claims to know where Marlowe can find Rusty Regan, Vivian
Sternwood's husband, who disappeared before the action of the novel
began. But Lash Canino, Eddie Mars's gunman, kills Jones before he
can tell Marlowe where. No matter, because Agnes knows where to

find Eddie Mars's wife, who had supposedly run off with Regan. (She hadn't.) Marlowe is captured by Canino, but Mars's wife falls in love with Marlowe and sets him free. Marlowe kills Canino. Carmen tries to kill Marlowe, confirming his suspicion that she killed Regan, which made it necessary for Vivian to team up with Eddie Mars to cover it up. Mars, thinking that General Sternwood knew about the murder and cover-up (he didn't), then hired Geiger to blackmail the general in exchange for their silence about the crime. Nobody knows who killed the chauffeur.[11]

I exaggerate only slightly in my retelling of the events of the novel. At the close of this book, not only am I not sure whodunit, I am in a great deal of doubt as to what "it" is—murder, blackmail, pornography, dope dealing, homosexuality, whatever. Faulkner and Hawks fared no better, leaving the *New York Times* film reviewer to lament: "If somebody had only told us . . . just what it is that happens in . . . *The Big Sleep*, we might be able to give you a more explicit and favorable report. . . . But with only the foggiest notion of who does what to whom—and we watched it with closest attention—we must be frankly disappointing about it."[12]

Reviewers of the period in "reputable" publications seem to have been preoccupied with the inordinately complicated plots of hard-boiled fiction and film, and the almost tangential nature of what readers of classical fiction would call the central puzzle. The novels are "confusing," "involved," "a bit too puzzling," and "a bit illogical"; "only the inoculated and inured can follow . . . all the details."[13] What so troubled readers from elite backgrounds, however, would have had a great deal of resonance for those who performed scientifically managed work.[14] As the jobs of skilled workers were broken down into minute, repetitive tasks requiring little skill, an individual worker had less need to understand the entire process through which labor and raw materials became finished goods. Just as one could read and enjoy the loosely linked scenes of action in hard-boiled fiction without being particularly concerned with the larger story, one could do one's scientifically managed task effectively without having any sense of how it fitted into the whole.[15]

Tania Modleski makes a similar argument about the narrative form of soap operas and the structure of women's work in the home.[16] Soap operas, like housework, never end. Plots are episodic and repetitive, capable of being followed by a woman simultaneously performing repetitive household chores. The interlocking domestic crises of soap characters resemble the interpersonal negotiations that characterize daily life in many families, and the soaps' frequent close-ups of faces make it easier to read emotions, a skill crucial to women's work nurturing men and children. In part, soaps teach ways of thinking necessary for housework: "Daytime television plays a part in habituating women to distraction, interruption, and spasmodic toil."[17]

Similarly, reading hard-boiled fiction, which lacked a coherent narrative trajectory, was a training ground for the kind of thinking necessary for Taylor-ed jobs. Among other things, it habituated readers to working without an overview. Or, looked at from the other direction, the work experience of laborers allowed them to tolerate aspects of hard-boiled texts that troubled bourgeois reviewers. If structures of feeling are cultural, then what constitutes an unacceptable level of confusion or absence of a larger organizing principle must also be conditioned in part by one's occupational and intellectual training.[18]

Irvin Faust, who wrote the critical afterword to Paul Cain's aptly named *Fast One* (1933), prefers the term "interlocking action" to "plot" for discussing hard-boiled novels.[19] Rather than plots in the usual sense, these novels are composed of linked episodes—a sequence of action-packed scenes, violence, drinking, and tough talk—that resonated with everyday life in working-class communities. Reviewers' complaints notwithstanding, these are not necessarily failed plots; they are plots that do not respect the unities of bourgeois cultural organization and logic. Hard-boiled plots formalize or organize the strategies that Michel de Certeau discusses under the rubric of "poaching," inviting readers to make contact with the story at odd, isolated moments without concerning themselves with an overarching narrative.

Besides being unbelievably complicated, hard-boiled novels move at a fantastic rate—a consequence, no doubt, of the pace of their production. Memoirs of pulp writers are filled with accounts of how fast they wrote, how little they edited, how much prose they produced, and what tricks they used to keep the words flowing.[20] Reviewers from the 1930s and '40s inevitably commented on the "fastness" of these novels as a way of offering high praise.[21] Speed at this point in history had a great deal of cultural resonance. Theorists of modernity discuss how evolving technology and administrative practices changed how people experienced time and space.[22] Railroads, the telegraph, steamships, improved postal service, continuous-process machinery, and improved (and increasingly bureaucratized) administrative coordination of the flow of goods made manufacture and distribution faster. Profit came from high turnover at lower prices rather than from the sale of a few higher-priced items. In this kind of world, to move quickly was a good thing. The transition from the task-oriented time of agricultural societies to industrial work-time involved thinking of time as a currency—something that could be sold, spent, or saved.[23]

Fast novels participated in this reconceptualization of time. The rapid accumulation of murders in Dashiell Hammett's *Red Harvest*, originally serialized in *Black Mask* in the late 1920s, may be a record in the history of mystery fiction.[24] Moreover, the sense of speed in hard-boiled fiction is intensified by its terse, almost telegraphic language, its heavy reliance on taciturn dialogue, and its short, action-packed chapters. Speed may also make the reader less concerned about how complicated these worlds are. If one moves through them quickly, one is less likely to notice the loose ends. Moreover, having speed forced on them by managers and machines at work, these readers found that harnessing speed to bring them pleasure gave them a feeling of mastery. John Kasson argues similarly that workers who visited Coney Island around the turn of the century enjoyed the inversion of their usual relationship to technology: It did things *to* them at work, but it did things *for* them at Coney Island.[25]

The structure of hard-boiled stories—their complexity and the speed with which they move—was marked, then, by the social world of the working-class readers they targeted, a world homologous with the writers' piecework prose production. This form differed markedly from the structures of the classical detective fiction against which hard-boiled writers defined themselves. The (effeminate, genteel) classical fiction tied up all the loose threads and dispelled any remaining mystery at the denouement. The (manly, artisanal) fiction of hard-boiled writers featured fast-moving, incomprehensibly complex plots and corruption that persisted at the close.[26]

The English Country House Versus the Mean Streets

A comparison of two detective novels from 1933 will make this distinction clearer. Frederick Nebel's hard-boiled *Sleepers East* and Agatha Christie's classical *Murder on the Orient Express* highlight the structural and epistemological differences between the two types of detective fiction. Each centers on a murder that occurs on a stranded train, but the reading experiences they offer differ markedly. Whereas Christie's novel offers a coherent narrative connecting all the extraneous details of the plot—a managerial overview, so to speak—Nebel's novel is full of interesting explication but ultimately makes little sense.

Murder on the Orient Express, which earned such high marks for improbability from Raymond Chandler, takes place in a sleeping car on a three-day trip from Stamboul, Turkey, to Calais, France.[27] On the second night out, in Yugoslavia, the train is stopped by snowdrifts. In the morning, one of the passengers, a Mr. Ratchett, is found stabbed to death. Hercule Poirot, Christie's eccentric Belgian detective, happens to be traveling in the same car, and applies his "little grey cells" to solving the mystery. Poirot is pleased with the case for two reasons: First, this exercise in reason will help to while away the hours while the train remains stranded; and second, the murder is a particularly satisfactory little problem of deduction because Poirot is cut off from the more pedestrian forms of detection, such as background checks and police records, and forced to rely entirely on his wits (44). The three parts of the novel are titled in accordance with the deductive method: "The Facts," "The Evidence," and "Hercule Poirot Sits Back and Thinks." Poirot limits his exertions to making lists of the passengers' evidence, the unanswered questions, and the curious "suggestive points" on which the case hinges—a pipe cleaner, a broken watch, a grease spot on a Hungarian passport, a dropped handkerchief with an "H" monogram, a missing button, and a red kimono.

Each of the twelve suspects in the sleeper—supposed strangers, "people of all classes, of all nationalities, of all ages" (22)—turns out to have been connected in some way with a celebrated child-kidnapping in America, the Daisy Armstrong case. The murdered man, Ratchett (really a notorious gangster named Cassetti), had kidnapped and killed Daisy Armstrong, but had escaped punishment on a legal technicality. Constituting themselves as a jury of twelve, the Armstrongs' friends, relatives, and remaining household servants took turns stabbing Ratchett. In the final pages of the novel, Poirot presents the truth to the closed circle of passengers, explaining the extraneous pipe cleaners, red kimonos, grease-stained passports, missing buttons, broken watches, and other troublesome trivia. Those assembled decide that justice has been done, so they agree on a story for the Yugoslavian police that will close the investigation. All the loose ends are explained at the close, all the dissonance and confusion relieved. More important, justice is served. The truly guilty man is punished, the good go free, and the prelapsarian circle of innocents from the right kind of families is restored.

Sleepers East is a radically different type of tale.[28] Departing from the usual hard-boiled formula, it features two detectives—an official of the railroad and a sleazy, money-hungry private eye—but the protagonist is Everett Jason, a middle-aged car dealer on a business trip. At the start of the book, Jason is waiting for a train at the Avondale station. Unbeknownst to his wife, who has accompanied him to the station, he has liquidated $20,000 worth of bonds and is planning to hightail it to South America to escape her constant nagging about the health of his gums, his digestion, and his careless habit of wearing thin, silk socks in bad winter weather. She makes it clear to him that on this trip there will be no poker, no drinking, no smoking, no stag parties, and no lavish expenditures.[29]

The train that Everett Jason boards at Avondale is carrying a number of notable people. There is Martin Knox, a famous attorney returning from Chicago with a surprise witness who will clear his client, a gangster, of a murder actually committed by the governor's son. Lena Karelsen, the surprise witness, has been smuggled aboard the train with orders not to leave her compartment. Knox's ex-lover, Ada Robillard, a liberated journalist, is aboard as well, though no one knows exactly why. Representative Tom Linscott, secretly engaged to Ada Robillard, has boarded the train to convince Knox to let his innocent client go to the electric chair, since public knowledge that the governor's son was the real murderer would topple the political machine to which Linscott owes his career. Carl Izzard, a private detective who was following Knox in Chicago, wants to get a cut of the hush money that Linscott is prepared to offer Knox and Karelsen. Everett Jason stumbles into the whole political/sexual conspiracy accidentally when he enters Karelsen's compartment by mistake, and—very drunk—decides that the answer to her problems is to run away to South America with him.

During the night, the speeding train derails from the icy tracks, an accident that kills the engineman and slightly injures Lena Karelsen. Karelsen tells Ada Robillard the whole story while Robillard tends to her injuries. A substantial part of the middle of the novel consists of Robillard keeping the various men away from the injured woman. Knox wants to make sure his reluctant witness is fit and still willing to testify. (She's not.) Linscott wants to bribe her to keep quiet. Izzard, when he realizes that Linscott won't be able to bribe Karelsen, wants to do so himself, since his clients also want her silenced. Ducking them all, Karelsen flees the train in the dead of night with Everett Jason, whose hard-earned $20,000 will put them on easy street in South America. However, they are spotted leaving by the train detective, who, believing that the money is stolen, shoots and kills Karelsen.

Deductive logic plays only a tiny part in this novel. Nobody, in fact, appears to be thinking particularly clearly. The "mystery"—who killed the man that Knox's client is standing trial for murdering—is of little importance. Linscott, Knox, Karelsen, Izzard, and the reader know that the murderer is the governor's son, and Karelsen tells everyone else soon enough. The central action of the story is less detection than it is the corruption that results from covering up the initial crime and from the sexual liaisons of the key players.

This epistemological difference from Christie's model is also reflected in the ending. Whereas the truth emerges and justice is served at the close of *Murder on the Orient Express, Sleepers East* ends up seeming like much ado about nothing. Although there are many people aboard who have an interest in killing Lena Karelsen, the railroad detective kills her by mistake. As a result Knox will lose his case, an innocent man will die in the electric chair, the corrupt governor will retain his seat, the real murderer will go free, Robillard (disgusted by her fiancé's pleas for her help in bribing Karelsen) will break off her engagement, and Everett Jason, deprived of his true love by a mistaken shooting, will return to his nagging wife.

Nebel makes it additionally clear that the events of the narrative accomplish absolutely nothing by first offering and then removing the promise of progress. The political plot ends in disarray, but Nebel gives us a new Everett Jason studying himself in the mirror in the final chapter. Although Jason decides to return to his car dealership and his wife, he believes that he will go back a changed man. His (almost) love affair with Lena Karelsen has been a rebirth of sorts. "It just seems that out of her death I've built something new and strong inside me," he tells his reflection (282). This belief is radically undermined, however, by a wink from the narrator to the reader. In the final words of the novel, Jason says to the detective who will accompany him to the police station to give his evidence about Karelsen's death, "Just a minute, I think I'd better put on a pair of woolen socks" (283). With this self-conscious echo of Jason's wife's nagging words, nearly 300 pages of political and sexual machinations end exactly where they started—with Everett Jason's footwear. Nothing was accomplished—no justice served, no order restored, no personal transformation, and one innocent dead woman thrown in for good measure.

Workers' Control

If detection, at least in Christie's sense of the term, is not what happens in hard-boiled novels, what does happen? Among other things, these texts address contemporary debates between workers and managers over autonomy and control in the workplace. *Murder on the Orient Express*, stabbings aside, is an extremely genteel book. The passengers are all the right kind of people—a Russian princess, a Hungarian count and countess, an English military man returning from India, a governess, a few American businessmen, and the loyal valets, secretaries, and maids of these denizens of polite society. Poirot is aided in his efforts by the director of the railroad, and the evidence of one conductor figures importantly, but otherwise the staff of the train is invisible.

In contrast, there are workers in *Sleepers East*—many of them, with their own vividly drawn plotlines. Fully a third of the novel's exposition is given over to the employees of the railroad—the engineman, the fireboys, the porters, the railroad secretary, the conductor, the railroad detective. Nebel deals with the lives of the lower classes in detail—their complicated views of their work, their jealousy over love affairs, the frictions between coworkers. Moreover, the third-person narration is often replaced by the first-person narrative of the railroad secretary, Albert Cooke, whose letters home to his girl offer an alternative account of the passengers' lives. The initial description of the cast of characters comes in the form of one of these letters.

Work is a central and defining part of the lives of some of the railroad men in *Sleepers East*. In Chapter 2 alone, we meet Old Magowan the engineman, "a gaunt, rip-roaring, loud-mouthed, picturesque figure of a man, with the railroads in his spleen" (20); a character named McCarthy, who, though sidelined since losing his leg in an accident, continues to haunt the yards because the railroads are "in his blood" (16); and Dan Gibbons, the fireboy, who relishes the physicality of his work: "Heaving the scoop, opening and closing the butterfly doors with the pedal under his left foot, he felt a savage joy in his strength" (18). The arrival of the train at the Avondale station is seen through the eyes of an old porter, who licks his lips in expectation every time he hears a train whistle and feels the vibration of the platform under his feet, though he has been working the same shift and watching the same trains come in for more than fifteen years (22–23).

These workers were a select group. Railroad employees during this period were skilled workers, paid a wage that could support a family at a higher standard of living than the average worker's pay could. One of several railroad unions represented most of them, guaranteeing protection of promotion and seniority rights and providing health and accident insurance. They were overwhelmingly either native-born or children of immigrants from Britain, Ireland, and Germany. These immigrants increasingly set themselves apart from the newer arrivals from southern and eastern Europe, who held most of the unskilled and semiskilled jobs at the time.[30] These workers, in other words, constituted part of a "labor aristocracy," a class of workers distinguished by their skill, high wages, steady work, autonomy on the job, and leadership roles in working-class communities.[31] Significantly, workers of this type—disproportionately literate, with larger disposable incomes and often shorter hours—would probably have been more likely to buy and read the pulp magazines in which this fiction first appeared.

Even some of the "respectable" passengers riding the train in *Sleepers East* have proletarian skeletons in their closets. Tom Linscott does a lot of soul-searching before he can bring himself to try to bribe Lena Karelsen into withholding her testimony. Though such behavior is commonplace in the political machine of which he is now a part, it rankles in his conscience, which was formed by a working-class childhood: "His innate honesty, his proletarian sense of justice told him that what he was attempting to do was degrading and that he was abetting a vicious miscarriage of justice. This part of him, this code of honor, had its root in his childhood when, living among hoodlums, he had never been one of them. His father, a mail carrier, had had a high sense of honor and had talked it diligently to his son" (80–81). Linscott's view, that of an honest proletarian trying to wheel and deal like the big boys, gets a lot of space in *Sleepers East*, and his character is drawn with even more sympathy than is Everett Jason.

Beyond representing workers' lives and worldviews, *Sleepers East* investigates many of the central concerns of white, mostly native-born, skilled working men in the early twentieth century, notably autonomy, the pace of work, and manliness. Manliness remains in the forefront in

Sleepers East, from the suffering of Everett Jason at the hands of his emasculating wife to the fireboys boasting of their sexual prowess in the final pages. The novel carefully details the disciplined self-making of one man: Tom Linscott. Linscott's life story begins with a childhood incident in which he was called a "sissy" by the neighborhood bullies while walking home from school with a little girl. Rather than acquitting himself with physical and rhetorical courage, Linscott blushed and ran home crying. The story had a happy ending, however: "Seven years later, he had beaten the most obnoxious of his early tormentors in a three-round amateur boxing contest. Six years after that he had married the girl" (66).

The details of how the weeping little boy turned into a strong, virile man follow. Linscott performs a daily ritual of calisthenics, watches his diet, drinks only moderately, gets adequate rest, and spends his free time boxing, playing basketball, doing gymnastics, and engaging in other forms of physical culture. He stands very straight, "as if to take the full advantage of the last fractional inch of his five-feet-eight," and, although nearsighted, he "rebelled against glasses" (67). The text is littered with links between manliness and physical strength.[32] The fireboy's girlfriend is deeply impressed by the size of his biceps (18); he defends her honor in fistfights with men who defame her (275–76); the railroad secretary's contributions to the railroad magazine stress "square jaws, great muscles and feats of manly heroism" (38). These sections of the novel sound little different from Earle E. Liederman's bodybuilding ads, which filled pulp magazines during this period.

An emphasis on physical prowess is hardly surprising in a description of the making of men, but the second part of Linscott's cultivation of manhood may be: He reads. Linscott has a daily regimen of literary study, undertaken with a dictionary and a thesaurus open beside him (67). His daily linguistic workout is presented as analogous to his daily physical workout. The fistic duel and the public speech were, in fact, the two "structuring events in the history of manliness."[33] Dime novels and autobiographies of working-class men almost always included both a boxing match or other contest of strength and a major public speech that proved the hero to be a worthy leader. Like *Black Mask*'s guides to proper speech and writing, this hard-boiled fiction demonstrated the importance of regular practice with the appropriate rhetorical guide to social advancement.

All his reading notwithstanding, Linscott is no match for the glib defense attorney, Knox. Not surprisingly, Knox gets the girl—Ada Robillard. Robillard acknowledges that Linscott treats her better, involves her in his work, values her mind, worships her, but she returns to Knox at the end in spite of his dismissive and abusive behavior. She offers simply that Knox "dominated her" (280), and to be held in such powerful arms was a privilege indeed. In Robillard's eyes, Linscott has been reduced to "a plaster figure of a man that had somehow broken into fragments" (280), because while she was nursing Lena Karelsen, he pleaded for access to the injured woman in order to bribe her into not testifying. His breach of ethics was not a problem, but his need of Robillard, his asking for her approval and advice, was. This is Linscott's understanding, at any rate: "He felt he had to stand up for her in the manly manner, because his manliness had so crumpled before her but a short time back" (242–43). Robillard sends Linscott away without letting him see Karelsen, an act the other men on the train cannot comprehend. "Why didn't you *make* her let you speak with the woman?" Izzard asks. "What you need, Mr. Linscott, is just some plain, old-fashioned guts!" (235–36). Manliness here involves not only fighting back and talking back, but also patriarchal attitudes toward women. A man defends and protects his woman, but he never approaches her with anything but dominance and strength, or she will dismiss him for a more masterful model.

The speed of production and the presence or absence of white-collar supervision[34] are important subjects for the men in Sleepers East. Not only is it a fast novel in the sense that a great deal of action occurs in a very short space (no mere sitting back and thinking in *this* story), the narrative tension is heightened by the fact that more than two-thirds of the novel occurs on a train thundering over snow-covered tracks at lightning speed. Magowan's obsessive desire to arrive on time on his final run before retirement leads him to drive the engine faster than the poor condition of the machine and the blizzard outside warrant. "He was driving her like a fool," the fireboy says, "rolling her through the dark like a bat out of hell" (19). The narrative cuts back and forth among the engine, where Magowan and an exhausted fireboy urge the train ever faster, the dire predictions of the other train personnel about Magowan's fool desire to make it to the end of the line on time, and the machinations of the powerful passengers. Even when the action focuses on the passengers, the speeding engine is never far from the reader's mind. The passengers keep commenting on how fast they are moving and how the train moans and rocks on the tracks as it plows through enormous snowdrifts at unbelievable speeds.

Just before the accident that kills him and derails the train, Magowan hears a noise above the sounds of the storm and the engine: "The singing sound rose high, higher, until it became a whir like a dynamo, distant, but drawing nearer, coursing over him like an electric current. His blood pumped faster. Speed! That was it—that sound, growing, fast, faster. Speed! He rose, gripped the throttle with both hands, tried with all his might to advance it, but it would not budge; it could not be moved another inch" (202). The cause of the accident is a monomaniacal dedication to speed, to getting the job done faster regardless of the storm or the condition of the machinery. Both the fatality and the speed of the machinery that caused it would have had resonance for workers of the 1920s and '30s, since speedup during this period resulted in a phenomenally high rate of workplace injuries.[35] Anson Rabinbach calls this mind-set "productivism," defined as "a totalizing framework that subordinated all social activities to production." Productivism became the dominant ideology between 1870 and 1945, after a significant struggle between labor and management over the relative importance of production quotas and quality of life.[36]

A belief in productivism was one of the primary ideological props needed to instill what E. P. Thompson calls "work discipline" in workers with a different ("pre-modern" or "task-oriented") sense of time. Work under task-oriented time expanded or contracted according to the job at hand. It involved a long, porous workday in which labor and "passing the time of day" were by no means mutually exclusive, and in which "life" and "work" were difficult to separate. Industrial work-time, however, viewed time as currency and carefully distinguished one's employer's time and one's own.[37] Because successive waves of immigrants and rural migrants entered wage labor in the United States, the struggles between owners and workers continued into the twentieth century, long after industrial work discipline had been established in Britain.[38]

Sleepers East is a parable about the unproblematic embracing of industrial work discipline, clock time, and productivism. Magowan is, after all, a model employee in the eyes of the owners of the railroad, however much his coworkers curse him. He describes himself: "Forty-four years on the railroads, from yard messenger to engineman of a crack east-west run! Thirty-eight years married to the same woman! Never had touched liquor. Never had had a wreck, not even a minor derailment. Money in the bank, plenty of it" (200–201). Magowan might have been one of Ford's model workers, one who had earned the sociology department's stamp of approval for higher piece rates through the wholesome nature of his family life—its sobriety, monogamy, and fiscal prudence.³⁹ Nevertheless, this darling of the middle-class reformers and managers is the one who wrecks the train. The other men, those who drink on the job and get into fistfights over who is sleeping with whose woman, end up looking pretty good in comparison. It's particularly fitting that a fable about the dangers of clock time should take place on a train, since the impetus for the institution of standard time in the late nineteenth century came not from state or military authorities but from railroad companies needing uniform scheduling of arrivals and departures.⁴⁰

The other issue over which workers and management repeatedly knocked heads was the institution of scientific management practices. The use of time-and-motion studies to codify and systematize the technical knowledge once possessed and controlled exclusively by skilled workers had a number of disturbing consequences for them. By breaking the skilled workman's monopoly on expertise, Taylorism interfered with traditional lines of authority on the shop floor, weakened union bargaining positions, and gave management a powerful new way to exercise control over the entire manufacturing process.⁴¹ One consequence of Taylorism was the replacement of skilled artisans by unskilled workers performing a single, repetitive task under the detailed supervision of a small army of white-collar engineers and managers.

The railroad detective in *Sleepers East*, August Trautwein, has taken to this new logic of work with great enthusiasm. He is called to work on the train at the last moment by his supervisor, who promises to wire instructions at the first stop. Communications are held up first by the storm and then by the accident. Trautwein paces the train like a caged animal throughout the novel, ineffectually cursing his lack of instructions and consequent inability to do his job: "I been on this train for hours, thinking, worrying, trying to figure things out . . . me not knowing what's what, getting no wires, no nothing to straighten me out" (207). Although basically a good man—"an honest man, loyal to his job, conscientious"—he is rendered useless by his inability to "grab a telephone and communicate with his chief" (189). The only job-related action Trautwein takes in the entire novel is to shoot an innocent Lena Karelsen. It turns out, in fact, that Trautwein's entire assignment is a false alarm: The supervisor heard an incorrect rumor that the director's daughter would be eloping on that train. Karelsen's death seems particularly tragic and unnecessary given the circumstances. Trautwein's actions, then, can be read as a cautionary tale about the dangers of employing unskilled workers incapable of doing their jobs without minute supervision.

Surprisingly, hard-boiled fiction prominently features time-and-motion studies of a different sort—the ubiquitous, painstakingly detailed scenes of violence that fill its pages. The following confrontation between Sam Spade and Joel Cairo from Hammett's *The Maltese Falcon*, serialized in *Black Mask* in the late 1920s, is typical:

> Spade's elbow dropped as Spade spun to the right. Cairo's face jerked back not far enough: Spade's right heel on the patent-leathered toes anchored the smaller man in the elbow's path. The elbow struck him beneath the cheek-bone, staggering him so that he must have fallen had he not been held by Spade's foot on his foot. Spade's elbow went on past the astonished dark face and straightened when Spade's hand struck down at the pistol. Cairo let the pistol go the instant that Spade's fingers touched it. The pistol was small in Spade's hand.
>
> Spade took his foot off Cairo's to complete his about-face. With his left hand Spade gathered together the smaller man's coat-lapels—the ruby-set green tie bunching out over his knuckles—while his right hand stowed the captured weapon away in a coat-pocket.... His right shoulder raised a few inches. His bent right arm was driven up by the shoulder's lift. Fist, wrist, forearm, crooked elbow, and upper arm seemed all one rigid piece, with only the limber shoulder giving them motion. The fist struck Cairo's face, covering for a moment one side of his chin, a corner of his mouth, and most of his cheek between cheek-bone and jaw-bone.[42]

In hard-boiled fiction, rather than centering on production and efficiency, such scenes functioned as instruction manuals for effective brawling. They are also proof of the hard-boiled writer's he-manly credentials, evidence that although he was a writer, he had been in a few fights of his own. Significantly, many of these scenes of violence are directed at representatives of wealth and high culture. Sam Spade's wrong-side-of-the-tracks brawling messes up both Cairo's face and his fancy clothes. Cairo may rub elbows with international art dealers, but he is powerless when faced with a routine display of proletarian manliness, carefully codified for the reader in that quintessentially bourgeois form, the time-and-motion study.[43]

There is a filmic quality to these scenes.[44] Huge numbers of hard-boiled crime stories were made into Hollywood films, often within a year or two of publication. Further, much film noir was not only based on hard-boiled fiction but written by hard-boiled writers who turned to more lucrative screenwriting.[45] One "Behind the Mask" column called *Black Mask* "a breeding station for the movies," since in one year the stories of Frederick Nebel, Theodore Tinsley, George Harmon Coxe, W. T. Ballard, Dashiell Hammett, Erle Stanley Gardner, Raoul Whitfield, Horace McCoy, and Paul Cain were bought by Hollywood studios.[46] The overlapping communities of writers made it possible to write hard-boiled fiction with the screenplay in mind from the start.

The connection between film and hard-boiled crime stories may have been additionally significant for readers outside traditional book culture, those working-class and immigrant audiences originally targeted by the movies.[47] It seems likely that reading hard-boiled crime stories after seeing the films based on them forged an important link between oral and print cultures for those less at home in the world of print.

Hard-boiled crime stories were conduct manuals of a sort, offering step-by-step guidelines to manly demeanor on the job and off. They were also cautionary tales about the de-skilling (read unmanning) of production work. This fiction provided a he-manly mold by which the reader could shape himself, but it also reassured him that his employer's failure to honor his manly skill and autonomy came at considerable cost. In *Sleepers East*, the productivism characteristic of management is literally fatal.

The Autonomous Craftsman and His Code

The manly demeanor of the hard-boiled hero was part of a larger ethos, a code of behavior characteristic of American skilled workers in the nineteenth and early twentieth centuries. Three related ideals—functional autonomy, a mutualist ethic, and a manly bearing toward supervisors and colleagues—constituted the code under which such autonomous craftsmen worked.[48] George Harmon Coxe's "Murder Mixup," first published in *Black Mask* in May of 1936, easily lends itself to readings centered on the sanctity of this code.[49] Although it is nominally a crime story, its preoccupation with competing models of work takes center stage. Coxe's hero, Jack "Flash" Casey, and his assistant, Wade, two newspaper photographers, represent the residual ideals of nineteenth-century autonomous craftsmen.[50] The city editor, Blaine, represents the emergent industrial work discipline with its time clock and close managerial supervision. Blaine's struggle with Casey and Wade intervenes in larger debates between skilled workers and white-collar engineers and managers about the pace of work, methods of production, and the length of the workday.

After Casey and Wade return from a job, Blaine confronts Casey: "We've been looking for you for nearly an hour. Somebody saw you and Wade go out, but nobody knew where. . . . Now where the hell were you? . . . You should have been here on call" (188–89). Blaine makes it clear that he considers his workers' time his time, and that they ought to remain under managerial supervision during those hours. Casey replies that he was doing his job, but doing it on his own terms: "We get paid to take pictures, and we take 'em. How we get 'em is our business" (189). At this point Wade enters with exclusive photographs of a crime scene, and the editor storms out, unable to refute this evidence that his workers are more capable of handling their business than he is.

Casey displays the manly demeanor toward the boss that the autonomous craftsman's code demanded. A manly worker "refused to cower before the foreman's glares—in fact, often would not work at all when a boss was watching."[51] When Blaine enters the office, Casey reacts in time-honored fashion: He "swiveled the chair, and . . . he straightened his legs and clasped his hands behind his neck in a gesture of sheer laziness" (188). He'll work on his own terms, Casey's body language seems to say, and if Blaine wants any work to get done, he'd better stay out of the way.

Similarly, when Elihu Willsson of Hammett's *Red Harvest* hires the Continental Op to clean up the corruption plaguing his city, he cautions, "It's a man's job. Are you a man?" The Op answers by making some demands of his own: "I'd have to have a free hand—no favors to anybody—run the job as I pleased. . . . That's the way it'll have to be. Take it or leave it."[52] A man's working conditions, this conversation suggests, involve not only adequate money (the "family wage" that unions of the period demanded for their male members), but also autonomy—respect for his intelligence and artisanship. That being one's own boss is a chief criterion for manhood in hard-boiled worlds is emphasized by the diminutive terms used to characterize jobs lacking in autonomy. For instance, the chief of police in *Red Harvest*, a man at the beck and call of Elihu Willsson, is "an errand boy."[53]

The Continental Op resists corporate authority of all kinds, including the daily reports demanded by his boss in San Francisco. "It's right enough for the Agency to have rules and regulations, but when you're out on a job you've got to do it the best way you can," he says.[54] A "man" gets his job done, whereas an "errand boy" provides his supervisor with the petty details and depends on instructions.[55] Such a definition of masculinity might make it increasingly difficult for men to be "men," particularly if they were members of a skilled labor aristocracy rapidly losing caste through the efforts of white-collar managers and time-and-motion men.

Casey's relations with his colleagues and underlings in "Murder Mixup" are in accord with this older model of work. Rather than being part of a bureaucratic system of control with a carefully delineated chain of command, Wade and Casey rely on personal relationships with other workers. Casey gets his information from what he calls his "Bureau of Investigation"—street hustlers, newsboys, and other stooges (182). Nor does Casey think of his colleagues and subordinates as operatives, as interchangeable parts of a production process. When Casey goes to eavesdrop on some kidnappers, leaving Wade outside to watch the door, he cautions: "I can't draw you a map . . . use your head if you can stand the strain" (195). Wade's tasks are not spelled out with the expectation that he will perform as ordered. The job involves Wade's experience, his knowledge, and his judgment rather than merely his laboring body.

The mutualist ethic characteristic of craft unions is also manifested in "Murder Mixup." Just as men on the shop floor plotted to slow down production when the time-and-motion man was there, tricking supervisors into setting lower production quotas,[56] Casey and Wade plot to get around the police so they can do their job as they see fit. Tipped off that a counterfeiter has been murdered, Casey shows up at the scene to grill the police and the federal investigators about the circumstances, winning permission to stay by promising not to take any pictures. He then rattles the doorknob and opens the door, signaling Wade to snap a picture through the open door. Casey then stands in the doorway, blocking the pursuit of Wade, and complains to the police that they've let him be "scooped" by another photographer (187). Later, when Wade's amateur snooping allows the criminals they are tracking to get away, Casey sees no reason to tell the police, who blame him for the escape (199).

Like autonomous craftsmen, Casey and Wade have a porous work-day, the mingling of "life" and "work" testifying to the persistence of a task-oriented notion of time.[57] After getting their pictures of the dead counterfeiter and a witness, they stop and have two drinks. They develop the pictures, then they have another round. After they are beaten up by the men who kidnapped the witness, they have fourteen more drinks before continuing their pursuit of the suspects. After the resolution of the case, Wade and Casey follow the tradition of "Blue Monday," getting so drunk to celebrate the end of a job that they find themselves unable to come to work the next day. Missing work on the day after a weekend or holiday was common in some industries before the institution of industrial work discipline.[58] "Won't be in tomorrow—me and Wade," Casey tells the managing editor. "We're gonna take a day off and sleep." He then goes off to get drunk (223).

Drinking was a critical part of the ties that bound working men to one another. Late–nineteenth-century saloons were the center of working men's communities, all-male spaces where men drank, discussed politics, enjoyed recreation, and networked about jobs.[59] Many working-class citizens interpreted Prohibition (1920–33) as part of a larger attempt by the privileged classes to control these other aspects of working-class life.[60] Since white, middle-class women dominated much early temperance activity, Prohibition also seemed to challenge male supremacy.[61]

This vision of work was profoundly nostalgic. Autonomous artisans who ran their shops as they saw fit, the practice of drinking on the job, and blue Mondays were not just disappearing; they had been more or less gone for fifty to 100 years, no longer a part of living memory. By the last third of the nineteenth century, the transition from craft production to management control and advanced division of labor was complete. Mary Ann Clawson calls the defeat "decisive" by the late 1890s.[62] Drinking during the workday or at the workplace had come under fire by the 1830s in most cities, and most employers considered the issue long settled in their favor by the late nineteenth century.[63] As early as 1825, preindustrial work patterns—fairs, days off, drinking during the day, long meal breaks, and the like—were under attack, and skilled tasks once performed by artisans had increasingly been divided among a few well-paid journeymen and many unskilled, poorly paid hands.[64] The artisan republic was history by the 1850s, if not before—almost seventy years before hard-boiled detectives appeared in the pages of *Black Mask*.

Nevertheless, the ideal of an artisan republic, complete with preindustrial notions of time and autonomy on the job, was a significant part of the collective memory of workers, part of the cultural inheritance handed down from generation to generation. Lawrence Glickman states that the figure of the independent craftsman was "a symbol deeply etched in labor's collective memory" long after the realities of working life made this model of work untenable.[65]

By the early twentieth century, however, labor activists were no longer particularly interested in the artisan ideal in which hard-boiled detective fiction trafficked. After the Civil War, consumerist rhetoric— support for a "living wage"—increasingly replaced the producerist rhetoric of "wage slavery" that had marked the antebellum period. The producerist rhetoric had distinguished manly producers—artisans, farmers, shopkeepers—from effeminate consumers—millionaires, bankers, and others who produced nothing of value to the republic. By the 1870s, more than two-thirds of the male population spent their lives in wage labor. The "consumerist turn" in labor's rhetoric was intended to reimagine the artisan republic for an industrial age, to use high wages to insure what earlier artisans had sought: patriarchal self-esteem, leisure to participate in civic life, a living to support a family.[66]

Hard-boiled detective fiction wanted nothing to do with labor's new paradigm. Workaholic private eyes had little, if anything, to say about union labels, the eight-hour day, or organized consumption as a form of working-class self-employment. They were too busy wresting control over their investigations from effeminate employers and corrupt cops to bother with organizing. Moreover, hard-boiled detectives never showed much interest in the size of their paychecks.

The hard-boiled investigator was a man of modest means. More often than not, as John G. Cawelti notes, he worked out of an office "associated with unsuccessful dentists, small mail-order businesses and shyster lawyers." His class status was lower middle-class at best, and Leslie Fiedler was probably right to label him an "honest proletarian."[67] Yet he was clearly not out to make a fast buck. Without exception, hard-boiled detectives refused bribes, rewards, hush money, and remunerative cases that would compromise their principles or their autonomy. The motto of Chandler's fictional private eyes was "I'm on straight salary and expenses."[68] Jo Gar, Raoul Whitfield's Filipino detective, wouldn't leave his small, seedy office for a better one because it would have required taking uninteresting though better-paid cases.[69] Perhaps Hammett's Continental Op best explained the unshakable fiscal ethics of the hard-boiled hero in "The Gutting of Couffignal," published in *Black Mask* in 1925. The Op declined a bribe offered by a corrupt Russian princess:

> Now I'm a detective because I happen to like the work. It pays me a fair salary, but I could find other jobs that would pay more. Even a hundred dollars a month would be twelve hundred a year. Say twenty-five or thirty thousand dollars in the years between now and my sixtieth birthday. Now I pass up

about twenty-five or thirty thousand of honest gain because I like being a
detective, like the work. And liking work makes you want to do it as well as
you can. Otherwise there'd be no sense to it. That's the fix I am in. I don't
know anything else, don't enjoy anything else, don't want to know or enjoy
anything else. You can't weigh that against any sum of money. Money is good
stuff. I haven't anything against it. But in the past eighteen years I've been
getting my fun out of chasing crooks and tackling puzzles, my satisfaction out
of catching crooks and solving riddles. It's the only kind of sport I know anything about, and I can't imagine a pleasanter future than twenty-some years
more of it.[70]

The Op's choice of the pleasures of work over the income it could bring
him is profoundly old-fashioned, an emphasis disappearing from the
agendas of most labor unions by the 1940s.

Most American companies that embraced scientific management
offered high wages or shorter hours to compensate workers for the dis-
comfort and unpleasantness of increasingly standardized, routine
work.[71] Robert and Helen Lynd found that workers in 1920s Middletown were concerned with the disappearance of intrinsic motivations
for work—"a sense of craftsmanship" and "group solidarity." Instead,
they reported, they increasingly went to work for the paycheck that let
them participate in consumer culture.[72] The working-class swing toward
consumerism was particularly prominent among skilled workers, who
shared in some of the 1920s prosperity denied to more recent immigrant laborers. As James R. Green puts it, "Denied dignity as a worker,
the wage earner could gain a measure of self-respect, as well as personal
satisfaction, as a consumer."[73]

After World War II, unions increasingly ceded control over working conditions to management in exchange for higher wages.[74] During
the 1920s, '30s, and '40s, then, many companies were "buying off" their
workers, seeking to quiet protest over speedup and the loss of autonomy at work through higher wages. The acquiescence of unions to this
plan during the 1940s compounded the situation. Autonomous craftsmen, it seemed, were a dying breed, perfectly content to become scientifically managed operatives if the bribe were large enough and the
consumer goods that it could buy were impressive enough.

The hard-boiled hero kept the faith. Clinging fiercely to his autonomy and his disdain for authority figures of all sorts, he continued to
practice his manly craft in a world increasingly filled with corrupt
authorities, powerful rings of gangsters (read corporations), and errand
boys of all types. Moreover, hard-boiled heroes were lousy consumers.

They *never* went shopping. Sometimes, if in danger of being spotted while shadowing a suspect, they would duck into a tobacco shop or a drugstore and buy a package of cigarettes. The department stores that became increasingly common in American cities from the 1920s on are completely absent from hard-boiled fiction, probably because they were populated by women (designated consumers) and the "errand boys" who bankrolled their purchases.[75]

Faced with the de-skilling of men's work and the growth of a consumer economy that centered on women, hard-boiled heroes did not "sell out," agreeing to put up with deadening work in exchange for a larger paycheck. Instead, they did valiant battle to protect their autonomy on the job from wealthy clients and corrupt authorities of all sorts, proving their manhood through feats of physical prowess and some very tough talk. Though the artisan republic was increasingly irrelevant, both to corporations and to labor, it lived on in the pages of pulp detective magazines and paperbacks.

To view hard-boiled detective stories as parables about workers' control and autonomy requires a certain kind of interested reading. Surveys done by library researchers, such as the work Douglas Waples did at the University of Chicago in the 1930s, suggest that workers were predisposed to read in exactly this way. Readers of all classes reported wanting to read about people like themselves; reading interests, in other words, were dependent on such variables as gender, education, occupation, age, and living circumstances.[76] Most relevant to my purposes is the fact that young working men were overwhelmingly interested in reading about labor, the labor market, and other topics related to the social and economic status of their occupational group. Men who had finished high school and women of all classes reported very little interest in this topic.[77] Waples and his colleagues thought these interests shaped not only the texts readers selected, but also the ways in which they read them. They were arguing for something resembling reading as poaching. Moreover, they thought that readers with very constrained choices of reading material sometimes had to "do their best to make imaginary adjustments and compensations."[78] White, working-class men would have read their concerns about labor and the labor market, their interest in what would further their group's social and economic status, into hard-boiled fiction.

In interviews with Ken Worpole, British labor leaders frequently spoke of the American hard-boiled writing they had read in their youth.

Worpole argues that this fiction was important in the making of working-class militants because it unpatronizingly represented life in large cities, the corruption of big business, and the everyday practices and speech of the working class in a way that postwar British fiction (particularly murder mysteries preoccupied with aristocrats bumping one another off at family estates) did not.[79] Hard-boiled mysteries gave the men of the British working class materials to think with, an idiom through which to represent and express their world.

Hard-boiled fiction, then, emerges as a highly ambivalent proletarian literature—one whose Taylor-ed plots nonetheless addressed the everyday lives of its working-class readers. The readers who appropriated hard-boiled crime stories as proletarian literature, however, were not necessarily powerful.[80] Because workers did not control the means of cultural production, they had to psychically remake mass cultural texts in ways that resonated with their own experiences. They "made do" with these texts, creating a proletarian literature of sorts from the raw materials offered them by piecework prose producers in the employ of large corporations. Making themselves at home in the nostalgic worlds of hard-boiled magazines, workers were nonetheless habituated to ways of thinking necessary for the scientifically managed work that was their lot.

4

Dressed to Kill

An affair with Raymond Chandler, what a joy! Not because of the mangled bodies and the marinated cops and hints of eccentric sex, but because of his interest in furniture.

Margaret Atwood

erle Constiner's "The Turkey Buzzard Blues," which ran in the July 1943 issue of *Black Mask*, introduced Lute McGavock, a private eye who pays obsessively close attention to interior decoration. In one passage, McGavock studies a wealthy client's library: "The mansion's library reeked wealth. The powder-blue rug had a two inch nap. The walls were pressed leather and the rare colonial furniture gave off a lustrous, shimmering patina. There were alabaster figurines and oriental vases and busts of famous poets—but, as far as McGavock could observe, there were no books in the Layton library."[1]

This description demonstrates how wealth and power are communicated through the display of consumer goods. One reads wealth from thick carpets, handcrafted furniture, leather, and art objects whose cosmopolitan points of origin and lack of utilitarian value testify to the owner's aesthetic worldview and his ability to afford significant travel.[2] Moreover, the mere appearance of genteel learning is enough, at least in this passage. A finely furnished library need not actually contain any books to communicate wealth and education.

McGavock attends to less luxurious furnishings with equal interest. Charlie Lusk, secretary to the murdered Layton

103

patriarch, lives in markedly different surroundings: "Lusk's tiny room was cramped, but somehow cozy. There was a Spanish daybed, a small bureau and a friendly-looking, broken-down Morris chair with a shelf of books beside it. Three thread-bare suits hung from a broomstick bar in the corner. The detective picked up the books, examined them one by one. The first was a paperback affair titled: *1001 JOKES, Fun for Young and Old*. The four others were instructional volumes on how to become a self-taught cartoonist."[3]

There is little wealth in the secretary's "cubbyhole," but a great deal of comfort. McGavock, who refers to himself as "riffraff" at one point in the story, is clearly more at home here than in the ostentatiously furnished library. Moreover, there are books in this room—the kinds of books advertised in *Black Mask*. Lusk puts these books to good use. He uses his cartooning skills and the fancy pens and ink that came with the books to forge checks on the Laytons' bank account.

McGavock's work as a private detective takes him into the homes of wealthy and poor alike. This universal access, Fredric Jameson argues, makes the figure of the detective a significant narrative innovation. Traveling from the exclusive worlds of the rich to the slums of the underclass, the detective draws the entire class-fractured society into the tale.[4] Early twentieth-century cities were split into geographic enclaves separating rich from poor, black from white, immigrant from native-born. "Such a city," according to John Kasson, "could not be grasped as a totality, since it lacked any moral, social or physical center."[5] Different classes increasingly encountered one another only through journalism, sociology, and other forms of representation. The inability to create a single account of the entire social world, which had troubled writers of the 1880s and 1890s, only intensified for writers of the 1920s and 1930s.[6] The gulf between rich and poor had become wider,[7] and the successes of labor organizers during the Depression articulated more publicly and powerfully an alternative to corporate narratives about work.

Hard-boiled fiction represented the whole class-fractured social world and explained the different worldviews of each class. That is, it revealed how the other half lived—how they dressed, what their homes looked like, the rules that regulated their social intercourse. Elite readers encountering hard-boiled fiction as novels published by Knopf and other high-quality publishers could go slumming merely by opening a book. More important for my purposes, however, hard-boiled stories functioned as "how-to" manuals in class mobility for working-class readers, complete with stage directions on how to move, what to wear, and what to purchase.

Reading Class Through Commodities

Hard-boiled fiction's concern with class is most powerfully apparent in its obsessive interest in clothing and interiors, those apparently trivial matters that are deeply enmeshed with the (re)production of class hierarchies.[8] Philip Marlowe itemizes his wardrobe for us at the beginning of Raymond Chandler's *The Big Sleep* (1939): "I was wearing my powder-blue suit, with dark blue shirt, tie and display handkerchief, black brogues, black wool socks with dark blue clocks on them. I was neat, clean, shaved and sober, and I didn't care who knew it. I was everything the well-dressed private detective ought to be. I was calling on four million dollars."[9]

This passage makes it clear that those with family fortunes present themselves and conduct themselves differently from the working classes. They dress in matching, conservative colors and understated, repeating patterns; they place great importance on a close shave; they believe that one's appearance is intimately linked to one's success in life. Such modes of self-presentation differed markedly from those of the working class in the early twentieth century. Working men valued work clothes for their function rather than their appearance, and working-class women frequently made great sacrifices in order to have the money to "put on style"—flashy hats, gaudy-colored finery, obvious makeup—in which to go out on the town.[10]

Compare Marlowe's outfit in *The Big Sleep* with that of Moose Malloy in *Farewell, My Lovely* (1940): "He wore a shaggy borsalino hat, a rough gray sports coat with white golf balls on it for buttons, a brown shirt, a yellow tie, pleated gray flannel slacks and alligator shoes with white explosions on the toes. From his outer breast pocket cascaded a show handkerchief of the same brilliant yellow as his tie. There were a couple of colored feathers tucked into the band of his hat, but he didn't really need them. Even on Central Avenue, not the quietest dressed street in the world, he looked about as inconspicuous as a tarantula on a slice of angel food."[11]

Moose is the perfect opposite of Philip Marlowe, conservatively dressed to call on a millionaire. Moose's loud clothes call attention to him as he walks the anonymous byways of the city, a direct violation of the bourgeois conduct manuals of the late nineteenth and early twentieth centuries, which urged making oneself inconspicuous on the street.[12] His apparel makes perfect sense, however, when considered from a working-class viewpoint. Sunday clothes, as distinct from work clothes, "were visible displays of social standing and self-respect in the rituals of church-going, promenading and visiting" in working-class communities in the early twentieth century.[13] In the story, Moose has just been paroled after eight years in prison, and he is in search of his lost love, Velma, to whom he intends to propose marriage. His outrageous costume is a ritual adjunct to his wooing. He dresses in his ostentatious best to communicate the significance of the occasion to Velma and to any bystanders who may witness their reunion.

By dominant bourgeois standards, this social faux pas is particularly glaring. Moose is so loudly attired that he even calls attention to himself in a mixed neighborhood of blacks and southern and eastern European immigrants, such as the Greek barber whom Marlowe is trying to track down when he spots Moose. None of these groups, Marlowe notes dryly, is known for a subdued style of dress. We know that Moose, too, is such an immigrant from Marlowe's description of his features—"curly black hair and heavy eyebrows that almost met over his thick nose"— and bearing—"like a hunky immigrant catching his first sight of the Statue of Liberty." Moreover, Marlowe acknowledges the inadequacy of Moose's self-presentation by declaring "he would always need a shave."[14]

In this description of Moose Malloy, Marlowe is reading what Pierre Bourdieu calls "bodily hexis"—dress, bearing, speech, and manners as redundant and overlapping signifiers of class position.[15] Marlowe, fluent in reading clothing and manners, gives less savvy readers the benefit of his expertise.

Bourdieu argues that professionals and white-collar workers pay a great deal of attention to their appearance, investing much time and money in self-presentation, because professional labor markets reward these efforts. Working men reap next to no material benefit from meticulous attention to dress, which has nothing to do with one's promotion on the shop floor.[16] The bourgeois concern with the appearance of clothing should be juxtaposed with the working-class concern with its function, durability, and value for the money. A shave and socks with clocks on them are not likely to increase one's earning power in the mill, the mine, or the factory, so why bother? But there are real social and economic returns from such things among the managerial classes.

Hard-boiled fiction's lessons in self-presentation, then, were lessons in the rules of bourgeois life, a demystification of the games the ruling class played. The politics of such a project were contradictory, however. Mastering the bodily hexis of the hereditary bourgeoisie might further an individual worker's social mobility, but it did nothing to address the wages or working conditions of laborers as a class. The diffusion of bourgeois dress and manners theoretically had some socially destabilizing effects, however. If everyone possessed them, how could social hierarchies be maintained?

The flippant self-description at the opening of *The Big Sleep* has a pedagogical function, but its irony complicates how the lesson worked. Although he is dressed to please a millionaire, Marlowe's breezy description of the scene casts him as superior to the "dress for success" mentality. He plays the game, but he is careful not to take it too seriously. Similarly, his tone addresses readers as savvy analysts of clothing and other class cues, who are nevertheless superior to the game of impression management. The ironic tone might also encourage readers to feel that they were already in-the-know, bolstering their self-confidence while instructing them.

Marlowe's flippancy about self-presentation models the attitude of the bourgeoisie toward cultural capital. In Bourdieu's model, people who come by their cultural capital honestly (by birth and breeding) display self-confidence, casualness, and easy familiarity. The upwardly mobile lower classes, who get their cultural capital at school and from books, give themselves away through their angst-ridden attention to correctness.[17] Hard-boiled fiction codified and systematized the "legitimate" taste of the upper classes for workers, but its hard-boiled heroes are not at all intimidated by it. The detective has the same easy sense of privilege and self-confidence as an aristocrat from the best family. Marlowe and his colleagues taught not only "legitimate" modes of self-presentation, but also the legitimate way of deploying such knowledge—casually, with an air of entitlement, of "bluff."

Marlowe's sympathy for Moose in *Farewell, My Lovely* reveals a sense of class solidarity. Moose's old girlfriend takes advantage of him and the police consider him a dangerous criminal, but Marlowe thinks everyone should give poor Moose a break. Absent throughout much of the book (the police are unable to locate the right swarthy, six-and-a-half-

foot-tall man), Moose is nonetheless the most appealing of the characters. He is a simple man—not an astute manipulator of impressions, not
a savvy performer of the rituals of polite society, merely a man who is
what he appears to be. Marlowe may have become an astute reader of
the signs of upper-class distinction, but he is, at heart, a working man
whose functional aesthetic has affinity with Moose's own.

Hard-boiled fiction's attention to dress and interiors resonated with
the parable of the first impression in contemporary ads. One assembled
a self, so to speak, from consumer goods, read the social order by
becoming fluent in the language of commodities, and advanced according to one's skills at purchasing and displaying them. This worldview—
what Susman calls the "culture of personality"—ignored character traits
to emphasize social performance.[18] Hard-boiled stories attempted to
rethink identity in these terms, and the language of the theater fills
their pages as a consequence. Philip Marlowe finds himself using "the
quietly strained voice of a stage manager at a bad rehearsal" with a vic-
timized secretary in *The High Window*, and the client's son tells Marlowe his "tough guy act stinks"—both testimony to the collapse of categories between performance and reality.[19]

One of the characters in *The Little Sister* (1949), Chandler's Hollywood novel, is an actress named Mavis Weld. Marlowe's desire to pos-
sess something besides a Hollywood image is apparent in his response
to a query about whether he loves Weld: "That would be kind of silly.
I could sit in the dark with her and hold hands, but for how long? In
a little while she will drift off into a haze of glamour and expensive
clothes and froth and unreality and muted sex. She won't be a real person any more. Just a voice from a sound track, a face on a screen. I'd
want more than that."[20] The commodity version of Weld—the two-
dimensional images, the costumes and makeup, the scripted lines—do
not satisfy Marlowe, whose devotion to work and complete lack of
interest in consumption (in almost twenty years of sleuthing, he never
once goes shopping) belong to the culture of character. Moreover, this
passage reveals a good deal of fuzziness between Mavis Weld's screen
image and her physical presence, showing how difficult it was to distinguish between them.

However critical of the culture of personality and the commodities
that supported it, hard-boiled fiction trafficked in what Jean-Christophe
Agnew calls a "commodity aesthetic"—"a way of seeing the world in
general, and the self and society in particular, as so much raw space to

be furnished with mobile, detachable, and transactional goods."[21] Clothing and interior decoration became not just representations of or likenesses of selves, but "interchangeable with those selves, something out of which those selves were at once improvised and imprisoned, constructed and confined."[22] Hard-boiled fiction's engagement with commodities was an engagement with different worldviews and different ways of conceiving of selves. Moreover, these worldviews were articulated not only in terms of class and its embodiment in dress and decor, but also in terms of gender and sexuality.

Suspect Performances, Performing Suspects

The preoccupation with reading identities from appearances is clear from the first page of Chandler's *The Lady in the Lake* (1943). Philip Marlowe enters the headquarters of the Gillerlain Company to meet a new client named Derace Kingsley, an executive with the firm. Gillerlain, a cosmetics company, shows great concern with putting its best face forward for visitors:

> The Gillerlain Company was on the seventh floor, in front, behind swinging double plate glass doors bound in platinum. Their reception room had Chinese rugs, dull silver walls, angular but elaborate furniture, sharp shiny bits of abstract sculpture on pedestals and a tall display in a triangular showcase in the corner. On tiers and steps and islands and promontories of shining mirror-glass it seemed to contain every fancy bottle and box that had ever been designed. There were creams and powders and soaps and toilet waters for every season and every occasion. There were perfumes in tall thin bottles that looked as if a breath would blow them over and perfumes in little pastel phials tied with ducky satin bows, like little girls at a dancing class. The cream of the crop seemed to be something very small and simple in a squat amber bottle. It was in the middle at eye height, had a lot of space to itself, and was labeled *Gillerlain Regal, The Champagne of Perfumes.* It was definitely the stuff to get. One drop of that in the hollow of your throat and the matched pink pearls started falling on you like summer rain.[23]

The Gillerlain Company uses its reception room to display its wealth and modernity, decking it out in imported rugs, elaborate furniture, and art that testifies to the company's prosperity and cosmopolitan tastes. Unlike the overstuffed clutter of Victorian parlors, the reception room features the clean lines of modern design—hard metallic and glass surfaces, abstract art, and cold colors that evoke the sharp, shiny surfaces of planes, trains, and other aerodynamic, modern machines.[24]

The sculptures, art for art's sake, are displayed on pedestals that raise them above the economic work of the office into an aesthetic realm. The actual products of the company are likewise displayed above the utilitarian world. Though it is the business of the company to produce these goods, they are presented to the world as having no relation to the labor and raw materials from which they came. Presented as aesthetic goods rather than economic ones, the creams and soaps and toilet waters are displayed in expensive containers on mirrored glass, again focusing attention on image rather than use. Moreover, the function of these products is to create attractive surfaces on people, to present beautiful faces that may or may not reflect the souls within.

Marlowe recognizes the evidence of material wealth in the decor and the customary distanced, aesthetic way of interacting with the world that arises from it. Pierre Bourdieu calls this the "aesthetic disposition" or "the pure gaze," and argues that it is the fundamental factor distinguishing the hereditary bourgeoisie from the lower classes, whose functional aesthetic/ethos refuses the distinction between art and life, the elevation of form over function.[25]

However, the tone of Marlowe's final comment deflates the image of beauty, ease, and leisure created by the prior description. "Matched pink pearls . . . falling on you like summer rain" are so ridiculous that they call the reality of the entire set-piece ino question. "You can't tell anything about an outfit like that," Marlowe muses, while waiting to see his client. "They might be making millions, and they might have the sheriff in the back room, with his chair tilted against the safe" (6).

Marlowe's immunity to the spell of consumer culture and the spectatorship it encourages arises from his own economic and social situation. As an independent entrepreneur, Marlowe belongs to an older economic order. The slick, modern surfaces created by big corporations for their consumer goods are nothing to him. When Kingsley complains that he doesn't like Marlowe's less than cordial manner, Marlowe replies, "That's all right, I'm not selling it" (7). That Kingsley *is* selling his own manner and appearance quickly becomes clear. He begins the interview by "march[ing] briskly behind about eight hundred dollars' worth of executive desk and plant[ing] his backside in a tall leather chair," but by the end of the conversation he is admitting that "I have a good job here, but a job is all it is. I can't stand scandal. I'd be out of here in a hurry if my wife got mixed up with the police" (8, 14). Marlowe does not have a posh, air-conditioned office, but at least his seedy place of business is his for keeps.

It's no accident that Gillerlain is a cosmetics company. The cosmetics industry came of age with commodity culture, experiencing phenomenal growth between 1890 and 1930.[26] The beauty culture of the early twentieth century, centered in expensive, urban salons designed to serve elite white women, was at first critical of visible cosmetics. Rather than painting the face, entrepreneurs such as Helena Rubinstein and Elizabeth Arden focused on beauty regimens that, through diet, exercise, breathing, rest, and appropriate cleansing, would allow one's natural beauty to become apparent. Visible cosmetics were at best a stopgap measure to cover the imperfections in one's skin while one excised the imperfections in one's life that had caused them.

The "mass" lines of cosmetics sold in drugstores, however, abandoned "true" beauty principles to embrace visible artifice, particularly that made popular by film actresses, whose close-ups were used to promote the lipstick and mascara they wore in films. Makeovers focused on creating different "looks" through the obvious use of color. These looks, the fashionable faces that women in the 1920s and 1930s could change at will, were like the roles of screen stars. A woman of the 1920s could choose any number of fashionable faces, each designed to please a particular audience.

The Lady in the Lake focuses on the disappearances of two such fashionable women: Derace Kingsley's wife, Crystal, and Muriel Chess, wife of the caretaker at the Kingsleys' mountain cabin. They disappear on the same night, and neither is found until more than a month later. One body, identified as that of Muriel, is found under a pier in the lake near the mountain cabin. Marlowe spends most of the story tracking the other woman. He eventually finds her, but she is strangled in her apartment shortly after meeting with him. At the center of the novel is a case of reversed identities. The lady in the lake was actually Crystal Kingsley; the other was Muriel Chess. Their various cuckolded husbands, ex-husbands, and lovers cannot distinguish between these two reckless blondes, who continually alter their appearances with makeup and costumes.

The two women are, in fact, quite different. Everyone thinks of Crystal Kingsley as "a reckless little idiot with no brains and no control," but Marlowe describes Muriel Chess as a "cold-blooded little bitch" (208–9). The Crystal Kingsley her husband describes is "young, pretty, reckless, and wild," prone to drink and easily seduced by men who take advantage of her (15). She is such a poor crook she cannot even get away with petty shoplifting. Muriel Chess has a previous life as Mildred Haviland, an accomplished liar, murderer, and blackmailer. She is clever enough to fool most of the men in the novel. Only a bellhop whom Marlowe questions understands how easily men can be manipulated: "These small blondes are so much of a pattern that a change of clothes or light or makeup makes them all alike or all different" (97).

Recognizing his wife's clothes and her jade necklace, Bill Chess promptly identifies Crystal Kingsley's corpse as Muriel. Even Marlowe fails to identify Muriel Chess. In their first encounter, she introduces herself as Mrs. Fallbrook, a landlady. She claims to have been poking around the house of Crystal Kingsley's playboy lover, Chris Lavery, trying to collect her overdue rent. Marlowe describes her as "a slender woman of uncertain age, with untidy brown hair, a scarlet mess of a mouth, too much rouge on her cheekbones, shadowed eyes. She wore a blue tweed suit that looked like the dickens with the purple hat that was doing its best to hang on to the side of her head" (107). When Marlowe encounters her again, masquerading as Crystal Kingsley, he does not recognize her: "I tried to make up my mind whether her face was familiar or just such a standard type of lean, rather hard, prettiness that I must have seen it ten thousand times" (199). He tells her that he'd been given "a rather different idea of you" by Kingsley and Lavery, but he fails to make anything of the discrepancy. She looks enough like Crystal Kingsley to let him dismiss her sharper intellect and "quiet secret face" (203). Marlowe talks to Muriel for more than half an hour before realizing that she is the "landlady" he saw at the scene of Chris Lavery's murder. He could not connect the "slim, brown-haired girl in coal black slacks and a yellow shirt and a long gray coat" with the landlady in a loud purple hat, blue tweed suit and "messed-up makeup" (199). Having assembled different selves for each occasion from clothing and cosmetics, Muriel/Mildred in effect makes herself a different person so far as the unsophisticated male observers are concerned.

There are, in fact, way too many cosmetics for Marlowe's comfort in *The Lady in the Lake*, evidence of the duplicitous nature of the consuming women at the center of the case. When searching through the contents of Muriel Chess's dressing table, Marlowe notes that "There was the usual stuff women use on their faces and fingernails and eyebrows, and it seemed to me that there was too much of it" (87). The murder scene in Lavery's apartment is also marked by an excess of cosmetics and costuming. Face powder is spilled on the dressing table, and a towel is smeared with dark lipstick. Even after Lavery's body has grown cold, so much perfume lingers in the air that it's clear that too much of it had been used (114).

All sorts of important epiphanies hinge on costuming in this novel.[27] The key to discovering Muriel Chess's double life as Mildred Haviland is an anklet from her ex-husband, which she has hidden in the powdered sugar at her new husband's cabin. "A woman's hiding place," Marlowe calls it, and the local sheriff admits that he would never have found it had he not knocked over the box of sugar accidentally (84). The police pin the murder of Chris Lavery on Crystal Kingsley because the black-and-white suit in which she was last seen is hanging in Lavery's closet. Marlowe begins to suspect that Muriel Chess has met with foul play when he finds a peach-colored, silk-and-lace slip in her drawer: "Silk slips were not being left behind that year, not by any woman in her senses" (87). The high-heeled dancing slipper of a dope doctor's wife suggests that her death was a murder, not a suicide; its heel shows no signs that she walked down the rough concrete path to the garage where she died (188). Marlowe is finally tipped off that Muriel/Mildred was Chris Lavery's "landlady" by another detail of costuming: The dark landlady must be Muriel, he decides, since the loud purple hat, so awful with dark hair, would have looked quite sharp on a blonde (208).

On the most literal level, these epiphanies suggest that costuming and self-presentation are a matter of life and death, pointing to larger issues that one must not ignore. Although hard-boiled fiction demonstrated how to read and manipulate appearances, it distrusted commodity culture and the feminized consumers who were its most enthusiastic subjects.

Marlowe prefers men—slightly scruffy men, whose rough edges testify to their lack of interest in misleading self-presentation. In *The Lady in the Lake*, the sheriff of the isolated mountain community where the Kingsleys' cabin is located appeals to Marlowe for precisely this reason. "He had a sweat-stained Stetson on the back of his head and his large hairless hands were clasped comfortably over his stomach, above the waistband of a pair of khaki pants that had been scrubbed thin years ago. His shirt matched the pants except that it was even more faded. It was buttoned tight to the man's thick neck and undecorated by a tie.... The star on his left breast had a bent point.... I liked everything about him" (53). The sheriff's lack of pretension, his willingness to represent himself exactly as he is, is a refreshing contrast to the outrageously costumed, outrageously dishonest, consuming women at the center of Marlowe's case.

In *The Lady in the Lake*, Chandler articulates class through gender, setting the virility of working-class men and women against the effeminacy of wealthy women and men. The "working men" include Marlowe, the rural sheriff in his weathered khakis, and Kingsley's secretary, Adrienne Fromsett, who qualifies as a "man" in Chandler's world. She costumes herself in a steel-gray business suit, a blue shirt, and a man's tie, and her tough-guy act keeps Marlowe effectively in his place. Her manly credentials are evident not only in her masculine apparel and tough demeanor, but also in her frugally furnished apartment. Her paycheck, she tells Marlowe, is so small that she cannot afford the cosmetics that her company sells (129). Her income, if not her gender, has placed her outside consumer culture.

These residual remnants of artisan culture are increasingly beset by consuming "women" of all sorts—carefully costumed playboys (Lavery), executives in fancy offices (Kingsley), and the little blondes with their too-full closets and excessive makeup who are at the center of the novel. However successfully these "women"/consumers dupe the commodity-illiterate men, they are ultimately killed off in acts of violent narrative retribution. Lavery is shot in his shower while primping to go out, and the two murdered blondes end up in decidedly unpretty poses—a ghastly, waterlogged corpse in the lake and a strangled and mutilated body on a pull-down bed.

This novel, then, clearly set out the rules by which a residual artisan culture of manly producers and an emergent commodity culture of feminine consumers operated. Like hard-boiled fiction in general, it served as both a guide to reading the social order inscribed in differently classed bodies and homes and a critique of consumer society. Hard-boiled fantasy prefers a working man's weathered khakis to the designer suits of society women, and the hero's monastic domicile to the ostentatiously furnished homes of the wealthy.

Hard-boiled writing's profound distrust of the impeccably groomed is particularly noticeable in Dashiell Hammett's paired short stories "The Big Knockover" and "$106,000 Blood Money," published in *Black Mask* in February and May of 1927.[28] The stories center on a bank heist of unprecedented proportions, involving hundreds of gangsters, grifters, and ex-cons who come to San Francisco from all over the United States. Once the robbery has taken place, the crooks turn on one another and gang warfare ensues. The Continental Op is assisted in this case by Jack Counihan, a novice who comes from a wealthy family. The Op describes him:

Jack was a tall, slender lad of twenty-three or four who had drifted into the Continental's employ a few months before. It was the first job he'd ever had and he wouldn't have had it if his father hadn't insisted that if sonny wanted to keep his fingers in the family till, he'd have to get over the notion that squeezing through a college graduation was enough work for one lifetime. So Jack came to the Agency. He thought gumshoeing would be fun. In spite of the fact that he'd rather catch the wrong man than wear the wrong neck-tie, he was a promising young thief-catcher. A likable youngster, well-mus-cled for all his slimness, smooth-haired, with a gentleman's face and a gen-tleman's manner, nervy, quick with head and hands, full of the don't-give-a-damn gaiety that belonged to his youthfulness. He was jingle-brained, of course, and needed holding, but I would rather work with him than with a lot of old-timers I knew (360–61).

The Continental Op takes Counihan under his wing, showing him the nuts and bolts of the detective business. The Op, uncharacteristically, is full of benevolent paternalism, calling Counihan "son," "youngster," and "child," and offering advice and good-natured ribbing. His benev-olence evaporates in a hurry, however, when he and the Old Man—owner of the Continental Detective Agency—discover that Counihan is selling out the agency to Papadopoulos, the gangster who master-minded the heist. Although Counihan's betrayal is not revealed to the reader until the end of "$106,000 Blood Money," Hammett critiques Counihan's impeccable grooming, and by extension his penchant for dissembling, throughout the two stories.

When Counihan calls the Op for backup after getting a hot tip, the Op comments dryly that the information must be tremendous indeed, since Counihan's usually impeccable collar is askew (415). When Couni-han complains that the director of the agency never sends him out on exciting or dangerous jobs, the Op replies: "He is afraid to risk some-thing happening to you. He says in all his fifty years of gumshoeing he's never seen such a handsome op, besides being a fashion plate and a social butterfly and the heir to millions. His idea is we ought to keep you as a sort of show piece . . ." (433). Setting Counihan up to be killed when the criminals are arrested, the Op tells him that they are going out on a job for which he should be "all dressed up—evening duds . . . every-thing but the high hat" (433). The thug accompanying them to the final shoot-out makes a point of ridiculing Counihan's evening dress. "Your friend's a waiter, huh?" he says (434).

When the Op accuses Counihan of double-crossing the agency, he blames the young man's dishonesty not on his desire for a cut of the

crooks' money or on his love for a millionaire's daughter who has got-
ten mixed up with Papadopoulos, but on his "vanity." Counihan's pride
made him an easy target for the gangster's machinations. "So you were
meat to Papadopoulos' grinder," the Op says. "He gave you a part you
could play to yourself—a super-gentleman-crook, a mastermind, a desperate suave villain, and all that kind of romantic garbage. That's the
way you went, my son" (448). The slope to a life of crime, the Op
implies, is greased with concern for impression management and social
performance, with attention to "playing a part."[29]

Still, the story resists easy closure. The Op is sickened by his part in
Counihan's death. Counihan was not a bad young man, just too eager
to cut a figure in the world to remain loyal to his coworkers. The Op
refuses the agency director's thanks for taking Counihan out of com-
mission, and goes home at the end of the story "tired" and "washed out"
to nurse his psychic wounds for a couple of weeks before returning to
work (451).

Black Mask's invective against "dandies" such as Counihan sounds a
little hysterical to modern ears. The August 15, 1923, issue of *Black Mask*
carried an editorial piece entitled "The Fancyman," in which the author
noted the number of recent news stories about slickly groomed con
men who sweet-talked wealthy women out of large sums. We know the
type, the author told his readers—the "macaroni," the "lounge lizard,"
the "male beauty"—those "dandified little brothers of the rich" whose
charming exteriors hide the hearts of predators. "Between an 'honest,'
out-and-out highwayman with blackjack and automatic and a simper-
ing fancyman with perfume and guile," the author concluded, "I prefer
the yegg!"[30] Over the course of its thirty-one years in print, *Black Mask*
seldom ventured into social commentary,[31] yet its editors considered
"fancymen" enough of a threat to devote this column to them.

Reading Queerness, Performing Manliness

Someone properly trained in the arts of reading clothing and manners
could identify not only an individual's class but his or her sexuality. The
introduction of Joel Cairo from Dashiell Hammett's *The Maltese Falcon*,
originally a *Black Mask* serial, is a case in point. Effie Perine, Sam Spade's
secretary, presents Cairo's card to Spade, declaring "This guy is queer."
The description follows: "Mr. Joel Cairo was a small-boned dark man
of medium height. His hair was black and smooth and very glossy. His

features were Levantine. A square-cut ruby, its sides paralleled by four baguette diamonds, gleamed against the deep green of his cravat. His black coat, cut tight to narrow shoulders, flared a little over slightly plump hips. His trousers fitted his round legs more snugly than was the current fashion. The uppers of his patent-leather shoes were hidden by fawn spats. He held a black derby hat in a chamois-gloved hand and came towards Spade with short, mincing, bobbing steps. The fragrance of *chypre* came with him. . . . He sat down primly, crossing his ankles, placing his hat on his knees, and began to draw off his yellow gloves."[32]

The passage begins with the conclusion that Cairo is "queer"; the evidence follows. He has a woman's mincing steps, her way of sitting, her fondness for jewels and perfume. His colorful, unconventionally cut clothing is a fashion statement about sexuality. George Chauncey lists a variety of sartorial cues through which "fairies" could be identified in early–twentieth-century working-class communities: flamboyant clothes, green suits, tight-cuffed trousers, half-length flaring topcoats, red ties, suede or high-heeled shoes, bright feathers in hatbands.[33] "In the right context," Chauncey argues, "appropriating even a single feminine—or at least unconventional—style or article of clothing might signify a man's identity as a fairy."[34] Cairo is a walking assemblage of such cues. To read such a passage pedagogically would be easy; it models the process through which conclusions about sexual identity could be reached.

Costuming and performance signaled sexual identity in working-class communities at this time, when gender, the performance of masculine or feminine behaviors, rather than the sex of one's partner, was the determining factor.[35] George Chauncey explains: "The fundamental division of male sexual actors in much of turn-of-the century working-class thought . . . was not between 'heterosexual' and 'homosexual' *men*, but between conventionally masculine males, who were regarded as men, and effeminate males, known as fairies or pansies who were regarded as virtual women. . . . The heterosexual-homosexual binarism that governs our thinking about sexuality today, and that, as we shall see, was already becoming hegemonic in middle-class sexual ideology, did not yet constitute the common sense of working-class sexual ideology."[36]

A fairy was effeminate, then, not only in his desire for men but also in his clothing and conduct. A man, even if he engaged in sexual activity with other men, was manly as long as he performed the "masculine" part. The plasticity of sexual identities in this worldview does a great deal to explain the compulsive manliness of hard-boiled fiction, its con-

viction that manhood was earned through its more or less continual performance. This performance was becoming more difficult for working-
class men as the bulwarks of their gender identity—all-male work and
leisure spaces, skilled work and the family wage that used to accompany
it—eroded.

Moreover, gender and sexuality mapped easily onto the class sym-
pathies of hard-boiled fiction. There was a fine line between effeminacy
or dressing like a fairy and upper-class gentility. Cairo is offensive not
only because of his she-manliness but because of his expensive clothes
and jewelry. His class background and his sexuality are arguably insep-
arable. Just as virile manhood in hard-boiled worlds was inevitably artisanal, effeminacy had everything to do with gentility. Gender styles
were taken as markers of class status, and class styles were read in gendered terms.

Hard-boiled fiction between the wars is full of homosexual male
characters. Chandler's *The Big Sleep* oozes hatred for Carol Lundgren,
who kills Joe Brody for murdering his queen. Marlowe himself imper-
sonates a fairy in a rare-book shop, costuming himself in horn-rimmed
sunglasses and a falsetto,[37] but queerness does not pay in hard-boiled
fiction. The gay men are always linked to other transgressions—pornography, theft, drug dealing, whatever—and they are usually murdered or
marched off to prison at the close.

The homophobia of hard-boiled fiction arises in part from its own
focus on the bonds between men. For example, until quite late in his
career, Chandler's Marlowe lived a monastic life.[38] Hard-boiled fiction
is often structured by love triangles in which the love of two men for
each other is mediated through the body of a woman.[39] In *The Big Sleep*,
Rusty Regan marries General Sternwood's daughter as the closest accessible love object to the general himself. Hammett's *The Glass Key*
involves the love between Ned Beaumont and his mobster boss, Paul
Madvig, mediated through Janet Henry, whom they both love.

As early as the late 1940s, the vivid homoerotic descriptions in Chandler's fiction had captured the attention of critics. Gershon Legman
went so far as to suggest that Chandler's Marlowe was "clearly homosexual," a charge to which Chandler and numerous fans responded with
outraged denials and blustering.[40] The evidence is hard to deny, however. In *Farewell, My Lovely*, Marlowe, who has been resisting his attrac-
tion to Anne Riordan, the red-haired daughter of an ex-cop, does not
resist the charm of "Red," an ex-cop who helps him sneak aboard a

gangster's gambling boat. Red has a "soft, dreamy" voice, "so delicate for a big man it was startling." He has "eyes like a girl, a lovely girl," and his skin is "as soft as silk."⁴¹ In a moment of vulnerability, Marlowe confides to Red that he is "scared stiff," then tells him all about the case he's working on: "I told him a great deal more than I intended to. It must have been his eyes" (251). Marlowe finds Red a great comfort: He "leaned close to me and his breath tickled my ear" (255), and "He took hold of my hand. His was stern, hard, warm and slightly sticky" (257). Contrast this vision of intense, physical camaraderie with Marlowe's refusal of Anne Riordan's aid after he suffers narcotic poisoning. He demands that she take him home, and once there, he savors the smell of dust and tobacco, expressing his appreciation for "the smell of a world where men live" (190).

Lesbians, on the other hand, were unrepresentable in the hard-boiled imagination. The manly women who littered the pages of hard-boiled fiction between the wars were adamantly heterosexual, often predatory in their pursuit of the hero. Although queerness (manly women, womanly men) often brought violent retribution (murder, imprisonment, or execution), the penalties followed gender lines. Effeminate (often gay) men were almost never sympathetically drawn and were usually dispatched rapidly. Manly women (never lesbians) fascinated the hard-boiled imagination, getting a great deal of space before being shut down. Chapter 6 discusses these women at greater length. Suffice it to say here that a worldview that conceived of gender and sexuality as a matter of costuming and performance rendered men both anxious about their own he-manliness and profoundly nervous about she-men. Performing and reading heterosexual manliness mattered so much to white, working-class readers during this period precisely because the workplace autonomy and homosocial bonding that had anchored their gender and class identities were increasingly untenable.

Race and the Commodity Aesthetic

Just as hard-boiled fiction simultaneously condemned commodity culture and offered lessons in how it worked, it participated enthusiastically in racisms of its time while portraying race as yet another identity that one could perform. Chandler's *The Little Sister* features Dolores Gonzales, a high-class Mexican whore, who flaunts a stereotypically aggressive Latin sexuality. In the closing pages of the novel, however, she turns out to be the Anglo lover of a petty gangster from Cleveland who taught herself a few words in Spanish and affected a vaguely foreign way of speaking.[42] Her performance was good enough to fool almost all of the people all of the time. In Chandler's *The Long Goodbye* (1953), Terry Lennox, a fine specimen of Anglo-Saxon manhood, bears the scars of eighteen months as a prisoner of the Germans in the Great War on his even, aristocratic features. When, after supposedly having died in Mexico, he returns at the close of the book disguised as a Mexican, only Marlowe's brotherly affection for Lennox sees past the surgically altered features. [43]

The running gag in Chandler's *The High Window* is Marlowe's sense of solidarity with a statue of a little black boy in livery in his client's front yard. "He looked a little sad," Marlowe says, "as if he had been waiting there a long time and was getting discouraged." After an ill-tempered housekeeper has taken his card and slammed the door in his face, Marlowe muses: "I thought that maybe I ought to have gone to the back door." He pats the "little Negro" on the head with the words, "Brother, you and me both."[44] Race here is less a matter of skin color than a power relationship. Marlowe is "black" in this scenario because he is a poorly paid hireling of a wealthy white woman.

The most powerful tales of ethnic masquerade came from Erle Stanley Gardner, whose private eye Ed Jenkins spent large portions of his eighteen-year career in *Black Mask* in drag as a Chinaman. In the June 1930 "Hell's Kettle," Jenkins leases two adjoining flats—one as Dr. Chew, a Chinese herb doctor and fortune-teller, the other as the ethnically unmarked Colonel Grayson. "There was a connecting stairway," he explains, "I could shift instantly from one personality to another."[45] Jenkins has all he needs to pass himself off as Chinese: "an ability to speak Cantonese dialect like a native, strips of adhesive tape under a skullcap, drawing my eyes in a slant, a quickly removable face stain, Chinese silk clothes" (104). Moreover, he has mastered the "shuffling gait of a Chinaman" and "the lilting singsong with which an educated Chinaman masters the English language" (104, 105).

Jenkins describes his transformations as a process of remaking himself, with no sense of a true identity on which to anchor his constructions. "I walked to the back of the flat, took off the Chinese clothes, climbed the stairs, unlocked a door, adjusted my spectacles and mustache, put on a suit of tweeds that were distinctive, picked up my cane and broad-brimmed hat, and became Colonel Grayson" (111). Jenkins describes his change of clothes and role not as a disguise but as "becoming," a formulation that fits with the culture of personality and its commodity aesthetic. Moreover, Jenkins's skill at costuming and performance makes him better at doing his job—just what the ads for Lee's "promotion clothes" promised *Black Mask* readers. In this story, Jenkins's masquerade helps him foil "The Full Dress Kid," an Anglo gangster who always appears in evening dress. In others, his service to members of the Chinese community and his deep knowledge of their culture win him membership in it.

Black Mask argued for the authenticity of Gardner's Chinatown mysteries in its writers' column, "Behind the Mask."[46] Citing Gardner's ability to speak Chinese like a native, his travels to southeast Asia, and his law practice defending Chinese-American clients, *Black Mask* offered Gardner's fiction as an insider's account. Gardner later shored up his own credibility with readers of Street & Smith's *Clues* in a January 1939 column: "I always stuck with the Chinese and they stuck with me," Gardner wrote. "I learned something of their language and psychology, and, later on, when I had entered the writing profession and was able to break away from an office, I went over to China. By that time, I had a host of friends and was able to speak their language well enough to get by. . . . I didn't see the things which the ordinary tourist in China does see, but on the other hand, I saw things the ordinary tourist could never see. I returned from China with notebooks bulging with local color, adventures, and experiences."[47]

As in much popular fiction of the period, the racism in hard-boiled fiction seems blatant to a modern reader. Gardner's Chinatown mysteries, in particular, depend on assumptions about the devious nature of the Chinese and their fondness for ostentatious display. But these assumptions coexist uneasily with a worldview that conceives of selves as a matter of performance and costuming, a worldview in which identities—on which racisms depend—could be quite slippery.

Dashiell Hammett's "Dead Yellow Women," which ran in *Black Mask* in 1925, has an assimilated Chinese-American woman at its center. The story opens with a description of Lillian Shan, who is hiring the Continental Detective Agency to solve the murder of her maid and to find her missing servants: "She was sitting straight and stiff in one of the Old Man's chairs when he called me into his office—a tall girl of perhaps twenty-four, broad-shouldered, deep-bosomed, in mannish gray clothes. That she was Oriental showed only in the black shine of her bobbed hair, in the pale yellow of her unpowdered skin, and in the fold of her upper lids at the outer eye-corners, half hidden by the dark rims of her spectacles. But there was no slant to her eyes, her nose was almost aquiline, and she had more chin than Mongolians usually have. She was modern Chinese-American from the flat heels of her tan shoes to the crown of her untrimmed felt hat."[48]

Shan's American image is an acquired one, however. The Op reconstructs the process through which a small Chinese girl, arriving in California in 1912, became the imposing American woman sitting in his boss's office: "She had been ten-year-old Ai Ho, a very Chinese little girl, when her father had brought her to California. All that was Oriental of her now were the features I have mentioned and the money her father had left her. Her name, translated into English, had become Water Lily, and then, by another step, Lillian. It was as Lillian Shan that she had attended an eastern university, acquired several degrees, won a tennis championship of some sort in 1919, and published a book on the nature and significance of fetishes, whatever all that is or are" (190).

In the Op's description, Lillian Shan's identity is mostly a matter of packaging. She becomes an almost ethnically unmarked New Woman once she dons a man-tailored suit and flat shoes, and adds a college degree and some championship tennis to her résumé. Very little of her Chinese childhood is still legible in her dress and conduct. Shan is no giggling child with bound feet. Hammett makes this distinction clear by introducing just such a character, a tiny, terrified slave girl named Hsiu Hsiu: "She wasn't four and a half feet high—a living ornament from somebody's shelf. Her face was a tiny oval of painted beauty, its perfection emphasized by the lacquer-black hair that was flat and glossy around her temples. Gold earrings swung beside her smooth cheeks, a jade butterfly was in her hair. A lavender jacket, glittering with white stones, covered her from under her chin to her knees. Lavender stockings showed under her short lavender trousers, her bound-small feet were in slippers of the same color, shaped like kittens, with yellow stones for eyes and aigrettes for whiskers" (224). The Op tells the reader that he offers all these sartorial details, all this "our-young-ladies'-fashion stuff," to convince us that Hsiu Hsiu is "impossibly dainty," a powerful contrast to the imposing and Americanized figure of Lillian Shan at the start of the narrative.

The metamorphosis from little Chinese girl to American New Woman, however, is little more than skin-deep. Shan reappears at the end of the story having taken up her ethnic birthright. The Op describes her as "the queen of something" as she stands before him in her traditional costume: "She was a tall woman, straight-bodied and proud. A butterfly-shaped headdress decked with the loot of a dozen jewelry stores exaggerated her height. Her gown was amethyst filigreed with gold above, a living rainbow below" (237). When he asks her what she is doing in the Chinatown hideout of gangster Chang Li Ching, she tells him: "I am here where I belong. . . . I have come back to my people."

The Op is no great believer in the claims of blood and culture, however. He calls this explanation "a lot of bunk," and substitutes an explanation of an alliance based on self-interest: It is profitable for both Chang and Shan to be allies at this particular moment (224). The account Shan gives the Op—that Chang was using her home to smuggle guns out of the country to aid the Chinese in their struggle against imperialist Japanese forces—is shown to be untrue. Chang was smuggling opium, guns, and illegal immigrants to finance his own personal empire. Race and ethnicity are powerful organizers of the world, the story seems to suggest, but race is less a matter of having a true, ethnic self than it is a makeover that one can take up or cast aside at will.

The Op causes a breach between Chang and his Anglo gangster ally, The Whistler, by showing Chang a faked photograph of his ally wearing a Japanese medal of honor. The story closes with a note sent to the Op by Chang, saying that he had discovered the trickery and that he felt foolish for letting his "patriotic fervor" interfere with an otherwise lucrative partnership (246). Sean McCann argues that "Dead Yellow Women" offers race as "an empty, but potent social fiction"—yet another idiom through which personal interests are articulated.[49] Although this story, like most hard-boiled tales, is full of ethnic and racial stereotypes, the action calls into question the reality and integrity of the identities on which such stereotyped representations are based.

In this way, hard-boiled detective stories were Americanizing narratives. They invoked familiar racial and ethnic distinctions, but suggested that such distinctions could be emphasized or deemphasized as one's interests dictated. For working-class readers enmeshed in networks of kin and ethnic culture, hard-boiled fiction modeled other ways of life: "American," bourgeois. In the hard-boiled world, a person had an ethnic identity but was first and foremost a self-serving individual. If race and ethnicity were merely social conventions, the world looked very different than it did from within the ethnic enclave. The exploitation of ethnic differences by corporations to keep wages low and workers unorganized looked a good deal more suspect if ethnicity were merely a social fiction. Moreover, reserving a larger proportion of one's wages for personal consumption rather than family support made more sense. This is not to suggest that certain ethnic groups did not have a more difficult time "becoming white" than others, but to point out that this fiction offered readers different ways of thinking about whatever ethnicity they embraced or were assigned.

The slipperiness of racial and ethnic identities in hard-boiled detective fiction was also about the loss of white, male privilege in the workplace. In the United States, working-class consciousness arose in the nineteenth century in opposition to slavery. Workers' sense of themselves as working-class and "white" were mutually constitutive. "They were free laborers because they were not slaves," David Roediger explains. "They considered themselves manly/respectable/Americanized/mature/middle class because they were not allegedly degraded and dissolute people of color."[50] Whiteness functioned as a psychological wage that, in part, compensated white workers for their powerlessness at work and the increasingly alienated nature of their labor. The status and privileges conferred upon them because they were white eased the psychic burdens of class exploitation and capitalist work discipline that shaped life in their working-class communities.

The anxieties over racial and ethnic categories expressed in hard-boiled detective fiction would have resonated with native-born and first-wave immigrant readers' experiences with the de-skilling of craft labor. Even men with solidly Anglo-Saxon names—"Philip Marlowe," for instance—had, in a sense, been reduced to black boys in livery by Taylorism. Hard-boiled detective fiction assured readers that they were superior to blacks and recent immigrants, but also anxiously rehearsed how unstable the line between "them" and "us" was.

Raymond Williams closes his 1958 *Culture and Society* by suggesting that working-class culture is basically collective in nature, whereas bourgeois culture is characterized by ideas, institutions, and structures of feeling that are profoundly individualistic.[51] If Williams is correct, pulp detective magazines were an uneasy class mélange. In hard-boiled fiction, the private eye was an "honest proletarian," but above all he was an individual. The celebration of proletarian worldviews was offset by careful instructions in consumerist ways. Hard-boiled fiction recognized consumption—the strategic purchase and display of commodities—as important to the reproduction of class hierarchies, but hailed workers as *individual* consumers. In contrast, the contemporaneous labor movement's strategy of encouraging shoppers to "look for the union label" emphasized class solidarity in the face of structural and institutional inequalities. Hard-boiled fiction's interest in clothing, furniture, speech, and manners, then, was evidence of a larger concern with how identities are formed and read. Readers of this fiction were hailed simultaneously as savvy creatures of commodity culture and defenders of artisanal character in a world increasingly overrun by (effeminate) consuming/performing subjects. Maintaining this mutually contradictory position required some fast talking—the kind of rhetorical prowess that perhaps only hard-boiled heroes possessed.

5

Talking Tough

It is doubtful if even Ernest Hemingway has ever written more effective dialogue than may be found within the pages of this extraordinary tale of gunmen, gin and gangsters. The author displays a style of amazing clarity and compactness, devoid of literary frills and furbelows, and his characters, who race through the story with the rapidity and destructiveness of machine guns, speak the crisp, hard-boiled language of the underworld.

Bookman review of Hammett's *Red Harvest*

Frankly, Erle . . . nothing has worried me so much since I have been here as a suggestion, or rather an impression, of our being in any way "high-brow." It has been my bête noire.

Joseph Thompson Shaw, editor of *Black Mask*, to Erle Stanley Gardner

ashiell Hammett's *Red Harvest*, serialized in the late 1920s in *Black Mask*, begins with a meditation on issues of class and language. "I first heard Personville called Poisonville by a red-haired mucker named Hickey Dewey in the Big Ship in Butte," says Hammett's narrator, the unnamed Continental Op. "He also called his shirt a shoit. I didn't think anything of what he had done to the city's name. Later I heard men who could manage their r's give it the same pronunciation. I still didn't see anything in it but the meaningless sort of humor that used to make richardsnary the thieves' word for dictionary. A few years later I went to Personville and learned better."[1]

The Op takes different kinds of language as his topic in this passage. He first calls attention to differences in pronunciation related to the speaker's class origins. He notes next that the vocabulary of thieves differs from Standard English. The Op himself is fluent in different class and cultural codes. He is both a self-conscious crafter of language, one who recognizes the importance to social standing of pronouncing one's r's, and a man who is at home conversing with thieves and other lowlifes. His comments about the dictionary also suggest the intimate relationship between language and power. The Op's protests aside, there is a good deal of meaning in the thieves' humorous appropriation and renaming of the dictionary, a book that privileges an upper-class form of speech as normative.[2] Invoking the tendency of higher-class speakers to use more formal language, and that of thieves to use abbreviated slang, the thieves' joke makes it clear that the dictionary is probably more accurately described as Richard's rather than Dick's. Finally, the Op concedes that the mucker's language more accurately represents the city of Personville, which is overrun by crime and corruption.

This passage is fairly representative hard-boiled prose. As a genre, hard-boiled fiction was highly self-conscious and sophisticated about how language might be used in a variety of situations. Though "proper" speech was good for promotion into white-collar work, it was not particularly useful in negotiating with illiterate, armed thugs down by the docks. Grammatical or even literary language could ingratiate a private detective with millionaire clients, but not with underworld informants. Moreover, it was not always a good idea to address a person in the code that he or she best understood; confusing a listener sometimes served one's interests better. Hard-boiled fiction demonstrated that language was one of the primary means through which class, gender, and power hierarchies were (re)produced. Powerful speakers mastered a number of different speech codes and knew when and to whom each should be spoken.

The hard-boiled detective's mastery of several types of speech does not minimize the importance of his native tongue, that of American working men. Reviewers in literary gatekeepers of the period, *The New York Times Book Review*, *The Saturday Review of Literature*, and others, were preoccupied with the language of these texts—their "grand line of lowdown lingo"[3]—and its difference from Standard English or the literary prose with which regular book-buyers were more familiar. The

"Americanness" of the prose won praise from the American press and petulant complaints from the British about the "obscurest American slang" one encountered in this fiction.[4] Inflected by class and gender, this talk was, as one reviewer put it, "not the sort that was used in drawing-rooms in the good old days that grandmother so fondly remembers."[5] The coarseness of hard-boiled language, however appealing to the (male) ear, was not fit for polite society, particularly the society of respectable women. Dennis Porter links this language to the rugged individuals at the center of canonical American literature: "Bad grammar, slang, and even a strong regional accent, like cussing, blaspheming, hard drinking and tomcatting, were the prerogatives of men and boys, defensive reactions against the encroachments of civilizing womankind and the tyranny of hearth and home."[6]

Porter claims that the publication of hard-boiled fiction conferred "the dignity of print on what sounded like the language of ordinary people."[7] For working-class men, seeing their language (or something like it) in print gave it a form of legitimacy usually reserved for bourgeois speech, the Standard English in which most of the nation's official business was carried out. Ken Worpole found that British labor leaders after World War II remembered American hard-boiled fiction vividly, having found "the 'tough guy' vernacular style of writing" a particularly fruitful language through which to make sense of contemporary class experience.[8] Like the ads with which it shared space in *Black Mask*, this fiction offered readers demonstrations of the mutually constitutive relationship between language and class position. The hard-boiled hero's rhetorical prowess schooled readers in bourgeois speech, but reassured them that the terse, colorful, working-class vernacular more accurately described the world.

Education and Cultural Capital in Hard-Boiled Writing Culture

Frederick Nebel's 1933 *Sleepers East*, discussed at length in Chapter 3, demonstrates how one goes about learning and using a variety of different class codes. Representative Tom Linscott, recognizing that his working-class upbringing has not prepared him for the political wrangling in which he is now engaged, sets aside time each day to read with a dictionary and a thesaurus open beside him.[9] This suggests that for readers like Linscott, cultured speech and writing must be mastered, like a foreign language, through sustained practice and study. Linscott also rehearses for conversations with the bourgeoisie. Preparing to ask Knox, the defense attorney, to sacrifice his client for the benefit of Linscott's political machine, Linscott "had put words on paper, hundreds of them, memorized them and then torn them up" (71). Face-to-face, however, he is stymied by Knox's "easy going barrage of eloquence," and is unable to tell whether the "hodgepodge of words" directed at him is insulting or complimentary (70). Linscott's experience demonstrates that the kinds of self-help encouraged by pulp ads—reading such books as *How to Work Wonders With Words*, for example—are no match for men like Knox, whose middle-class upbringing gives them a formidable rhetorical advantage.[10]

This ambivalence about education typified hard-boiled fiction and the writing culture that surrounded it. *Black Mask* writers held a variety of seemingly contradictory positions with regard to schooling and the cultural capital that came with it. Few hard-boiled writers were well educated, and in this respect they resembled the average American. In 1920, the median number of years of school completed by Americans over the age of twenty-five was 8.2.[11] Nebel announced in *Black Mask*'s "Behind the Mask" column that he had "walked out" of school at fourteen and had "never set foot in a classroom since."[12] Dashiell Hammett left school at the age of fourteen to work odd jobs; Erle Stanley Gardner was booted out of several schools and colleges before teaching himself enough law to pass the California bar exam.

Perhaps because of their minimal schooling, many of these writers ridiculed book learning and regarded it as useless for anything but learned posturing. Hammett, according to Lillian Hellman, his longtime partner, read almost everything he could get his hands on—mathematics, Hegel, Icelandic sagas—but ridiculed her for reading literary and cultural criticism. "Carrying books," he called them—good only for keeping one's balance on the stairs on the way up to bed.[13] Carroll John Daly behaved as though mastery of the conventions of educated discourse were a waste of time. In his profile in "Behind the Mask," the editors introduced him as follows: "Like all geniuses, Mr. Daly places little importance on such slight matters as authentic spelling, but he says that after wasting a half hour searching for 'chaos' under 'k,' he gave up the matter and has since put the responsibility on the editor."[14]

Hard-boiled writers did value practical knowledge, whether derived from reading or experience. Nebel differentiated being a student of "life," who studied people at work and at play in the world, from being a student at school, for which he had no patience.[15] Hammett's autodidacticism gave him an amazing variety of practical information—such as how to stop leaks in swimming pools, how to build a trap for snapping turtles, and the basics of plasma physics.[16] The importance of "useful" knowledge in *Black Mask*'s culture was also evident in its ads, most of which offered training for "practical people" or taught what was required by "practical business" rather than information whose value was less obvious.[17]

Black Mask repeatedly reminded its audience that its writers had received their education in life, not school, citing their experience as journalists, detectives, soldiers, travelers, pilots, or whatever as evidence of the realism of its fiction. Raoul Whitfield, who wrote aviation mysteries, flew fighter planes in the war. Dashiell Hammett had been a Pinkerton private detective. Erle Stanley Gardner spoke Chinese and was completely at home in Chinatown, where he set many of his stories.[18] *Black Mask* culture sought to claim the practical experience possessed by laborers as knowledge—knowledge to be valued at least as highly as the kind obtained at school. Not only was practical experience central to manly, artisanal ideology, the high value placed on it was a compensatory strategy. By telling working men that the only education to which they had had access was superior, it gave them a measure of dignity and a way of competing with better-educated men.

Black Mask itself was more than a little ambivalent about cultural capital. The letters printed in the early years were anxious assertions of the magazine's appeal to an elite audience. Most of them came from doctors, lawyers, journalists, bankers, businessmen, professors, and the like. Many letters had headlines identifying the social and economic status of the writer: "From an Eminent English Author" or "From a Professor in America's Biggest School of Journalism," for example.[19] One column asserted that some of the most important men in the world were readers of detective stories: Woodrow Wilson, Frank B. Kellogg (Secretary of State under Coolidge and Hoover), King George, and others.[20] Some headlines equated *Black Mask* stories with the classics of Western civilization: "Reads Thackeray and *Black Mask*" or "*Black Mask* and Shakespeare."[21] Many letters contained literary allusions or learned phrases—a comparison to Poe, a reference to the "je ne sais quoi" of a particular story.[22]

At the same time, *Black Mask* took pains to distance itself from the world of "highbrows." One review of a book of ghost stories by a college professor reassured readers that "there is nothing of the usual professor's dulness [sic] about them."[23] Inaugurating a new feature about psychoanalysis (specifically the interpretation of dreams) entitled "Your Own Mysteries," the editors offered this justification for the seemingly academic undertaking: "It is not a highbrow experiment. It is a practical, helpful application of one of the newest sciences—psychoanalysis—by a recognized expert who knows what he is talking about."[24] "Science" and "expertise" name the knowledge valued in hard-boiled writing culture, knowledge that was both class- and gender-specific. Science and technology—virile pursuits—opposed such feminine and aristocratic subjects as art and literature. Rather than addressing liberally educated gentlemen, *Black Mask* invited readers to identify with skilled experts who used their hands-on training to mold the world to their desires.

Hard-boiled writing often ridiculed high culture, pointing to the superiority of the practical knowledge possessed by working men. William Brandon's ironically titled "It's So Peaceful in the Country," first published in *Black Mask* in November of 1943, opens with the familiar clash of class codes.[25] Horse Luvnik, an ungrammatical ex-convict, sits in a neighborhood bar thumbing the pages of a leather-bound, academic book on Edgar Allan Poe. By way of explaining how this distinguished volume came to be dedicated to him—in learned prose, complete with Latin epigraph—Horse tells the narrator that two Poe scholars, Homer Dingle and Dr. Dorothy Mady, had hired him as a burglar. It's no coincidence that the story hinges on scholarly manuscripts about Poe, creator of the prototype for the classical mysteries penned by the London Detection Club between the wars. Just as *Black Mask* held hard-boiled fiction superior to the Poe-inspired English-country-house species, Horse's street smarts prove superior to the book learning of the Poe scholars in "It's So Peaceful in the Country."

Dingle has hired Horse to steal Dr. Mady's notes every evening and return them before dawn every morning. Mady, however, catches him snooping around her house. Although she suspects that he is after her pearls, she hires him to steal Dingle's notes every morning and put them back every evening. For a while, Horse does very well, earning $100 a day from Dr. Mady and $100 each night from Mr. Dingle, and the two scholars make liberal use of each other's material. One night, unfortunately, Horse has a little too much to drink and confuses the boxes. Having discovered Horse's double-dealing, the scholars make him return their money. They now have no choice but cooperation, so they decide to collaborate on a single study, which they dedicate to Horse, whose "invaluable assistance" brought them together in the first place.

Throughout the narrative, the literate classes are made to look silly for their petty concerns and effete ways. Dingle, introduced with a bruised jaw and a swollen eye, tells Horse that Dr. Mady attacked him with a croquet mallet (the blackjack of the literate classes) when he politely asked her for access to her sources. Mady and Dingle have been conducting a feud in the pages of academic journals for years. Horse knows how to ingratiate himself with these self-important scholars. When Dingle tells Horse that he is the world's foremost authority on Poe (whose name means nothing to Horse), the burglar assures Dingle that he understands the magnitude and gravity of this claim. Horse justifies this harmless little lie to the narrator: "Why should I look like a dope?" (359). By the time Dr. Mady tells Horse that *she* is the world's foremost authority on Poe, he is ready for her, and claims to have seen a first edition of Poe's work in a museum—"to get lush with her, see, and it works" (363). Manipulating the literate classes is easy, Horse demonstrates, if you are attentive to their cues and willing to feed their egos. In yet a further leveling tactic, Horse's descriptions erase the differences between illiterate thugs and classically educated scholars. With his bruised face, Dingle looks like Paddy Malone, ex-boxer-turned-junkie, and Mady is "strictly uptown," reminding Horse of Daisy Gross, who, Horse reminds the narrator, used to sing sad songs at the Empyrean meat show, where on occasion she would "bust out on a high note and her pants would fall down" (361).

Although it seems that Mady and Dingle, who publish their volume and get married, have benefited at Horse's expense, everyone gets something. Horse did have to return all the money, with which he had hoped to buy a cigar store and settle down in a legitimate business, but when the narrator expresses his outrage that Mady and Dingle have cheated Horse out of the cash he "rightfully earned," Horse reveals that he swiped Mady's pearls on his way back to the city, and that the necklace just covered the price of the cigar store (368). His street smarts prove more than adequate for negotiating with better-educated men and women.

One could use information gained in school to intimidate others, however. Chandler's Marlowe alludes to Shakespeare, Browning, Hemingway, T. S. Eliot, the Brontës, Arthurian romance, and other literary touchstones, not to align himself with a particular tradition but to assert his dominance over opponents with less cultural capital.[26] In *Farewell*,

My Lovely, Marlowe taunts a cop by referring to him as Hemingway, an allusion that is frustratingly beyond the cop's experience.[27] When he is conversing with highbrows who might understand his literary allusions, however, Marlowe invariably turns to street lingo as a refusal to negotiate on their terms.[28] His ability to choose different types of speech for different audiences resonates with the *Black Mask* ads that promised mastery of language as a way of dominating others.[29]

The ideas about education, knowledge, and language in hard-boiled writing culture had wider circulation between the wars. During this period an almost universal consensus was reached about the importance of education. School enrollments, which had been increasing steadily since the late nineteenth century, continued to grow at a much faster rate than the general population. Enrollments in high schools and colleges skyrocketed, and large numbers of working people were enrolled in evening schools, vocational schools, or correspondence courses.[30] Robert and Helen Lynd, coauthors of *Middletown*, the 1929 ethnography of Muncie, Indiana, described education there as "a faith, a religion," particularly among the working class.[31]

This faith in education seems paradoxical, however, since many observers agreed with hard-boiled writers that much of what one learned in high school was irrelevant to everyday life. Students, the Lynds wrote, had to take the value of their high-school courses "largely on faith," since their immediate usefulness was mysterious: "Square root, algebra, French, the battles of the Civil War, the presidents of the United States before Grover Cleveland . . . the ability to write compositions or to use semicolons, sonnets, free verse, and the Victorian novel—all these and many other things that constitute the core of education simply do not operate in life as Middletown adults live it."[32] The content of an education did not matter as much as what an education stood for—an "open sesame" to admit working-class children to worlds closed to their parents, a way of "getting ahead" socially and economically for the business class.[33] Education counted most importantly as cultural capital, and this is what made its inequitable distribution so important to hard-boiled writing culture.

Though faith in education was nearly universal, access to institutions of higher learning was not. "The United States, like many other industrial countries sixty-five years ago," Carl Kaestle writes, "had widespread basic literacy training in elementary schools and a much more exclusive group trained in higher literacy skills in high schools and colleges."[34] Because education and access to more sophisticated literacies were unequally distributed, schools were one of the primary sites at which social hierarchies were continually produced and reinforced. In 1920, for example, less than 3 percent of the twenty-three-year-olds had graduated from college, and only 16 percent of seventeen-year-olds had finished high school.[35] Since these credentials were increasingly necessary for entrance into professional or white-collar life, schools became the gatekeepers of the social order, which tended to replicate itself because finishing high school was highly correlated with the wealth and occupation of one's parents. Free, public, elementary education made access to Standard English nearly universal, but the cultural literacy and more sophisticated reading practices that marked one as a well-educated person were available only to those whose families could afford college—or who could afford to stay in high school instead of getting a job.

Like education, the expanding world of print was class-fractured. Book production doubled between 1890 and the early 1920s, public libraries' circulation increased more than twice as fast as the rate of population growth, and the number and variety of magazines entering people's homes increased dramatically.[36] Very few outside the business class were book buyers, however, and periodical reading was also divided along class lines.[37] The audience for *Atlantic Monthly*, for example, consisted of wealthy, college-educated readers who reproduced their class position in part through the sophisticated reading practices they had learned in universities. Working-class readers, because of their limited access to higher education, read a different set of periodicals (including pulp magazines), which did not require much schooling to enjoy.

Marginal readers between the wars had little reading material other than pulp fiction available to them. Librarians, adult educators, and reading researchers during the Depression estimated that because of the restricted diffusion of advanced literacy, approximately half of American readers found books on topics that interested them too difficult in style or vocabulary.[38] These teachers and librarians sounded an alarm that eventually led to the 1935 founding of the Readability Lab at the Columbia University Library School. The lab performed research on what made books accessible to readers with limited education, and published a series of books aimed at this audience.[39] Meanwhile, pulp magazines offered these underserved readers fiction whose vocabulary and simple syntax did not require a high-school education.

Most readability formulas combined three variables: sentence length, word length, and word familiarity.[40] Hard-boiled fiction met the criteria for highly readable prose: Its sentences were short; its vocabulary was easy, familiar, and often heard in casual speech; and it was grammatically uncomplicated, eschewing the passive voice and other complex constructions. William Marling's minute analysis of Dashiell Hammett's prose estimates that 77 percent of the words are monosyllabic, and that fully 98 percent are of Anglo-Saxon stock. Hammett's fiction, then, included few learned Latinate borrowings that might be difficult for marginal readers. The average sentence length is very short—thirteen words or so in the early work from the pulps, and as few as eight in fight scenes.[41] A recent assessment of the difficulty of prose in newspapers and magazines from 1920 found that *Argosy*, an all-story pulp magazine, was considerably more readable than most newspapers and elite and middlebrow magazines of the period.[42] In Gray and Leary's *What Makes A Book Readable* (1935), the authors ranked all the pulp magazines in their sample in the "easy" category, based on a readability index derived from sentence length, proportion of monosyllables, variety of vocabulary, and number of simple sentences.[43] They went so far as to urge authors attempting to write more accessible prose to study cheap wood-pulp magazines and second- and third-grade textbooks as models.[44]

At the opposite end of the readability scale from the pulps were the high modernist works published in little magazines, the publications in which much of the New Critical modernist canon originally appeared. In John Guillory's view, New Critics valued, above all, difficulty (meaning ambiguity and paradox). Difficulty was a form of cultural capital,[45] and the close reading taught (initially, at least) only in universities reproduced class distinctions.[46]

There is some evidence from contemporary sources that the difficult prose the New Critics valued so highly did, indeed, succeed in its gatekeeping work. The formal innovation of some proletarian fiction of the period alienated many working-class readers. In a 1934 article entitled "What the Proletariat Reads" in *The Saturday Review of Literature*, Louis Adamic discussed his yearlong study of the reading habits of workers. He concluded that the American working class read very little besides newspapers and cheap magazines, least of all the proletarian literature that was supposedly directed at them.[47] The most powerful parts of the article were workers' reactions to some of the best proletarian writing of the period. For the most part, workers were frustrated by the "over-subdued," "too flat" style, and by the difficulty of the prose, which made reading such books "hard going." Adamic quotes one worker, who failed to finish William Rollins's *The Shadow Before*, at length:

> I didn't finish it. I couldn't. It's full of queer spelling, queer paragraphing, italics, and words in big type and all jumbled up in places, like parts of John Dos Passos's books. . . . And Dos Passos, by the way: why does he write so queer? I read "1919," which everybody seemed to rave about when it came out, and, man, it was like solving puzzles from start to finish. Some of the things I solved were interesting and true, I don't say they weren't; but why should a writer want to turn reading into a game? Why should I spend a week or two puzzling over a book? Why shouldn't they write so a fellow who isn't altogether dumb could understand things right away? Do they want to make me feel stupid and humble before their genius, or is that art?[48]

Pierre Bourdieu's work offers a means of interpreting this worker's comments. Formal innovation makes workers uncomfortable because it is a poor fit with their worldview. Whereas people raised in privileged homes, surrounded by material plenty, tend to view the world in aesthetic, distanced, formalist ways, the popular aesthetic subordinates form to function, rejecting formal experiments or "specifically artistic effects" that interfere with the "substance" or "content" of the work.[49] In the quoted worker's view, the book's language is good only insofar as it communicates ideas clearly. The "queer writing," which calls attention to the form of the text without helping it communicate, is just silly—a "game" or a "puzzle." The popular aesthetic, however, is a dominated aesthetic, always aware that there are more privileged, bourgeois ways of reading. Rather than dismiss aesthetic objects, working-class readers tend to be pluralistic and conditional about their judgments.[50] This worker was quick to say that what he did puzzle out of *1919* was true and powerful, though he questions the need for all this puzzling in the first place. Finally, part of workers' suspicion of high art stems from a conviction that formal innovation and artistic obscurity are intended, at least in part, to exclude people like them.

In Adamic's view, however exciting and effective "queer" writing may have seemed to the radical intelligentsia, its value to workers was dubious. Adamic estimated that only half of 1 percent of workers outside radical circles in New York even attempted to read these books. This lack of enthusiasm for modernist formal experimentation among workers was particularly important given the findings of reading researchers in the 1930s that poor readers were more influenced by factors of style in the selection of reading materials than they were by their interest in the subject.[51]

In fact, most proletarian novels during the interwar period were abysmal commercial failures, a fact that much of the literary left found acutely embarrassing. Even after accounting for the prohibitive cost of hardcover books during the Depression and the possibility that proletarian novels were reaching a wider audience through lending libraries, Barbara Foley concedes that proletarian novels could not be said to have reached a mass audience by any stretch of the imagination. In a 1934 *Daily Worker* article, Mike Gold, perhaps the best public-relations man literary proletarianism ever had, admitted that not even radical workers bought proletarian novels. As a consequence, many cultural critics maintained that proletarian novels were a "hot-house creation," and that the real proletarian literature was the pulp Westerns and romances that huge numbers of workers actually did read.[52]

Although Frankfurt School theorists thought that only formally complex, experimental fiction that refused easy identification to readers could resist appropriation and incorporation by capitalism, much of the American literary left had more pragmatic views. If workers such as those quoted by Adamic had no desire to read the stuff, it could hardly have much political impact. Revolutionary intellectuals who wanted to reach a mass readership might be better served by the documentary or narrative styles they described as "realistic." Addressing the 1935 Writer's Congress, worker-writer Jack Conroy had little positive to say about the innovations of literary modernism: "The effect of this desperate striving for novelty of phrase and imagery is often that of achieving a semi-private terminology almost unintelligible to the masses and a lamentable dullness in the narrative the innovator has set out to enliven and enrich."[53] Some members of the literary left conceded that a proletarian literature that proletarians actually read might have to look a good deal more like pulp magazines and a good deal less like John Dos Passos' *1919*, but no one embraced the pulps.

In 1934, the Marxist periodical *Pen & Hammer Bulletin* published an article entitled "The Pulps and Shinies" that claimed that the influence of popular magazines accounted, in part, for the "ideological weakness" of American workers. The author singled out *Black Mask*, criticizing it for "the implicit demand for glorification of the police, detective and private operatives, those strike-breaking enemies of the working class," and for obfuscating the place of class in defining crime and punishment.[54]

There is some evidence from *Black Mask* book reviews and reader letters that its readers did read in accordance with what Bourdieu calls the popular aesthetic or ethos. The book reviews that appeared in the early years of *Black Mask* reveal alternatives to the bourgeois, aesthetic ways of reading that value form over function. The reviews are full of conditional statements. Rather than telling a reader that a particular book was good, they told a reader what a book was good *for*, what kinds of satisfactions it was likely to bring. "If the colorful life of the Far East appeals to you, here is something that you will want to read and keep on your library shelves," wrote the reviewer of Henry Milner Rideout's *The Foot Path Way.* Another book was categorized as "a conventional melodrama of the wild and wooly Western school."[55] In each case the reviewer made it clear that the book was good for meeting certain needs—vicarious tourism, emotionally charged adventure. The letters featured in the "Our Readers' Private Corner" column sound remarkably similar. Many were less opinions on the merit of the stories than careful categorizations of every tale featured in the previous issue. One reader offered that "'The Belgrade Assassinations' is interesting history," and "'The Wallet that Weighed Too Much' is a fair story of the underworld to read on a train."[56] The categorizing impulse and the conditional statements suggest that these readers and reviewers accepted a range of reasons for reading and made an effort to match readers' needs with acceptable material.

Classifying books by the kind of reading they allow resembles the editorial practices of the Book-of-the-Month Club, which was founded in 1926.[57] This middlebrow aesthetic bears some resemblance to the aesthetic operating in hard-boiled writing culture at the time. Both reassured readers that the literary fare they offered would lack the dullness and dry difficulty of more self-consciously literary work, and both promised readers a pleasurable, accessible education of sorts. Here, however, the two aesthetics part company. The middlebrow was "feminine"; its consumers were defined against the solitary male reader who made his own decisions.[58] Hard-boiled fiction was clearly niche-marketed to self-styled manly men. Middlebrow texts offered intense emotional identifications, what Janice Radway calls a "sentimental education,"[59] but hard-boiled detective fiction revealed a stunning absence of affect, even in the face of unspeakable violence. If the scandal of the middlebrow was "cultural miscegenation"—the conjoining of culture and commodity, aesthetic and commercial, high and low[60]—the scandal of hard-boiled writing culture was its complete failure to be impressed by claims about the transcendent possibilities of high culture and aesthetics in the first place. Hard-boiled fiction began in pulps widely held to be less respectable than the literature of Main Street, but the work of Hammett and Chandler, at least, ended up with a degree of literary legitimacy akin to that of the alienated (male) high modernists to whom they bear some resemblance. Either from above or from below, hard-boiled fiction defined itself against the middle-class fiction of slick magazines and the genteel, effeminate literature of Main Street in which they trafficked.[61]

We know that readers of pulp detective fiction did not read in literary ways—that is, with a great deal of respect for the text as a linguistic artifact possessed of some structural unity. We know this because *Black Mask*'s editor had to tell them to read this way in a high-handed editorial entitled "A Word With Readers: How to Read Black Mask Stories." "You must not read these stories the way you probably read most other fiction tales," it admonished. "If you skip quickly over the pages, you will miss the background and the details of the complete picture which each story presents. If you read the first paragraphs and then jump to the end 'to see how it comes out' you will cheat yourself out of a rare pleasure and defeat the very purpose for which you bought the magazine.... You cannot get the full force of these stories if you spoil your own pleasure by reading them the wrong end first."[62]

This editor, at least, was convinced that his readers were poachers, the kind of men who just skimmed a story or who skipped what did not interest them in order to get to the good parts. With none of the educated man's respect for the unity of the work or the rules for reading a finely wrought piece of literature, these unruly readers revealed themselves to be in need of discipline and instruction. In demanding the kind of attention reserved for "literature," the editor defended the quality of *Black Mask* stories but ignored the possibility that readers might have different uses for them.

Although *Black Mask* celebrated its well-educated readers and offered its other readers de facto lessons in bourgeois rhetorical prowess, it also celebrated the superiority of practical learning gained through experience over book learning. This eminently readable prose offered a solution to the conflict between the universal value placed on education and the working class's unequal access to it by promising working-class readers the benefits of higher education—rhetorical empowerment—without its substantial costs. Because the popular or working-class aesthetic of *Black Mask* readers was a dominated one, they accepted a variety of different ways of interacting with print, ways that better-educated editors often tried to limit.

Hard-Boiled Detectives Get Culture

Norbert Davis's "Red Goose," originally published in the February 1934 issue of *Black Mask*, skillfully juxtaposes working-class speech and bourgeois speech, and carefully delineates how dispositions toward aesthetic goods form the boundary between the two classes.[63] Ben Shaley, a hard-boiled detective, is hired by the curator of an art museum to recover a stolen sixteenth-century painting of a red goose. An attorney on the museum board has suggested that Shaley might be able to recover the painting, because "it takes a crook to catch a crook." The comment organizes the world into two classes—the "respectable" (who patronize museums) and the "dangerous" (who do not), the latter class embracing both thieves and marginally employed working men such as Shaley (159). The museum, as an institution of high culture, is the gatekeeper between the two classes. Two men whose altercation drew the guards away from the painting immediately before the theft are described as "a trifle out of place in a museum," having drawn attention to themselves by their appearance and bearing even before the fight broke out (160). This class bifurcation, centered on different relationships to high art, museums, and the aesthetic worldview with which they are implicated, is central to the story.

Shaley's initial conversation with the curator, Mr. Gray, introduces the social division between the aesthetically inclined museum-goers and the functionally inclined lower classes. The two men are examining a Rubens painting of a female nude. "Beautiful, isn't it?" Gray prompts Shaley. Shaley responds not to the formal properties of the painting, as an aesthete would, but to the the thing it represents—a female body. "Too fat," he answers (158), invoking the popular tendency to reduce art to life, a refusal of the aesthetic distance with which the bourgeoisie view art. That Shaley and Gray are talking at cross-purposes becomes even more obvious throughout the conversation, as Gray calls the nude "it" while Shaley repeatedly refers to it as "she."

The museum crowd and the dangerous classes have different vocabularies. Davis juxtaposes the curator's description of the two men who staged the fight with Shaley's repetition of that description over the phone to a fellow working man. One thug, a big, bald man with long arms, short legs, four gold teeth and a cauliflower ear, held the curator's interest particularly: "The man interested me as an example of arrested development in the evolutionary process. . . . He had certain definite characteristics— the small eyes sunken under very heavy brows, the flattened nose, the abnormally protruding jaw—that have come to be associated with the development of the human race in its earlier stages" (160–61). Shaley is puzzled for a moment, scratching his head, squinting a little, but he finally finds a translation: "You mean he looked like an ape?" (160). Gray's agreement sends Shaley to the phone to try to get an identification from an old acquaintance: "Pete, I want to ask you about a couple of guys. Number one is a big gook that looks like an ape. He's got gold front teeth, a flat snozzle, a thick ear, and he's bald. Know him?" (162).

The respectable classes use polysyllabic language, learned terms, and complete sentences with long strings of modifying subordinate clauses. The underclasses use slang—"gook," "snozzle"—and short, declarative sentences or informal questions that omit the understood subject.[64] The detective, like all hard-boiled private eyes, can speak both languages. He has mastered the codes of both classes and serves as a bridge between them. A reader of this story learns how different classes articulate a view of the material world, and how a smart man can increase his relative influence by mastering both his own kind of speech and that of the elite.[65] But however skilled Shaley is at decoding bourgeois speech, the text makes it clear that his own functional speech is better for getting the point across.

The differences between working-class and polite speech include formal differences that call attention to the competing modes of narration through which Shaley and Gray make sense of the world. Consider Shaley's first interview with Gray about the stolen painting:

"There was a picture stolen from the museum, then, three days ago. What kind of picture?"

"The Red Goose, painted by Guiterrez about 1523. A beautiful thing. It was loaned to us by a private collector for an exhibition of sixteenth century work. It's a priceless example."

"What does it look like?" Shaley asked.

Gray peered at him closely. "You never saw the Red Goose?"

"No," said Shaley patiently. "I never saw the Red Goose."

Gray shook his head pityingly.

Shaley took out his handkerchief and wiped his forehead. "Listen," he said in a strained voice. "Would you mind giving me a description of that picture?"

"Certainly," said Gray quickly. "It's twelve inches by fifteen. It's a reproduc-
tion of a pink goose in a pond of green water lilies. A beautiful work."
"It sounds like it," Shaley said sourly. "How was it stolen?"
"It was cut out of the frame with a razor blade. I never heard of such an act
of vicious vandalism! They cut a quarter of an inch off the painting all around
it!"
"Terrible," Shaley agreed. "When was this done?"
"I told you. Three days ago."
Shaley took a deep breath and let it out very slowly. "I know you told me three
days ago," he said in a deceptively mild voice. "But what time of the day was
it stolen—at night?"
"Oh, no. In the afternoon."
"Where were your guards?"
"They were stopping the fight."
Shaley made a sudden strangling noise. He took off his hat and dropped it
on the floor. He glared at Gray. Gray stared back at him in mild surprise.
Shaley picked up his hat and straightened it out carefully.
"The fight," he said, his voice trembling a little. "There was a fight, then?"
"Why, yes," said Gray. "I forgot to mention it. Two men got into a fight in
the back gallery, and it took four of the guards to eject them from the prem-
ises. And then we noticed that the picture was gone."
    "That's fine," Shaley told him sarcastically. "Now would it be too much
trouble for you to describe these men who fought?" (159–60)

This conversation is maddening to Shaley. Gray is so preoccupied
with aesthetic concerns—Shaley's vulgar taste, the beauty of the Red
Goose, horror at the defacement of art—that he is incapable of producing a coherent narrative. The most central and critical point of the
narrative for Shaley's purposes—that there was a fistfight that allowed
the theft of the painting—is not important to Gray, who mentions it
only in passing. Getting the story at all requires Shaley to prompt Gray
repeatedly and to stifle his impatience and frustration. The physical
evidence of this strain permeates the passage—Shaley's trembling voice,
his sweating, his taking his frustration out on his hat. Getting the tale
out of Gray is like "solving puzzles from start to finish," little different
from the reading labors of working-class readers faced with modernist
formal experimentation. Gray gives the high modernist "little magazine" version of the theft; Shaley wants the pulp version. The narrative
Shaley wanted—a chronological, "realistic" account of the events without any "queer" formal innovation—was (and arguably remains) the
dominant mode of most popular genres.
    The ability of the detective to speak (or at least decipher) the codes
of both the criminal underclass and the elite is undermined as a means

of upward mobility, however, by the ending of "Red Goose." Shaley recovers what he believes to be the Red Goose after a fistfight and shoot-out that leave two men dead and Shaley with head injuries and a broken nose. When he returns the painting to the museum, however, Gray tells him that it has already been returned. Gray examines the painting that Shaley has recovered, and says that although it's a clever copy, it is deficient in color, depth, and blending. Gray is amazed that Shaley could not tell the difference (180). The story closes, then, on the same note with which it opened—the juxtaposition of working-class and bourgeois ways of making sense of the world. According to an aesthetic worldview, the original and the copy are indeed very different, their formal properties distinguishing them clearly. According to the working-class worldview, both are representations of a red goose, and they perform that function equally well. Under a popular aesthetic, the two paintings are indistinguishable (and Shaley has therefore done his job).

Davis returns to language differences in the final line of "Red Goose," calling attention to the fact that these worldviews are, in part, created and maintained through speech. Gray, clearly pleased with himself, says, "I'm sorry you were deceived, Mr. Shaley. You could say that the Red Goose was a sort of red herring, couldn't you?" (180). The "red herring" reference resonated with bourgeois detective stories, with the puzzle mysteries written by the London Detection Club and serialized in slick-paper magazines in the early decades of the century—the stories against which hard-boiled fiction defined itself. Gray's sense of superiority over Shaley and men of his class is tangible in Gray's wordplay and the allusion to classical detective fiction.

Shaley is curiously reticent at the end. "I could say a lot worse than that," he states as the story closes (180), but he never does say any of it. Rather than bringing him professional advancement, manly self-assertion, and the capacity to dominate others, his foray into speaking the codes of the literate classes results in frustration, injury, and no money at all. Such an outcome calls into question the promises that pulp ads made about their speech and conduct manuals. "Red Goose," although it offers the same lessons in bourgeois language practices as the ads, is also a cautionary tale about the limits of class ventriloquism. The complexities of interclass conversation, "Red Goose" seems to suggest, are a little harder to finesse than pulp advertisers would like you to think.

These ads, discussed at length in Chapter 2, did promise a great deal: that social and professional advancement would inevitably follow one's mastery of bourgeois speech. What if someone took those ads seriously? What would happen if some thug did try to pass for respectable by refashioning his clothes, manners, and speech to match the hereditary bourgeoisie? Would fifteen minutes a day of at-home exercises from *How to Work Wonders With Words* do it? With a suit of expensive evening clothes and advice from an etiquette manual explaining how not to disgrace oneself in polite social circles, would such a person be able to fit in?

Raoul Whitfield's *The Virgin Kills* (1932) is a fictional test of this question.[66] Although this novel was published by Knopf as a hardback, Whitfield's first two novels, *Green Ice* (1930) and *Death in a Bowl* (1931) were serialized in *Black Mask*, as were two others he published under the name Temple Field. *The Virgin Kills* takes place on the yacht of millionaire gambler Eric Vennel. Cruising down the Hudson River on their way to a regatta are a party of high-society guests—an aviator, a screen actress, a best-selling author, and several journalists, among others. Vennel, heavily in debt to a gangster named Dingo Bandelli, fears for his life and asks Al Connors, the hard-boiled sportswriter who narrates the book, to bring along a bodyguard when he joins the yachting party. Vennel hopes to conceal his sense of danger from the other guests, so they plan to pass off Mick O'Rourke, a big bruiser with a bullet- and knife-scarred body, as a socialite.

Connors tells Vennel that he has taught O'Rourke some "highbrow" lines to drop into his conversation in order to "alibi" him with the high-society guests. As they are boarding the yacht, for example, O'Rourke alludes to the color imagery in Joyce's *Ulysses*, and Connors reminds him of the Greek translation in which O'Rourke is presumably engaged (11). Not only does Connors provide the little proofs of distinction he wants O'Rourke to drop into conversation, he offers advice on the best way to present one's cultural capital. He often warns O'Rourke that he has overdone his performance, that he needs to "tone down a little" if he is to be believed. "Don't make it too thick," he admonishes O'Rourke, "scatter the stuff a little" (15). The authenticity of the performance, then, depends not only on the content of O'Rourke's comments but on the manner in which he makes them. To try too hard or to be too correct gives one away as an anxious faker rather than someone whose cultural inheritance sits easily and naturally on him. This is not, however, to suggest that carelessness is acceptable. After correcting O'Rourke's grammar on one of many occasions, Connors tells him that "little things can assume considerable importance in the greater scheme of things" (131).

O'Rourke is never quite at home in the culture of wealth. He frequently forgets his lines, requires prompting, or gives himself away through his manner or bearing. He is unfamiliar with "Rabelaisian humor," Pirandello (an Italian playwright he mistakes for a boxer), and the Passion play ("the girls oughta like *that* one") (15).[67] Descriptions of the exotic cuisine sampled by the other guests on their travels—silkworm salad, shark's fins, pudding of pumpkin seeds and white worms—make him groan and clutch his stomach (52). He is completely stymied by his bow tie, and his pajamas are so loudly colored that even the narrator ridicules them (54).

O'Rourke's attempts to pass for upper-class structure the text. Staged scenes in front of the other passengers on the yacht alternate with backstage scenes in which O'Rourke and Connors evaluate the credibility of the last performance and begin rehearsing the next one.[68] "Did it go, Al . . . did it go?" O'Rourke asks anxiously after the *Ulysses* performance while boarding the yacht (15).

O'Rourke's performance is a good deal more self-conscious and deliberate than those of the other passengers, but everyone, to a greater or lesser extent, is engaged in demonstrating his or her cultural and educational attainments. In one scene, Carla Sard, an actress, reads a magazine with "high-sounding titles and foreign-sounding names on the cover," a magazine that looks "literary—and a little analytical" (150). Connors asks her whether Balzac appears in that issue, to which she responds that *she* does not. Rita Veld, Sard's arch-rival, immediately cuts in asking about George Sand—did he have anything in the magazine? (151). When Sard asks Connors whether he means the Balzac who wrote *Lost Ladies*, Veld cuts in again, telling her that that was "William Cather" (151).

Connors does not know what to make of this scene. "I wasn't quite sure who was kidding whom," he says, a comment that could have served as an epigraph to the novel. Was Carla Sard just ignorant, or was she pulling his leg? Was Rita Veld ridiculing Sard's ignorance, or was she not astute enough to understand that Sard might be giving Connors a hard time for trying to pass O'Rourke off as her intellectual equal? If Sard is, in fact, just ignorant, does she know that Veld is making fun of her, and if so, does she understand how? No one is sure who is patronizing or teasing or posturing to whom. That some sort of intellectual gamesmanship is going on becomes clear when Connors tries to recover the magazine that Sard has thrown on the ground in disgust at Veld's goading. She tells Connors to leave it on the floor, because the story was so "lousy" that she was "damn near asleep anyway" (151).

Furthermore, at some points O'Rourke seems to be enjoying the masquerade, taking great glee in surprising Connors with little bits of culture he has obtained without Connors's coaching. When Connors asks whether O'Rourke would like to join him on deck for breakfast, O'Rourke answers in French: "Avec plaisir" (69). He learned his French, he confesses, while in hiding at a Chicago speakeasy, waiting for his chance to assassinate a gangster. As time goes by, O'Rourke tires of the masquerade and Connors reasserts his authority to keep O'Rourke performing. "Stick in character," Connors says at one point, and he orders O'Rourke to use a line about liking to read Greek classics in Latin countries. O'Rourke cuts him off, swearing and claiming not to remember that line. "To hell with it," he says, "this other is better" (64). O'Rourke, clearly impatient with his lack of autonomy, would like to make some thoughtful choices of his own. He rebels, in short, against the logic of the advertisement (you need an expert to conduct yourself adequately), which is also the logic of scientific management. O'Rourke wants to craft a self as artisans crafted goods, using his knowledge and experience rather than moving mechanically through someone else's choreography. When Connors lectures O'Rourke in front of the other passengers on the proper plural of "shark," he responds with sarcasm.

> He took my right hand and shook it with enthusiasm. He nodded his big head.
> "That's how I'm going to get ahead," he said in a determined voice. "It's you that's givin' me my start, Al." (131)

O'Rourke's assertions here cast doubt on Connors's attempt to make him into a bourgeois citizen in a few easy lessons. Teaching him to "work wonders with words" will make little difference in his social and professional standing, O'Rourke's sarcasm suggests. However important clothes, language, and bearing may be in revealing and maintaining class hierarchies, a quick change of costume, diction, or carriage (even if possible) will not wipe out a long history of material inequities and barriers to social mobility. Although a self-improvement plan may seem liberating to men who lack access to power and wealth, it masks the need for structural change. Why organize unions and demand more egalitarian education when a change of clothes will suffice to improve your chances? If the good life is so easily obtained by an individual who applies himself for fifteen minutes a day, why bother to organize collectively to change the way society distributes material and cultural goods?

Although Connors tries to pass him off as his "find," a "roughneck reaching for higher things" (18), O'Rourke proves to have had his own agenda all along. The job as Vennel's bodyguard offered him an excellent (though ultimately unnecessary) opportunity to kill Vennel and implicate his own archenemy, Dingo Bandelli.[69] The class masquerade that occupies much of the novel proves to be just an entertaining game to pass the time from O'Rourke's point of view. His performance as a socialite may have been spotty, but his performance as a willing student takes them all in. The Anglo yachting party is only too ready to see the Irish lout as a ridiculous wannabe, a view that O'Rourke uses to his advantage. While the "effeminate" highbrows posture for one another, O'Rourke is plotting Dingo Bandelli's downfall.

Hard-boiled heroes could also speak different ethnic codes. In Dashiell Hammett's "Dead Yellow Women," published in *Black Mask* in 1925, the Continental Op engages in wordplay with Chang Li Ching, a Chinese gangster.[70] When the Op comes to call for the first time, Chang welcomes him with these words: "It was only the inability to believe that one of your excellency's heaven-born splendor would waste his costly time on so mean a clod that kept the least of your slaves from running down to prostrate himself at your noble feet as soon as he heard the Father of Detectives was at his unworthy door. . . . If the Terror of Evildoers will honor one of my deplorable chairs by resting his divine body on it, I can assure him the chair shall be burned afterward, so no lesser being may use it. Or will the Prince of Thief-catchers permit me to send a servant to his palace for a chair worthy of him?" (209).

Chang's English is deeply marked by Chinese ways with words (or, more accurately, by Hammett's stereotypical representation). The Op prepares himself for rhetorical battle in this unfamiliar territory: "I went slowly to a chair, trying to arrange words in my mind. This old joker was spoofing me with an exaggeration—a burlesque—of the well-known Chinese politeness. I'm not hard to get along with; I'll play anybody's game up to a certain point" (209). The Op recognizes that Chang has chosen this way of speaking because he is more practiced at it, giving him a formidable rhetorical advantage. The Op exchanges a few convoluted lines with Chang, but then, he says, "I tried to get away from this vaudeville stuff, which was a strain on my head" (210).

The Op manages to explain to Chang that he is in search of information about a murder, but Chang answers with more flowery words: "Does one ask the way of a blind man? . . . Can a star, however willing, help the moon? If it pleases the Grandfather of Bloodhounds to flatter Chang Li Ching into thinking he can add to the great one's knowledge, who is Chang to thwart his master by refusing to make himself ridiculous?" (210).

The Op offers a deflating translation: "I took that to mean he was willing to listen to my questions" (210).

The Op's next visit is characterized by "the same sort of nonsense" (222). He opens the exchange by apologizing for harming one of Chang's men in a melee the night before: "'Not knowing who he was until too late, I beaned one of your servants last night. . . . I know there's nothing I can do to square myself for such a terrible act, but I hope you'll let me cut my throat and bleed to death in one of your garbage cans as a sort of apology.' A little sighing noise that could have been a smothered chuckle disturbed the old man's lips, and the purple cap twitched on his round head" (222).

The Op is obviously bilingual, speaking Chang's overly polite, indirect language and his own. Rhetoric is a performance, a game one plays with an opponent rather than an authentic expression of one's identity. By forcing Chang to lose his composure, the Op demonstrates the rules of rhetorical gamesmanship, the self-conscious strategizing that goes into talking one's opponent into submission, but the terse, working-class commentary he offers about the process shows that his speech describes the world with more clarity and power.

There is a sophisticated critical tradition that maintains that hard-boiled narratives reflect self-consciously on how narratives are made.[71] Steven Marcus argues that Dashiell Hammett's short stories are self-reflexively concerned with fiction-making. Unlike classical detectives (who reveal the "truth"), hard-boiled private eyes are in the business of unraveling the narratives of others in order to spin an alternate narrative of their own without any claim of ontological priority.[72] The "truths" in hard-boiled fiction are always interested truths, marked by an actor's point of view.[73] Hammett's *The Thin Man* closes with Nick Charles expounding his "theory" about a crime to his wife, Nora, who is disappointed that Nick's account is so "unsatisfactory," so lacking in the certainties she has come to expect from reading classical detective stories.[74] Rather than "truth," hard-boiled fiction offers the rhetorical process (detection) through which "truths" are constructed.[75]

Such readings are one kind of poaching, a kind that requires the scholarly reader to ask epistemological questions. However, the philosophical meditations on the construction of truths do not explain the popular appeal of this fiction to pulp-magazine readers. The self-referentiality of these readings, the view of literature they imply (autonomous rather than connected to the material world), engage what Bourdieu calls the "aesthetic disposition." Though these texts were concerned with language, knowledge, and interpretation, they were concerned with these issues in a different way for working-class readers during the Depression than they were for critics trained in Continental philosophy. The "popular aesthetic," based on perceiving and affirming a basic continuity between art and life, would be more likely to view these narratives as stories about certain aspects of working-class life. For working-class readers between the wars, hard-boiled fiction offered, among other things, lessons in rhetorical craftsmanship as a form of power, along with reassurances that these readers' worldview and the language characteristic of it were superior.

The analysis of language in hard-boiled fiction, then, is more complicated and contradictory than that offered by the pulp advertisements for such books as *Speechcraft, How To Work Wonders With Words,* and *How to Speak and Write Masterly English,* however similar their concerns with language and class mobility may have been. Whereas the ads unproblematically urged learning a single, correct (bourgeois) way of speaking and writing in order to win social and professional advancement, hard-boiled fiction offered a richer, more socially situated consideration of how and when different kinds of speech might be useful, and raised questions about the promise and value of passing for bourgeois.

6

The Office Wife

In the nineteenth century, men were confident ... but in the
twentieth century the men have no confidence and so they
have to make themselves ... more beautiful more intriguing
more everything and they cannot make any other man
because they have to hold on to themselves not having any
confidence.

Dashiell Hammett, as reported by Gertrude Stein

The hard-boiled private eye Ben Shaley and his secretary,
Sadie, graced the pages of the February 1934 issue of *Black
Mask* in Norbert Davis's "Red Goose." Ben and Sadie were
a fairly representative hard-boiled office duo, and their
respective roles and personalities are nicely encapsulated in
the following snippet of conversation:

> "And my mother was saying just last night," said Sadie right-
> eously, "that she didn't think this office was the proper place for
> a young girl to work. All these questionable people coming in
> and out all day long and you swearing and yelling at me all the
> time and—"
> "Shut-up," said Shaley absently.[1]

Sadie first appears "tapping away briskly on the typewriter
with glossy, pink-nailed fingers."[2] Linking her manicure and
her typing, the description suggests that part of her job is to
advertise through her attractiveness and employment the
virility of her boss and the prosperity of his practice.[3] Like

all relationships between hard-boiled detectives and their secretaries, this one is sexually charged. Sadie gets sulky and difficult when female clients phone Shaley, particularly when they sound like attractive blondes. Her mother's concern for Sadie's virtue also seems warranted, for in the promiscuous world of criminals and con men that provides Shaley with his living, work and sexuality are inextricably linked.

Secretaries figured prominently in pulp detective fiction between the wars. Dashiell Hammett's Sam Spade has his loyal Effie Perine in *The Maltese Falcon* (1929), originally a serial in *Black Mask*. Frederick Nebel's Jack Cardigan is ably assisted by spunky Patricia Seaward, who holds down the fort at the two-man Cosmos Detective Agency in forty-four stories published in *Dime Detective* between 1931 and 1937. The much tougher prototypes of Erle Stanley Gardner's Perry Mason and his loyal Della Street appeared in *Black Mask* and other pulp magazines. Even private detectives such as Raymond Chandler's Philip Marlowe, who can't afford or don't want a girl Friday, make time with their clients' secretaries.

Why all the secretaries? They are, in fact, something of a literary historical anomaly. "Where have all the secretaries gone?" a nostalgic Bill Pronzini laments in the 1979 mystery fan compendium *Murderess Ink*, noting their absence from detective fiction published after the 1950s.[4] Why did hard-boiled fiction feature secretaries so prominently during the years of its pulp origins, and why does it no longer do so? What did having a secretary or being a secretary mean between the wars? What can the hard-boiled way of representing them tell us about the way gender, class, and power were experienced by readers of pulp detective fiction?

Secretaries in History

In the early twentieth century, a complex set of anxieties about class, ethnicity, paid work, and manhood arose around the figure of the secretary. Until the late nineteenth century, secretaries were white men learning the business before ascending the corporate ladder, but the rationalization of production around the turn of the century changed that. The increasingly complex scale of operations required a large number of clerical workers to coordinate the flow of documents. Both men and women entered clerical work in increasing numbers, but better opportunities for educated white men led to the "feminization" of typing, stenography, and clerical work in general. By 1930 the overwhelming majority of secretaries were women.[5]

The feminization of clerical work intersected with issues of class and ethnicity in complex ways. Women became clerks only after an increase in the size of commercial bureaucracies made clerical work a good deal less autonomous, more routine, and less likely to lead to managerial positions. Margery Davies summarizes: "The nineteenth-century clerk had not turned into a proletarian; he had merely turned into a woman."[6] Pre–Civil-War male clerks were like skilled craftsmen in their autonomy and knowledge of the business; the female clerks of the early twentieth century were the office equivalent of workers under scientific management. Moreover, the de-skilling of clerical work was less controversial than the de-skilling of factory work, because organizations cloaked the transition in the naturalizing rhetoric of sex. Women were "naturally" suited to mindless detail work, while working men were entitled to manly autonomy.

This increasingly proletarian work nonetheless required literacy, a wage-less period of education and training, and an expensive office wardrobe. In this way, clerical employment was "conspicuous employment"—work that advertised a family's status and prosperity.[7] Most students training for clerical work around the turn of the century were the children of skilled laborers. Forming a labor aristocracy of sorts, these men had reasonably steady work, high wages, autonomy on the job, and leadership positions in working-class communities. Clerical workers throughout the early twentieth century were overwhelmingly native-born (more than 90 percent), and their employment in immigrant-free offices was a mark of their higher status.[8] While the new immigrants from southern and eastern Europe filled unskilled and semiskilled jobs created by technology and the subdivision of labor, this native-born labor aristocracy of northern European stock filled skilled manual jobs and clerical and sales positions. What Ileen DeVault calls the "collar line" (the distinction between white-collar people who work with their heads and blue-collar people who work with their hands) was remarkably fluid in the early twentieth century. Siblings and spouses of clerical workers found employment not only in clerical work, sales, and teaching, but also in the needle trades (women) and skilled manual labor (men).[9]

The secretary, then, was a woman doing what had until recently been a man's job, someone whose education, wages, familial ties to the labor elite, and ethnic purity gave her high status in white, working-class communities. At the same time, skilled, white male workers were losing status as their autonomy in the workplace and access to a family wage eroded.

Her presence (and sometimes omnipresence) in hard-boiled texts produced for and read by white, working men with the means to purchase
cheap books and pulp magazines should come as no surprise. Hard-boiled
fiction offered male, working-class readers a way to confront the transformation of all-male workplaces into mixed-sex settings. Though these
texts adamantly returned women to their traditional roles as sexual
objects, domestic nurturers, and vulnerable figures in need of a chivalrous male rescuer, hard-boiled stories muddied the boundaries between
men and women by reimagining identity as performance or masquerade.

Theorizing the Hard-Boiled Office Wife

The transformation of the secretary's job from men's work into women's
work was highly disruptive. "Women's presence in what had been
defined as a masculine space upset the nineteenth-century dyad of pub-
lic-private," writes historian Angel Kwolek-Folland. "It broke the ideological boundaries between them and invited inversions and mingling
in the social understanding of male and female roles."[10] This is to say
that slotting female bodies into male jobs created what Judith Butler
calls "gender trouble,"[11] making the arbitrariness of the sexual division
of labor visible and thus open to debate.[12] Enter the manly women and
womanly men of hard-boiled fiction.

Hard-boiled fiction is concerned with (among other things) negotiating an uneasy rapprochement between an artisanal model of identity,
based on production work and patriarchal family values, and an emergent model based on the purchase and display of commodities, in which
women played a major part. The restoration of patriarchal power
arrangements at the close of these novels coexists uneasily with hard-
boiled fiction's fascination with womanly men (sometimes overt homosexuals) and manly women (always predatory heterosexuals).

The shifting border between what men and women did and were led
to a frantic attempt to reinvent male privilege. Although women were
performing men's jobs, often working side by side with men, different
job titles and different access to wages and promotions preserved the
distinction between women's and men's work. Hard-boiled fiction
shored up male privilege by effacing the work of secretaries, emphasizing their sexuality and redefining work for pay as domesticity.

Erle Stanley Gardner's "Leg Man," from the February 1938 issue of
Black Mask, is an example.[13] The title's double entendre refers to Pete

Wennick, the detective and attorney who is the protagonist, as both someone who does the legwork on cases and someone who appreciates women's legs. In the opening scene, Mae Devers, Wennick's secretary, enters his office to give him his mail and tidy up his desk. Her mind may be on her (domestic) work, but his is not. "There was a patent leather belt around her waist, and below that belt I could see the play of muscles as her supple figure moved from side to side," Wennick says. "I slid my arm around the belt and started to draw her close to me" (201). Devers chides him for being "fresh," tells him she has work to do, and tries to extricate herself from his embrace. She doesn't try all that hard, however. Instead, she plants a large, lipstick-covered kiss on Wennick's lips just before his colleague bursts in to discuss a point of law. The lipstick on Wennick's face is a three-page–long gag, keeping Devers's sexuality in the forefront long after she has left the scene. Wennick has to keep his hand over his mouth while talking to his colleague, he smears lipstick all over his handkerchief trying to get it off, and when he's called to the boss's office he is caught with both lipstick on his face and a smeared handkerchief. Wennick's boss decides that the appropriate way to handle the situation is to fire Miss Devers, whom he has always considered "a bit too . . . voluptuous" in spite of her positive recommendations from the employment agency (204).

Unlike women in factories, women in offices had to spend a great deal of money on clothes and makeup that made them appear feminine and desirable to men. As Sharon Strom argues, secretaries were caught between two competing sets of demands: They "were expected to contribute to an atmosphere of heightened sexuality but not be explicitly sexual."[14] This double standard demands that only Devers suffer the consequences of the office romance. In the end, she keeps her job because Wennick threatens to quit if she is let go. Wennick values her both for her attractiveness and for her professional competence, apparently making no distinction between them. Sexuality is so deeply enmeshed with the structure of work that having a sexually attractive secretary probably enhances Wennick's image.

Young working women's sexual availability could be assumed in offices before World War II, because most companies enforced the so-called marriage bar. Women were expected to quit their jobs once they were married, particularly if they had children. Unions focused on winning a family wage for male workers so that women could stay at home; many companies had rules requiring the dismissal of women who got married; and most of the middle class assumed that marriage and work for pay were incompatible for women.[15] Material consequences followed from the marriage bar. First, since all working women were potential wives, they were viewed as temporary employees, who could be passed over for promotion and paid less than men. Second, the marriage bar fractured the workplace by gender and age, making unionization less likely.

The links between work and sexuality are obvious in a phrase coined around the turn of the century to describe a woman who worked for a man in an executive position: "office wife." Simultaneously commercial/public/masculine and domestic/private/feminine, the term showed the way in which secretaries straddled two formerly separate spheres. It also made it clear that sexuality, family, and personal life, rather than being ancillary to the world of work, were central to its structure. Even if not sexually involved with her boss, an office wife owed him the other duties of her sex—"domesticity, passivity, charm, and endless patience."[16] A personal secretary's job, in fact, could be seen as very traditional—maintaining interpersonal harmony at the office and performing detail work assisting men, rather than doing proletarian work that would put her in competition for jobs with male clerks.[17]

Dashiell Hammett gives us such a dutiful office wife in Effie Perine of *The Maltese Falcon* (1929).[18] Effie is indeed a right-hand woman, whose "feminine intuition" and attention to detail are at Sam Spade's service. It is Effie who notices that Iva, the wife of Spade's partner, has not been to bed at all on the night of her husband's murder, and Spade repeatedly asks for Effie's opinions of his clients. Effie is always on call. She tells Iva of her husband's death, although Spade has told the police that he would do it, and she spends the night with Iva. Later, Effie agrees to let an endangered client stay with her and her mother for a few days. She remains at the office into the wee hours of the morning, waiting worriedly for Spade to return so she can nurse his wounds, comfort him, and offer him support and sympathy. Spade calls her by all sorts of terms of endearment: sweetheart, darling, angel, precious. Spade also seems to have proprietary rights over her body—stroking her hair, embracing her, kissing her, being physically nurtured by her. These rights extend to physical roughness when he is having a bad day.

If Effie is earning wages in what used to be a man's job, she nonetheless does not get the independent living and the control over her body and her leisure time that once came with the job. Rather than being a source of autonomy or artisanal pride, Effie's job is merely domestic work taking place in an office. Moreover, Effie's office marriage is distinctly patriarchal, resembling the marriages of the previous generation more than the companionate marriages advocated in women's magazines from the 1910s through the 1930s.[19]

Merle Davis, the secretary in Raymond Chandler's *The High Window* (1942), is an entirely different story. As a "woman adrift"—one who lives independently of a spouse or family of origin—she might live the liberated life of a woman who makes her own way in the world. But Merle is a thin, pale woman who is afraid of men. She was the victim of sexual abuse of an unnamed sort by her employer's first husband, demonstrating the sexual vulnerability of women without protectors. Merle reflects one of two modes of representing "women adrift" that were current around the turn of the century, according to Joanne Meyerowitz. Late–nineteenth-century reformers portrayed them as vulnerable, passive victims of employers and other sexual predators. By the 1920s, however, commercial culture was portraying such women as active, opportunistic exploiters of naive men—"jazz babies" and "gold diggers."[20] The young, single women in hard-boiled fiction take both forms. Active, sexually predatory characters such as Brigid O'Shaughnessy of *The Maltese Falcon* and Vivian and Carmen Sternwood of *The Big Sleep* recall the 1920s jazz babies. Merle Davis and Gabrielle Leggett of *The Dain Curse* are passive victims of male sexual aggression, in need of rescue by the hard-boiled hero, who has no sexual designs on them. By the end of the 1930s, Meyerowitz argues, anxieties about women adrift had all but disappeared, but they persisted in hard-boiled fiction. Chandler's portrayal of Merle Davis as a vulnerable victim, recalling reformers' views earlier in the century, underlines the nostalgia of his vision, the backward-looking nature of the homosocial world that hard-boiled novels re-create.

After Merle suffers a breakdown brought on by finding the body of a murdered blackmailer, Marlowe returns her to the protection of her parents in Kansas. The last time we see Merle, she is in a thoroughly domestic setting: "When I left Merle was wearing a bungalow apron and rolling pie crust. She came to the door wiping her hands on the apron and kissed me on the mouth and began to cry and ran back into the house, leaving the doorway empty until her mother came into the space with a broad homey smile on her face to watch me drive away."[21]

Merle's linen work dress has been replaced by an apron, and instead of checking references by phone, a small pistol handy in her desk drawer, she is rolling out pie crust. At the end she has disappeared completely from public view. The image of the (more or less) autonomous working woman has been replaced by a mother with a homey smile, an older, far more familiar and less threatening image. "I had a funny feeling as I saw the house disappear," Marlowe says, "as though I had written a poem and it was very good and I had lost it and would never remember it again."[22] There is recognition here that this vision is a nostalgic one, an evocation of a situation whose time has passed, but one whose reenactment nonetheless brings reassurance and pleasure. Moreover, Marlowe is the agent in this construction. As the author of the poem, he decides what is to become of Merle Davis, regardless of what she may desire for herself.

Throughout his career, Marlowe has a good deal of trouble knowing what to do with women adrift. In *Farewell, My Lovely*, Anne Riordan, an ex-cop's daughter who carries a gun, finds Marlowe after he has been knocked unconscious by jewel thieves. In spite of her ability to hold her own, Marlowe leaves her out of the story he tells the police, suspecting that an interrogation by the authorities would be too rough for her. Although she has a good working relationship with the police because her father was a cop, and though she has information about the theft that got Marlowe involved with the case, Marlowe refuses her help at every turn. Significantly, he refuses her suggestion that he hire her as an assistant, though she insists that her only pay would be "a kind word now and then."[23] Despite her considerable potential value to him, Marlowe will not allow Anne Riordan to define herself in professional terms. He does, however, use her house as a "sanctuary" when he is alone on the street at night after having been drugged.[24]

Long before critics began to take hard-boiled fiction seriously, Leslie Fiedler noted its "native birth-right of antifeminism," and the misogyny of these books has become a critical commonplace.[25] Largely ignoring the material social and economic context of this misogyny, these critics have invoked the figure of the New Woman as a particular threat to masculinity.[26] "New Woman," a term that came into general use around the turn of the century, refers to middle-class, usually college-educated women who sought a larger public role than women had traditionally been allowed.[27] In my view, however, the bourgeois New Woman has less to do with hard-boiled misogyny than the transformation of working-class communities as a result of the de-skilling of craft work, the entry of young, single women into once all-male jobs, and the rise of consumer culture. Often overlooked Utopian representations of gender also serve as a counterweight to the misogyny of this fiction.

Cross-Dressing, or the Office Wife as Good Man

If the boundaries between what men and women were and did were fluid, how could one identify a woman? Was a woman's body in men's clothing still a "woman," or was s/he something else entirely? Raymond Chandler's *The Lady in the Lake* raises these questions. There are two secretaries in the reception room of the Gillerlain Company, "a neat little blonde" with a kittenish manner and "a tall, lean, dark-haired lovely" named Adrienne Fromsett, who engages in no nonsense whatsoever.[28] There is nothing soft, feminine, or insubstantial about Adrienne Fromsett. Her eyebrows are "severe" and the corner of the handkerchief in her breast pocket looks "sharp enough to slice bread" (4). She is wearing a steel-gray business suit, a blue shirt, and a man's tie.

This description clearly allies Miss Fromsett with her boss, Derace Kingsley, who is "a tall bird in a gray suit" who "didn't want any nonsense" (6).[29] Like her boss, Fromsett treats Marlowe disrespectfully at first, grilling him about his business with Kingsley and waiting half an hour before presenting his card to her boss. If gender is indeed performance, a "style of the flesh," then Miss Fromsett has most certainly raided some tough guy's closet."[30] Her "masculinity" stands out against her kittenish blonde foil. Some women are "women," Chandler seems to suggest, but others—tough, willful, sexually aggressive—might better be described as "men."

Fromsett has an unusual relationship with her boss. However docile she may be in the office, her after-hours life seems more characteristic of men in industrial societies who sold their labor by the hour than it is of women, whose domestic work was never done.[31] Although Kingsley insists that she wear perfume at the office and keep him company after business hours while waiting for his wayward wife to return, his authority does not extend to her personal life. He tells Marlowe at one point that he would divorce his wife and marry Miss Fromsett in a heartbeat if he could, but she sleeps with whomever she wants, including Chris Lavery, a womanizing ex-employee of the firm suspected of running off with Kingsley's wife.

Countless other hard-boiled secretaries perform manliness of one sort or another. In Frederick Nebel's 1933 "Chains of Darkness," Patricia Seaward, secretary to a private eye named Jack Cardigan, faces down two police detectives who are trying to enter the agency.[32] She smiles a sweet, perky smile while giving the men a rhetorical runaround that would do Sam Spade proud. When that fails, she hurls a heavy paperweight at an officer's head and threatens to tell her short-tempered boss that he made a pass at her. Seaward's power in this scene is of a contradictory type. She is in charge of the agency, quite capable of defending herself rhetorically and otherwise. Nevertheless, she is clearly acting as Cardigan's agent. The officers' response to her tough talk is laughter. "Come on," says one as they try to walk past her into the office. "She learned those cracks from Cardigan!"[33] However convincing such talk might be from him, it does not win Seaward much respect. Her threat to tell Cardigan that one of the policemen made a pass at her is also ambivalent. Although they take it seriously, it equates their invasion of Cardigan's office with sexual advances toward her, effectively casting her as Cardigan's property.

In a sense, all of these tough women are "men."[34] They work in small offices characterized by personal relationships rather than bureaucratic organization. Their jobs, then, are nineteenth-century men's secretarial jobs, marked by a knowledge of the entire business, a great deal of autonomy, and interesting, exciting work. Furthermore, these secretaries are usually the only woman in the office, so a women's culture of work never materializes (as it might in the typing pool) to challenge the masculine hegemony of the workplace.[35]

The most provocative point of all is that the dutiful office wife and the manly woman could be one and the same. Sam Spade, for example, calls Effie Perine "a damned good man" when he needs her to deal with the police after a profusely bleeding man with the priceless Maltese falcon in his arms dies on the floor of her office (160). "Lanky" with a "boyish face," Perine accurately identifies women whom her bosses will find sexually attractive (3). It's her "woman's intuition" that steers Spade wrong about Brigid O'Shaughnessy's character, but her ability to mislead the cops for Spade makes her "a damned good man." As a biological woman, Effie is nonetheless gendered masculine when she is competent, feminine when she screws up. However misogynist its value judgments, this state of affairs does make gender identity look remarkably fluid.

Hard-boiled representations of secretaries run along a spectrum, then, from docile office wives who are either rhetorically or physically contained in domestic spaces to feisty modern women whose power derives from their occupation of masculine positions or their capacity to stand in for their bosses. This is not to underestimate the cultural work of powerful women for readers of the time. The de facto assistant to Dashiell Hammett's Continental Op in *Red Harvest*, Dinah Brand, is proof of just how troublesome the disruption of traditional gender roles, however circumscribed, could be.

Reading Across Gender Lines

Red Harvest, originally a serial in *Black Mask*, has the labyrinthine plot characteristic of hard-boiled novels. The Continental Op is called to a small mining town called Personville by the publisher of the local newspaper, Donald Willsson. Before the Op can meet him, however, Willsson is murdered. His father, Elihu Willsson, owns most of Personville, but has recently lost control of his city to gangsters whom he originally called in to suppress a miner's strike. In one sense, the antics of the hired thugs of these rival gangs are just window dressing, since they turn out to have absolutely nothing to do with the murder of Donald Willsson, the crime that begins the novel. This murder, in fact, is solved less than a third of the way through, when Albury, a bank teller, confesses to shooting Donald Willsson in a jealous rage over Dinah Brand, a former lover of both. The Op nevertheless sticks around to clean up the city, the job Elihu Willsson hired him to do. The remainder of the book is dedicated to the Op's setting the rival gangs that run the city against one another to put them all out of business.

The Op is ably assisted in this matter by Dinah, who, though not an employee of the Continental Detective Agency, functions in this novel as the hard-boiled helpmate.[36] She plays Effie to the Op's Sam Spade, fighting and driving getaway cars to save his skin. It is her expertise in local scandals that provides the "spoon" the Op needs to stir up trouble in Personville. Like other hard-boiled girl Fridays, however, she has a great deal of trouble getting the Op to recognize her value as a professional. She is forever berating him for his failure to pay her for the information she provides, although his expense notebook is full of sizable payments to other informants. She finally gets $200.10 out of him when one of her lovers has the Op at gunpoint and she refuses to intervene on his behalf until he has made her a cash offer.[37] The same intermingling of sexual and professional alliances that characterizes relationships between office wives and their hard-boiled private eyes is present here. All of Personville assumes that Dinah is "his woman," and the Op's fear of losing her informs his tortured dreams, if not his daily conduct.

The "gender trouble" in this novel emerges from a larger reconceptualization of identity as performance or masquerade. In Chapter 1, the Op goes digging through his extensive collection of business cards, each a document testifying to a different identity, and selects one that identifies him as a sailor and a member of the Industrial Workers of the World. He presents this card to Bill Quint, the local labor organizer, who is not convinced by it. The Op offers some alternatives. He could just as easily be a lumberman or a miner, he says, asking Quint which he'd prefer. The multiplication of identities reappears when the Op is unable to remember which of his many names—"something like Hunter or Hunt or Huntington"—he has given another man (71). The Op's carelessness is important: It shows that he is equally ready to take up and inhabit any one of many identities.

Because disguise is a fundamental part of a detective's job, such scenes can be regarded as examples of the work of private detectives rather than as evidence of how identity has been reconceived as performance. The slippage between what the Op does and what he is is much more profound, however. As *Red Harvest* progresses, it becomes increasingly hard to tell the Continental Op from the natives of Personville. Ridding the city of thugs involves him in their activities—shoot-outs, murders, bootlegging, car chases. The Op explains the slide from investigator to participant: "This damned burg's getting me. If I don't get away soon I'll be going blood-simple like the natives" (154). He sends Dick Foley, another operative, back to San Francisco because Foley has an irritating habit of pointing out that the Op is no longer doing his job catching murderers, being too busy murdering people himself.

This reconceptualization of identity as performance complicates the definitional boundaries between men and women. In a particularly significant passage, Dinah Brand tells the Op about an Englishman named Holly, "a funny sort of old woman," whose gender identity here is apparent in his habit of wearing his white, silk socks inside out, so his sensitive skin will not be troubled by the loose threads (87). In this formulation, anybody who is not tough enough to face his fabrics right side out is a "woman," regardless of his anatomy. This view of gender identity has two consequences. First, there are the manly women and the womanly men who are ubiquitous in hard-boiled fiction. Second, the he-men must perform their machismo with great gusto so as not to be confused with the she-men they are always in danger of becoming or being mistaken for.

The Op's manliness is overdone. With no wife, no children, no home to speak of, and no personal attachments, he is strictly an economic transactor.[38] Assuring Elihu Willsson that the $10,000 retainer he demands is not intended for his personal use, the Op says, "When I say *me*, I mean the Continental" (44). On some level, the Op *is* the company; certainly there is little in him that would overflow the confines of this corporate role. If American culture was split into private (domestic, feminine) spaces and public (economic, political, masculine) spaces, the Op is entirely defined by and contained in the latter. He seeks the men he wants to talk to and spreads information to the gangsters who run the city in homosocial spaces—boxing matches, poolrooms, saloons, cigar stores, street corners, "wherever I found a man or two loafing" (70). These public spaces were controlled by working-class men, who did their socializing, politicking, networking, and attending to community affairs there. The saloon, in particular, was a hostile place for women to pass by, let alone enter.[39]

Manliness in *Red Harvest* is constituted by violence. Physical prowess here testifies to the hard bodies and hard hearts of the he-men who inhabit hard-boiled worlds. Social historians of the nineteenth century make clear the importance of physical strength and courage in defining manhood for working-class men,[40] whose economic manhood was clearly under fire from the Taylorization of their once-skilled artisan jobs. The Op keeps running into hails of gunfire, car chases, and vividly drawn fistfights. Sixteen people are killed by the time we reach Chapter 20, in which Hammett feels compelled to have the Op list the victims, many of whom the reader has probably forgotten. Many more killings are to follow. His role in the bloodbath disturbs the Op, as seen above, but the murders themselves have not. "I've got hard skin all over what's left of my soul, and after twenty years of messing around with crime I can look at any sort of a murder without seeing anything in it but my bread and butter, the day's work" (157). Not much feminine sentiment there.

The biggest threat to *Red Harvest*'s world of traditional gender arrangements is the reversal of roles enacted by Dinah Brand and her permanent houseguest, Dan Rolff. Dinah is the most manly of women. She is physically intimidating—taller than the Op, with "a broad-shouldered, full-breasted, round-hipped body and big muscular legs" (32).

She fails miserably at the arts of dress and makeup that are so crucial to gender masquerade. Her hair needs a trim and isn't parted straight, and her lipstick is crooked. She is forever falling out of her ripped, torn, or buttonless clothing and complaining about the runs in her stockings, continually reminding the reader that her powerful body will not be contained by traditional feminine costume. Nor does her behavior fit the feminine mold. Dinah eats with gusto, polishing off not only her dinner but half of the Op's when they go out to eat (80). The Op reports that she has "a very respectable wallop—man-size" (105) when she punches a thug in the stomach, but confesses he is less than thrilled when she tries to "manhandle" him, since she is probably strong enough to shake his 190 pounds hard enough to hurt (132).

Rather than getting indirect access to commerce through a man, Dinah insists on being a participant. Albury, a former lover, calls her "money-mad" (27), and the police chief describes her as a "big-league gold-digger" (22). The clutter on the kitchen table of her poorly kept house includes racing charts and bulletins from assorted stock and bond forecasters (31). She constantly snipes at the Op for his failure to offer her money for the information she has on the assorted gangsters who run the town. "It's not so much the money," she says. "It's the principle of the thing. If a girl's got something that's worth something to somebody, she's a boob if she doesn't collect" (35). This obsession with money is noteworthy, since the information she wishes to sell came from her numerous lovers. Dinah has crossed the boundary between private and public life by offering lovers' confidences for sale.

Dan Rolff is nearly as womanly as Dinah is manly. One informant reports that Dinah "keeps" Rolff, a "down-and-outer" who has tuberculosis (28). The kept woman here is a man, and he is suffering from that most feminine and romantic of ailments, consumption, which created the thin, weak, pale ideal of feminine beauty so popular among the nineteenth-century leisure classes.[41] When Rolff castigates her for preparing to sell out her friends to the Op, Dinah grabs him by the wrist, twists his arm until he is forced to his knees, and slaps him silly while the Op looks on (82). Rolff then pulls a gun and fires not at Dinah but at the Op. The Op explains why to Dinah: "Because I'd seen you maul him around. . . . You can't expect him to enjoy having another man see you slap his face" (83). Dinah does not understand that manhood is something produced for other men, and that women, however manly, are just incidentals, though necessary ones.[42]

This scene is central to the text, and the Op takes the time both to make Rolff back into a "man" and to explain to Dinah why this is necessary. The Op knocks Rolff out, though he could have disarmed him more gently, and explains his act as one of kindness: "I poked him to give him back some of his self-respect. You know, treated him as I would a man instead of a down-and-outer who could be slapped around by girls" (64). The whole process seems unduly complicated to Dinah, whose manliness sits on her more confidently and with a great deal less self-consciousness.

Dinah gets hers, however. The Op, before doping himself up on laudanum, decides the hundreds of men running around the city with firearms killing one another have everything to do with Dinah. "You seem to have a gift for stirring up murderous notions in your boy friends," he tells her, and provides a partial list: "There's Albury waiting trial for killing Willsson. There's Whisper who's got you shivering in corners. Even I haven't escaped your influence. Look at the way I've turned. And I've always had a private notion that Dan Rolff's going to have a try at you some day" (159).

When the Op comes out of his twisted, drug-induced dreams, he finds Dinah dead on the floor, her ice pick embedded in her heart and his hand around the handle. We don't learn who actually did kill Dinah until the end of the novel. The ambiguity is important. She so deserved it, we are to believe, that the actual culprit is of passing importance. In the final pages, a gangster named Reno Starkey confesses that he killed her in a scuffle, but the admission is anticlimactic.

Although by the close of *Red Harvest*, all of the surviving men are "men" and the women "women," we should not underestimate the importance of the gender disarray in the middle of the novel. For most of the story, the most sympathetic character in this overwhelmingly male world is a strapping, sexually assertive, financially ambitious young woman who is not attractive by accepted standards. She is, paradoxically, both a liberated woman and one of the guys. One of the probable consequences of hard-boiled representations of gender as masquerade is that male identifications with female characters become easier to make. For some readers, Dinah may well have been a "man"—a figure through which male readers could vicariously take part in her manly activities—gambling, drinking, fighting, and driving fast cars.

In suggesting male reader identification with anyone but the male private detective, I am swimming against the tide of critical tradition.

Most current research suggests that although women read themselves into masculine subject positions with ease, men seldom take up feminine subject positions.[43] According to Glenn Most, the effect of the detective's marginal position and lack of a distinctive personal history is to strengthen reader identification with him, a character whose blank personal history freely accepts the reader's projections. The detective, Most insists, *is* the figure for the reader in the text—"the one character whose activities most closely parallel the reader's own, in object (both reader and detective seek to unravel the mystery of the crime), in duration (both are engaged in the story from the beginning and when the detective reveals his solution the reader can no longer evade it himself and the novel can end), and in method (a tissue of guesswork and memory, of suspicion and logic)."[44]

Even female readers, in Judith Fetterley's view, would be likely to identify with the male private eye, because women and girls learn to read as men, because the valued texts of their culture demand it. I want to argue, however, that the historical context of pulp detective fiction and the texts themselves invite other identifications as well.

The ambiguous gender of characters in much hard-boiled fiction and the embattled nature of working-class manhood during the period encourages cross-gender identification. The de-skilling of manual labor, the loss of workplace autonomy, and the increasing number of visible, wage-earning women in jobs once reserved for men rendered the social and economic position of working-class men increasingly "womanly" in the traditional sense. A "feminine" position at work is compatible with the identification with female characters in fiction, and all the more likely if such a character is engaged in manly activity.[45]

Some of the cultural work of hard-boiled fiction, then, may have been a loosening of gender strictures, letting male readers take up both masculine and feminine subject positions. This practice (however unconscious) at thinking of gender as performance rather than as an immutable part of men's and women's nature had a great deal of transgressive potential, however overshadowed it might have been by the violent retribution against manly women enacted at the close of these texts. The fact that these stories returned women to their proper, subordinate places (or death or prison) at the end may have made such identifications less threatening because they were temporary; the traditional order was always restored.

Moreover, popular reading practices—"poaching," to use Michel de Certeau's term—place far less emphasis on the endings of texts than do academic readings. Barbara Sicherman argues, for instance, that the tomboy heroine of Louisa May Alcott's *Little Women*, Jo March, motivated powerful and transformative identification on the part of progressive women readers, who ignored her marriage to a middle-aged professor and her resignation to domesticity at the close of the book in favor of celebrating her adolescent ambition.[46] This kind of popular reading, this way of using cultural products, has less to do with the formal logic of the text than with the needs and histories of its readers. They become active creators of meaning—appropriating scenes, characters, settings, and language that speak to their concerns—rather than passive consumers of mass cultural texts.

Since the readers who concern me—white, working-class men with the means to buy pulp magazines or cheap paperbacks—were outside the record-keeping classes, they have left few diaries, letters, or autobiographies testifying to the ways they brought this fiction to bear on their lives. The social and economic situations of these readers, the ambivalent understandings of gender roles that the texts provided, and theoretical work on popular reading practices, however, provide suggestive ground for some informed speculation. This fiction returned women to their traditional, domestic spaces, nostalgically re-creating the order of an earlier generation. Even as these stories enacted profoundly conservative plots, however, they allowed readers to take up and discard masculine and feminine subject positions as they read. Like the figure of the office wife, who embodied so many contradictions, hard-boiled fiction simultaneously embraced conservative gender politics and undermined the categories on which such a politics was based. What good were conservative politics if some of the women were were really "men"? Implicit in these overtly misogynist texts, then, was the potential to think gender in new and possibly less confining ways. The "gender trouble" in pulp detective fiction between the wars also inspired powerful appropriations and rewritings of the genre by gay and lesbian writers in the past ten or fifteen years.

Afterword

The hard-boiled private eye is a special figure in American mythology.... It's a staple of the myth that he should be a cynical loner, a man at odds with society and its values. That is not something women normally relate to. Women aren't cynical loners—that's not how they like to work. It seems to me that if they want to go into the profession seriously, women writers will have to change the myth itself, instead of trying to fit themselves into it.

Lawrence Block, hard-boiled writer

Women are not interested in homoerotic sadism in the way that men are.

Sara Paretsky, hard-boiled writer

lack Mask stopped publication in 1951, only slightly before the rest of the pulp market collapsed in 1953, killed by competition from paperbacks, comic books, and television. Hard-boiled fiction, however, is alive and well. The tough-talking private eye is an American icon, continuing to appear in books, on television, and in the movies, but an increasingly large number of these tough detectives no longer look or sound much like Sam Spade. The most interesting examples are African-American, ethnic, female, gay, and/or lesbian—possibilities unthinkable to the "real, honest-to-jasper" he-men who walked the mean streets in the pages of *Black Mask* between the wars. In *Black Mask*, women who acted like Sara

Paretsky's V. I. Warshawski or Sue Grafton's Kinsey Millhone were killed off in graphic ways for their manly behavior. Chester Himes's African-American police detectives, Coffin Ed Johnson and Grave Digger Jones, would not have been detectives in *Black Mask*, though they might have had bit parts, like the ethnic characters who pump gas or work as bouncers in the rough bars that the white, hard-boiled heroes patronized. The lesbians in *Black Mask* were all safely closeted, and the "she-men" either died violently or, like Joel Cairo in *The Maltese Falcon*, wandered off (with mincing steps) into the sunset, forever in search of jewel-encrusted birds.

How did a genre historically marked by sexism, racism, and homophobia become such fertile ground for protesting sexism, racism, and homophobia? What reading practices, and what characteristics of the founding texts of the genre, made such appropriations possible?

Hard-boiled fiction between the wars was concerned with rethinking identities in light of emergent consumer culture, with reconciling a residual culture of manly, autonomous craftsmen and an emergent commodity culture. As a consequence, hard-boiled stories were loaded with contradictions. They offered the hero as an honest proletarian and a champion of unalienated labor, but their tortured plots followed the logic of scientific management. They offered object lessons in reading how class, gender, and power were embodied in clothing, furniture, and other commodities, but violently killed off effeminate consumers. They demonstrated the rules of bourgeois rhetoric, but ultimately dismissed it as silly, effeminate posturing that was inferior to working-class ways with words. They repeatedly returned manly women to subordinate places, but called into question exactly what "men" and "women" were in a culture where white men's wages and autonomy on the job were eroding and large numbers of women were working in positions once reserved for men.

Hard-boiled fiction's anxieties about identity in a consumer society, its representation of class, gender, sexuality, and ethnicity as matters of performance, were what proved so appealing to writers from a variety of marginal backgrounds after World War II. The way in which modern hard-boiled fiction calls the construction of identities into question was implicit in the founding texts of the genre. In this sense, ethnic, female, gay, and lesbian writers are poachers—readers who appropriated complex and often contradictory texts in ways that addressed their own needs, goals, and situations.

Studying the rewritings of the hard-boiled genre by marginalized writers since World War II is another project entirely, but a few examples suggest the kinds of appropriation that may have been at work. Erle Stanley Gardner's disguising of his Anglo sleuth, Ed Jenkins, as an elderly Chinese herb doctor gets a twist in Chester Himes's 1965 *Cotton Comes to Harlem*. Coffin Ed Johnson and Grave Digger Jones bust a light-skinned black woman out of jail by putting her in blackface. "Make yourself into a black woman and don't ask any questions," Grave Digger tells her, "You'll find everything in there you'll need—make-up, clothes and some money. Don't worry about the dye; it'll come off."[1] If the ease with which Gardner's sleuth passes for Chinese calls into question the naturalness of ethnic identity, disguising a black woman in blackface makes race seem nothing more than a matter of disguise, with no authentic origin.

Identity in Himes's novels, as it was in interwar detective fiction, is fluid. In the opening scene of *Blind Man With a Pistol* (1969), for example, two white police officers question an elderly black man living in a broken-down house with twelve black women and more than fifty children whom he has presumably fathered. The elderly man, Reverend Sam, explains to the police officers that the women are Roman Catholic nuns. They are also his wives, an arrangement he explains by appealing to his Mormon faith. The police are clearly baffled by the way identity works in this world: "You mean they were virgins in the morning, nuns during the day, and wives at night?"[2] The old man allows that the white cops' formulation is a reasonably accurate one. Identity, he says, just works differently for black folks than for white ones.

By the late 1970s and early 1980s the gender trouble that had been implicit in interwar hard-boiled fiction had come to the forefront. Effie decided she'd had it with Sam Spade and went into business for herself. Marcia Muller's Sharon McCone, Sara Paretsky's V. I. Warshawski, and Sue Grafton's Kinsey Millhone were the first women to occupy the unambiguously masculine position of hard-boiled private eye. Their impressive sales figures spawned what Kathleen Gregory Klein calls a "mini-explosion of women detectives" by the late 1980s.[3] However, as in the case of the interwar office wife, putting women's bodies into men's jobs proved highly disruptive. The titles of early reviews of women's hard-boiled crime novels suggest as much: "Female Dick" and "When the Dick is a Dame."[4] Moreover, these early novels were full of men who were sure that private detection was an unsuitable job for a woman. In Sara Paretsky's *Indemnity Only* (1982), Lieutenant Bobby Mallory tells V. I. Warshawski that "(b)eing a detective is not a job for a girl. . . . If Tony [her father] had turned you over his knee more often instead of spoiling you rotten, you'd be a happy housewife now, instead of playing at detective."[5]

Gay and lesbian rewritings of the genre were even more dramatic.[6] What if Wilmer and Joel Cairo, the homosexuals in hot pursuit of the Maltese falcon, had decided to go into business and beat Sam Spade at his own game? What if Effie's "woman's intuition" had told her that she and Brigid O'Shaughnessy could take better care of each other than the abusive Sam Spade ever could? What happened to a genre grounded in male homosocial bonds when the main character was a woman who had no sexual interest in men? Would such a text even count as hard-boiled fiction?[7]

The destabilizing of gender categories implicit in hard-boiled fiction between the wars and increasingly central to the fiction of contemporary writers reaches a logical end point in Barbara Wilson's 1990 *Gaudí Afternoon,* which centers on a custody battle over a child with too many mothers.[8] The investigator, Cassandra Reilly, is hired by a "woman" named Frankie, who is transgendered, to track down her gay "husband," Ben, a radical-feminist dyke. Ben's "girlfriend," April, is also transgendered, though Ben doesn't know this. April is seeing her gay, cross-dressing stepbrother. Cassandra Reilly, a lesbian, gives herself a bad haircut early in the story and is frequently mistaken for a man. The central question of the novel—who is the mother of the child?—seems far less important by the end than the larger, unanswerable question of just who the "men" and "women" are, and whether biological sex and gender are necessarily linked at all.

Although these new heroes look different from their virile ancestors, modern hard-boiled fiction resembles interwar hard-boiled fiction in striking ways. The stories are usually set in neighborhoods on the wrong side of the tracks, although working for Legal Aid often gets the modern detective there. Like Raymond Chandler's novels, modern stories are deeply interested in the details of everyday life. Readers of Sara Paretsky's V. I. Warshawski novels get to know Warshawski's wardrobe better than they may know their own. Violence continues to figure prominently, although modern private eyes are just as likely to be victims or victims' advocates (assisting battered women and children, counseling rape victims) as investigators.

These novels frequently nod to the founding texts of the hard-boiled tradition. In Barbara Wilson's *Murder in the Collective* (1984), lesbian detective Pam Nilsen and her partner have enthusiastic, Chandler-esque visions of what their investigation of a colleague's murder would be like if real life weren't so low-budget: "Seedy motels and luxurious estates.... Dazzling blondes answering the door in negligees.... Just trying to corrupt us."[9]

Cassandra Reilly introduces herself to the cast of ambiguously gendered figures in *Gaudí Afternoon* as Brigid O'Shaughnessy, the murderess who seduces Sam Spade in Dashiell Hammett's *The Maltese Falcon*.[10] The allusion places Wilson's work within a tradition of hard-boiled fiction that reaches back to the pulps, but it also marks her rewriting of that tradition from the position of a lesbian writer. Although Wilson is invoking, echoing, and paying tribute to that older tradition, she is also remaking it and parodying its masculinist conventions.

Mary Wings's *She Came Too Late* (1987) ends with a pastiche of Sam Spade's famous "I won't play the sap for you" speech to Brigid O'Shaughnessy at the end of *The Maltese Falcon*. Although he concedes that he may love her, Spade hands O'Shaughnessy over to the police, even though she may hang for her crimes. "I'm going to send you over," he says, and then: "You're taking the fall. One of us has got to take it, after the talking those birds will do."[11] In Spade's long list of reasons for turning O'Shaughnessy in, her untrustworthiness figures prominently: "I've got no reason in God's world to think I can trust you and if I did this and got away with it you'd have something on me that you could use whenever you happened to want to.... Since I've also got something on you, I couldn't be sure you wouldn't decide to shoot a hole in *me* some day."[12]

At the end of *She Came Too Late*, private eye Emma Victor stages a showdown with Stacy Weldemeer, the photogenic director of a successful women's health clinic and the star fund-raiser for women's causes in Boston. Weldemeer admits to having committed two murders, but assumes that Victor will not turn her in because they are both feminist activists. Victor sets her straight: "I'm sending you over, Stacy. I can't be your accomplice, I can't cover for you, and if I did I'd never be sure of you when the night is dark and I'm alone and you feel panicked and I become an object in the way of your future. No, Stacy, I'm sending you over. It's the only way.... It's either you or me, and I'm afraid it's going to be you."[13] The echoes are striking—the refusal to honor misplaced bonds of relationship, the lack of trust, the compelling nature of the murderer's distress. "I'm sending you over" is the declaration of both Spade and Victor, although they are separated by gender, sexuality, politics, milieu, and nearly sixty years. In each case, the investigator recognizes that the love invoked by the murderer is a cover for the treacherous pursuit of self-interest.

The meaning of these texts for readers is, of course, closely tied to the conditions under which they are written and read, their social framing and infrastructure. There was a significant resurgence in sales of detective fiction in general in the late 1980s. Mystery writers made it onto hardcover best-seller lists, publishers began to acquire more mystery fiction, the Book-of-the-Month Club chose a crime novel as its main selection, and membership in mystery book clubs increased dramatically. *Publishers Weekly* christened the 1980s a "new golden age of mysteries," and the growing market made the industry particularly hospitable to new writers, including those whose main characters were women.[14] Although publishers usually do not make public the results of demographically based market surveys, the common wisdom is that most of the readers of today's mystery fiction are women—significantly more than half, according to booksellers, authors, agents, and editors.[15] Although mysteries, unlike Westerns and romances, are regularly read by both men and women, the membership of the Mysterious Book Club (the Book-of-the-Month Club's mystery wing) and the Mystery Guild is more than 50 percent female.[16] The knowledge that women dominate the mystery audience could certainly make novels about female private eyes appear particularly marketable.

The social framing and infrastructure of gay and lesbian detective fiction is quite different. Most of it is published by small, alternative, and/or feminist presses. Since the 1970s, feminist presses such as Naiad, Seal, and Virago have offered an increasing number of books about lesbian investigators by such writers as Barbara Wilson, Eve Zaremba, Katherine Forrest, Mary Wings, Claire McNab, Jaye Maiman, and Kaye Davis. These avowedly feminist presses are driven not only by profits but by a desire to challenge accepted ideas and empower certain classes of readers. They are probably preaching to the choir. There is little evidence that gay and lesbian detective fiction interests significant numbers of mainstream readers. Fully 70 percent of gay and lesbian detective novels are bought in gay or specialty bookshops. Barbara Grier, a co-founder of Naiad Press, maintains, "There is no real crossover market ... I'm still trying to get the one in ten women who are lesbians to read my books."[17]

There is some evidence of crossover reading, however. A number of prominent writers of lesbian detective fiction have either begun publishing with mainstream houses (Phyllis Knight, Laurie R. King), or switched over from small, feminist presses to commercial publishing houses (Katherine Forrest, J. M. Redmann, Mary Wings). Once they have adopted/adapted the mainstream genre and proven there is an affluent market for their books, they gain access to publishing outlets and larger audiences through the appeal of the genre.[18] There are limits to the kinds of crossover reading one can achieve, however. "Some of my most avid readers are straight women," says gay writer Michael Nava, "but heterosexual men don't read my books. . . . Straight men see the word 'gay' on the cover and their minds close—they're too threatened. Straight women have fewer hang-ups and are more interested in plot and character."[19]

The best example of gay detective fiction's move to the mainstream is John Morgan Wilson's *Simple Justice*, the winner of the Mystery Writers of America's 1997 Edgar Award for best first novel by an American author.[20] Wilson's investigator, Benjamin Justice, is an ex-reporter for the *Los Angeles Times* who has lost his lover to AIDS and has lost his job and a Pulitzer Prize to a scandal over a faked story that he wrote six years ago. His editor calls him back to investigative reporting to do background work on a piece about an apparent hate killing outside a gay bar. To solve the case, Justice must explain why the admitted killer would have confessed to a crime he did not commit. Justice's empathetic reconstruction of the supposed killer's life reveals him as a young man coming to terms with his sexuality in a homophobic culture. Rather than admit to his family that he was at a gay bar because he was gay, he confessed to the murder. To read this as a detective story, to make sense of the clues and bring the narrative to a coherent close, a reader, regardless of his or her sexual identity, has to come to some understanding of the deforming power of homophobia.

Recent writers have given Dashiell Hammett's taciturn, middle-aged Continental Op some dramatic makeovers. Carlotta Carlyle, the private eye of contemporary hard-boiled writer Linda Barnes, is a six-foot-tall, red-haired woman who has inherited a seemingly inexhaustible supply of Yiddish proverbs from her maternal grandmother.[21] Michael Nava's hero, Henry Rios, is a gay, Hispanic public defender who narrates the death of his partner with great sensitivity and recognizes that his obsessive work habits come at significant personal cost.[22] The continuing relevance of hard-boiled detective fiction to modern life is testimony, then, to both the complexity of the founding texts of the 1920s, '30s, and '40s and the ingenuity of the readers and writers who reinvented this seemingly hostile genre on their own terms.

Notes

Introduction

Epigraphs: Dorothy Parker, "Reading and Writing: Oh Look—Two Good Books!" *The New Yorker,* 5 Apr. 1931, pp. 83–84; "New York in Prohibition Days," rev. of *The Thin Man* by Dashiell Hammett, *Saturday Review,* 30 June 1934, p. 773; Will Cuppy, rev. of *The Dain Curse* by Dashiell Hammett, *New York Herald Tribune Books,* 11 Aug. 1929, p. 11.

1. William F. Nolan, *The "Black Mask" Boys: Masters in the Hard-Boiled School of Detective Fiction* (New York: Morrow, 1985); David Madden, ed., *Tough Guy Writers of the Thirties* (Carbondale: Southern Illinois University Press, 1968); Ron Goulart, ed., *The Hardboiled Dicks: An Anthology and Study of Pulp Detective Fiction* (Los Angeles: Sherbourne, 1965).

2. Quoted in Marilyn Stasio, "Lady Gumshoes: Boiled Less Hard," *New York Times Book Review,* 18 Apr. 1985, pp. 3, 39.

3. Raymond Chandler, *Farewell, My Lovely* (1940; reprint, New York: Vintage, 1992), p. 190.

4. Carroll Smith-Rosenberg, "The Female World of Love and Ritual: Relations Between Women in Nineteenth-Century America," *Disorderly Conduct: Visions of Gender in Victorian America* (New York: Knopf, 1985), pp. 53–76.

5. Dashiell Hammett, *The Maltese Falcon* (1929, 1930; reprint, New York: Vintage, 1992), p. 145.

6. Kenneth Burke, "Literature as Equipment for Living," *The Philosophy of Literary Form,* 3d ed. (Berkeley: University of California Press, 1973), pp. 293–304.

7. Cathy N. Davidson, in *Revolution and the Word: The Rise of the Novel in America* (New York: Oxford University Press, 1986), similarly redefines "literature" as "not simply words upon a page but a complex social, political, and material process of cultural production" (viii). See also Jerome McGann's *The Textual Condition* (Princeton, NJ: Princeton University Press, 1991), in which he argues that a text's meaning is "a set of concrete and always changing conditions: because the meaning is in the use and textuality is a social condition of various times, places and persons" (21).

8. Fredric Jameson, "Reification and Utopia in Mass Culture," *Social Text* 1 (Winter 1979): 132.

9. Jerry Palmer, *Thrillers: Genesis and Structure of a Popular Genre* (New York: St. Martin's, 1979), p. 66; John G. Cawelti, *Adventure, Mystery, and Romance: Formula Stories as Art and Popular Culture* (Chicago: University of Chicago Press, 1976), pp. 35, 105. For a sampling of theorists arguing for the conservative politics of the form, see Slavoj Zizek, *Looking Awry: An Introduction to Jacques Lacan through Popular Culture* (Cambridge, MA: MIT Press, 1991), Chap. 3; Cynthia S. Hamilton, *Western and Hard-Boiled Detective Fiction in America* (Iowa City: University of Iowa Press, 1987), Chap. 1; Michael Holquist, "Whodunit and Other Questions: Metaphysical Detective Stories in Postwar Fiction," in *The Poetics of Murder: Detective Fiction and Literary Theory*, ed. Glenn W. Most and William W. Stowe (New York: Harcourt, 1983), pp. 149–74; Stephen Knight, *Form and Ideology in Crime Fiction* (Bloomington: Indiana University Press, 1980), Chap. 5; and Ernest Mandel, *Delightful Murder: A Social History of the Crime Story* (Minneapolis: University of Minnesota Press, 1984), pp. 71–73. For further discussion of the complicity of detective fiction and other "realist" texts with the bourgeois order, see Catherine Belsey, *Critical Practice* (New York: Routledge, 1980), Chap. 3; and Mark Seltzer, "The Princess Casamassima: Realism and the Fantasy of Surveillance," in *American Realism: New Essays*, ed. Eric J. Sundquist (Baltimore: Johns Hopkins University Press, 1982), pp. 95–118.

10. On the way changes in form invest texts with new meaning, see Roger Chartier, *The Order of Books: Readers, Authors, and Libraries in Europe between the Fourteenth and Eighteenth Centuries*, trans. Lydia G. Cochrane (Stanford, CA: Stanford University Press, 1994), p. 3.

11. Jameson, "Reification and Utopia," p. 141.

12. Alison Light, "'Returning to Manderley'—Romance Fiction, Female Sexuality and Class," *Feminist Review* 16 (Summer 1984): 8.

13. There are a few exceptions. Priscilla L. Walton and Manina Jones, in *Detective Agency: Women Rewriting the Hard-Boiled Tradition* (Berkeley: University of California Press, 1999), report the findings of a survey posted to the e-mail discussion list DorothyL, which is dedicated to women's mystery fiction. See also "Some Readers Reading," R. Gordon Kelly, *Mystery Fiction and Modern Life* (Jackson: University Press of Mississippi, 1998), Chap. 7.

14. Erin Smith, "'Both a woman and a complete professional': Women Readers and Women's Hard-Boiled Detective Fiction," in *Reading Sites*, ed. Elizabeth Flynn and Patrocinio Schweckart (Baltimore: Johns Hopkins University Press, forthcoming).

15. Michel de Certeau, *The Practice of Everyday Life*, trans. Steven R. Rendell (Berkeley: University of California Press, 1984).

16. See Light, "'Returning to Manderley'"; Cora Kaplan, "'The Thorn Birds': Fiction, Fantasy, Femininity," in *Sea Changes: Essays on Culture and Feminism* (London: Verso, 1986), pp. 117–46; and Smith, "'Both a woman and a complete professional'."

17. Roger Chartier, "Culture as Appropriation: Popular Cultural Uses in Early Modern France," in Steven Kaplan, *Understanding Popular Culture:*

Europe from the Middle Ages to the Nineteenth Century (New York: Mouton, 1984), p. 233. Chartier's redefinition of "popular" as a way of using artifacts resonates with Pierre Bourdieu's work on the differences between the "aesthetic disposition," which values form over function and recommends aesthetic distance as a worldview, and the "popular aesthetic," which asks what cultural artifacts are good *for*. See Pierre Bourdieu, *Distinction: A Social Critique of the Judgment of Taste*, trans. Richard Nice (Cambridge: Harvard University Press, 1984).

18. Elizabeth Long, "Textual Interpretation as Collective Action," in *The Ethnography of Reading*, ed. Jonathan Boyarin (Berkeley: University of California Press, 1993), pp. 180–211.

19. Long, "Textual Interpretation," pp. 191–92.

20. For a provocative attempt, see Carlo Ginzburg, *The Cheese and the Worms: The Cosmos of a Sixteenth-Century Miller*, trans. John and Anne Tedeschi (Baltimore: Johns Hopkins University Press, 1980).

21. Chartier, *The Order of Books*, p. 5. See also Robert Darnton, *The Forbidden Bestsellers of Pre-Revolutionary France* (New York: Norton, 1995), p. 187.

22. Davidson, *Revolution and the Word*, pp. 4–5.

23. Darnton, *Forbidden Bestsellers*, p. 184.

24. Harold Hersey, *Pulpwood Editor: The Fabulous World of Thriller Magazines Revealed by a Veteran Editor and Publisher* (New York: Stokes, 1937), p. 87.

25. Paulo Friere, *Pedagogy of the Oppressed*, trans. Myra Bergman Ramos (New York: Continuum, 1970).

26. For a discussion of class ventriloquism in nineteenth-century dime novels, see Michael Denning, *Mechanic Accents: Dime Novels and Working-Class Culture in America* (New York: Verso, 1987), pp. 84, 171, 226.

27. Recent works on consumption and the working class include Kathy Peiss, *Cheap Amusements: Leisure in Turn-of-the-Century New York* (Philadelphia: Temple University Press, 1986); Dana Frank, *Purchasing Power: Consumer Organizing, Gender, and the Seattle Labor Movement, 1919–1929* (New York: Cambridge University Press, 1994); Lizabeth Cohen, *Making a New Deal: Industrial Workers in Chicago, 1919–1939* (New York: Cambridge University Press, 1990); Lizabeth Cohen, "The Class Experience of Mass Consumption: Workers as Consumers in Interwar America," in *The Power of Culture: Critical Essays in American History*, ed. Richard Wightman Fox and T. J. Jackson Lears (Chicago: University of Chicago Press, 1993), pp. 135–60; Lizabeth Cohen, "Encountering Mass Culture at the Grassroots: The Experience of Chicago Workers in the 1920s," *American Quarterly* 41 (Spring 1989): 6–33; Lawrence Glickman, *A Living Wage: American Workers and the Making of Consumer Society* (Ithaca, NY: Cornell University Press, 1997); and Lawrence Glickman, "Inventing the 'American Standard of Living': Gender, Race and Working-Class Identity, 1880–1925," *Labor History* 34.2–3 (Spring/Summer 1993): 221–35.

28. In their introduction to the seminal *The Culture of Consumption: Critical Essays in American History, 1880–1980* (New York: Pantheon, 1983),

Richard Wightman Fox and T. J. Jackson Lears argue that the study of consumer culture ought to begin by focusing on the activities of urban elites—wealthy, well-educated white men who created consumption as a cultural ideal and lobbied for its wide acceptance in the late nineteenth and early twentieth centuries (x–xi). See also Roland Marchand, *Advertising the American Dream: Making Way for Modernity, 1920–1940* (Berkeley: University of California Press, 1985) for a discussion of middle-class white women as advertising's target audience. For an overview of this literature, see Mark A. Swiencicki, "Consuming Brotherhood: Men's Culture, Style and Recreation as Consumer Culture, 1880–1930," *Journal of Social History* 31.4 (Summer 1998): 773–809.

    29. David R. Roediger, *The Wages of Whiteness: Race and the Making of the American Working Class* (New York: Verso, 1991).

    30. John G. Cawelti, *The Six-Gun Mystique* (Bowling Green, OH: Bowling Green State University Popular Press, 1970), p. 17.

Part I

    Epigraph: Michel de Certeau, *The Practice of Everyday Life*, trans. Steven R. Rendell (Berkeley: University of California Press, 1984), p. 174.

    1. Robert Darnton, *The Great Cat Massacre and Other Episodes in French Cultural History* (New York: Basic, 1984), p. 261.

Chapter One

    Epigraphs: Marcus Duffield, "The Pulps: day dreams for the masses," *Vanity Fair*, June 1933, p. 26; Margaret MacMullen, "Pulps and Confessions," *Harper's Monthly Magazine*, June 1937, p. 98.

    1. *Black Mask* XIV, No. 4 (June 1931), p. 7.

    2. On the history of pulp magazines, see Lee Server, *Danger Is My Business: An Illustrated History of the Fabulous Pulp Magazines* (San Francisco: Chronicle, 1993); William F. Nolan, *The "Black Mask" Boys: Masters in the Hard-Boiled School of Detective Fiction* (New York: Morrow, 1985); Tony Goodstone, ed., *The Pulps: Fifty Years of American Pop Culture* (New York: Chelsea House, 1970); Frank Gruber, *The Pulp Jungle* (Los Angeles: Sherbourne, 1967); Harold Hersey, *Pulpwood Editor: The Fabulous World of Thriller Magazines Revealed by a Veteran Editor and Publisher* (New York: Stokes, 1937); Ron Goulart, *Dime Detectives* (New York: Mysterious, 1988); and Ron Goulart, *Cheap Thrills: An Informal History of Pulp Magazines* (New Rochelle, NY: Arlington House, 1972). General histories of magazines include John Tebbel and Mary Ellen Zuckerman, *The Magazine in America, 1741–1990* (New York: Oxford University Press, 1991) and Theodore Peterson, *Magazines in the Twentieth Century* (Urbana: University of Illinois Press, 1956), although neither discusses pulp magazines at length.

    3. The figures are based on a survey by A. A. Wyn, a pulp publisher (Peterson, *Magazines*, p. 309).

    4. On the production and distribution of dime novels, see Michael Denning, *Mechanic Accents: Dime Novels and Working-Class Culture in America* (New York:

Verso, 1987), Chap. 2; and Christine Bold, *Selling the Wild West: Popular Western Fiction, 1860–1960* (Bloomington: Indiana University Press, 1987), Chap. 1.

5. On pulp magazines as business enterprises, see Hersey, *Pulpwood Editor*, pp. 11–28; Peterson, *Magazines*, p. 69; and Tebbel and Zuckerman, *Magazine in America*, p. 341.

6. On price-cutting and circulation increases around the turn of the century, see Peterson, *Magazines*, pp. 2–14, 21–29, 223–24; and Tebbel and Zuckerman, *Magazine in America*, pp. 66–68.

7. Peterson, *Magazines*, Chap. 1, p. 13.

8. Gruber, *Pulp Jungle*, p. 23; Server, *Danger*, p. 19.

9. Although not the customary arrangement, regulars were sometimes commissioned to write for a given pulp and paid a monthly salary or guaranteed highest word rates for their submissions, whose acceptance was guaranteed. In the early 1930s, Erle Stanley Gardner negotiated an annual contract with *Black Mask* to accept one story a month from him without revision at the highest rate (Erle Stanley Gardner, letter to Joseph Thompson Shaw, 23 Feb. 1931, Erle Stanley Gardner Papers, Harry Ransom Humanities Research Center, University of Texas, Austin (henceforth cited as "HRC"). Several writers for Street & Smith pulps, including Walter Gibson, were paid a fixed salary for their regular monthly contributions (Editorial Files, Box 27, Street & Smith Collection, Syracuse University Library Special Collections (henceforth cited as "Syracuse")).

10. Quoted in Server, *Danger*, p. 15.

11. See, for example, T. S. Eliot, "Tradition and the Individual Talent," *Selected Essays, 1917–1932* (New York: Harcourt, 1932), pp. 3–11.

12. The notion of authorship predominant in Hollywood screenwriting circles resembled that of pulp writing in some ways. Many writers were frustrated when they discovered that screenwriting was a collective labor for which they often received no screen credit; that they were employees of a studio that owned their creative output rather than proprietors of their own work; and that their new profession lacked the prestige accorded novelists and playwrights in New York. The lack of protest in pulp writing circles about similar working conditions is evidence that pulp writers felt themselves to be engaged in an enterprise that was fundamentally different from more self-consciously literary writing. On writers in Hollywood, see Richard Fine, *West of Eden: Writers in Hollywood, 1928–1940* (Washington, DC: Smithsonian, 1993).

13. Erle Stanley Gardner, letter to Joseph Thompson Shaw, 23 Aug. 1926, Erle Stanley Gardner Papers, HRC.

14. Erle Stanley Gardner, letter to Don Moore, 28 Sept. 1932; Erle Stanley Gardner, letter to Phil Cody, 27 Mar. 1925; Erle Stanley Gardner, letter to Joseph Thompson Shaw, 6 Aug. 1925 (all in Erle Stanley Gardner Papers, HRC).

15. Erle Stanley Gardner, letter to Don Moore, 18 Feb. 1931, Erle Stanley Gardner Papers, HRC.

16. Erle Stanley Gardner, letter to A. H. Bittner, 21 June 1928. See also Erle Stanley Gardner, letter to H. C. North, 27 Mar. 1925; Erle Stanley Gardner, letter to Phil Cody, 6 Aug. 1925 (all in Erle Stanley Gardner Papers, HRC).

17. See Day Books, Box 11, Erle Stanley Gardner Papers, HRC.

18. Leroy Lad Panek, *An Introduction to the Detective Story* (Bowling Green, OH: Bowling Green State University Popular Press, 1987), p. 159.

19. Gruber, *Pulp Jungle*, p. 105.

20. See, for example, Editorial Files, Boxes 6 and 27, Street & Smith Collection, Syracuse; Server, *Danger*, p. 19.

21. Server, *Danger*, pp. 14–15

22. *Black Mask* VI, No. 15 (1 Nov. 1923), p. 126; *Black Mask* VI, No. 7 (1 July 1923), p. 126.

23. See, for example, *Black Mask* XXIII, No. 1 (Apr. 1940), p. 97.

24. *Black Mask* VI, No. 5 (1 June 1923), p. 128. See also Street & Smith's *Clues* XLI, No. 2 (Feb. 1939) for a "Story Trail" writer's column by Paul Ernst about his efforts to dream stories in his sleep during a case of writer's block. This form of inspiration was so physically destructive (he lost more than 20 pounds in a very short time), that he began to ignore the stories he dreamed in the hope of returning to his old, workmanlike ways of writing (125–27).

25. *Black Mask* XXII, No. 8 (Nov. 1939), p. 112; *Black Mask* VI, No. 2 (15 Apr. 1923), p. 3.

26. Pierre Bourdieu, *Distinction: A Social Critique of the Judgment of Taste*, trans. Richard Nice (Cambridge, MA: Harvard University Press, 1984), pp. 4, 11–18.

27. *Black Mask* VII, No. 5 (July 1924), p. 127.

28. On pulp readership, see Hersey, Chap. 1; Frank Schick, *The Paperbound Book in America: The History of Paperbacks and their European Background* (New York: Bowker, 1958), p. 56; Panek, *An Introduction*, pp. 159–60; Goodstone, *The Pulps*, p. xii; Nolan, *"Black Mask" Boys*, p. 29; William S. Gray and Ruth Munroe, *The Reading Interests and Habits of Adults: A Preliminary Report* (New York: Macmillan, 1929), pp. 84, 150, 206–7; and William Frank Rasche, *The Reading Interests of Young Workers* (Chicago: University of Chicago Press, 1937), pp. 10, 12. Also Louis Adamic, "What the Proletariat Reads: Conclusions Based on a Year's Study Among Hundreds of Workers Throughout the United States," *The Saturday Review of Literature* XI, No. 20 (1 Dec. 1934), pp. 321–22.

29. Hersey, *Pulpwood Editor*, pp. 7–9; Bold, *Selling*, pp. 7–8; Hersey, *Pulpwood Editor*, p. 4.

30. The best summary and analysis of this material is Stephen Karetzky, *Reading Research and Librarianship: A History and Analysis* (Westport, CT: Greenwood Press, 1982). Those studies that focused specifically on the reading of factory workers include Gray and Munroe, *Reading Interests;* Rasche, *Reading Interests;* and Hazel Ormsbee, *The Young Employed Girl* (New York: Woman's Press, 1927), pp. 75–95.

31. Gray and Munroe, *Reading Interests*, p. 149; Douglas Waples, *People and Print: Social Aspects of Reading in the Depression* (Chicago: University of Chicago Press, 1938), pp. 150–52.

32. This claim was commonplace in both the popular press and the scholarly work of librarians and adult educators of the period. For examples from library research, see Gray and Munroe, *Reading Interests*, pp. 84, 150, 206–7; and Rasche, *Reading Interests*, pp. 10, 12. For an example from the popular press, see Adamic, *What the Proletariat Reads*. Adamic's findings are challenged by Robert Cantwell, "What the Working Class Reads," *The New Republic*, 17 July 1935, pp. 274–76.

Cantwell argues that most of the readers checking Twain, Shaw, Hardy, and the Greek classics out of the public library were working-class.

33. On the union label, see Lawrence Glickman, *A Living Wage: American Workers and the Making of Consumer Society* (Ithaca, NY: Cornell University Press, 1997), Chap. 6, "Producers as Consumers."

34. See, for example, *Clues* XLI, No. 1 (1 Dec. 1938).

35. On the use of this term in the nineteenth century, see Denning, *Mechanic Accents*, pp. 45–46.

36. Hersey maintained that the largest portion of pulp-magazine readers were children or adolescents (5). Erle Stanley Gardner thought high-school students were some of the biggest readers of the pulps (Erle Stanley Gardner, letter to Phil Cody, 1 Dec. 1929). See also Joseph Thompson Shaw, letter to Erle Stanley Gardner, 28 Mar. 1927, Erle Stanley Gardner Papers, HRC.

37. H. C. North, letter to Erle Stanley Gardner, 7 July 1924, Erle Stanley Gardner Papers, HRC.

38. Joseph Thompson Shaw, letter to Erle Stanley Gardner, 17 Mar. 1927; Erle Stanley Gardner, letter to Joseph Thompson Shaw, 27 Oct. 1927; Erle Stanley Gardner, letter to Joseph Thompson Shaw, 10 Mar. 1928 (all in Erle Stanley Gardner Papers, HRC).

39. Erle Stanley Gardner, letter to Joseph Thompson Shaw, 5 July 1933, Erle Stanley Gardner Papers, HRC.

40. For a discussion from reading research of the period, see Douglas Waples, Bernard Berelson, and Franklyn R. Bradshaw, *What Reading Does to People: A Summary of Evidence on the Social Effects of Reading and a Statement of Problems for Research* (Chicago: University of Chicago Press, 1940), p. 94.

41. Hersey, *Pulpwood Editor*, p. 8.

42. Erle Stanley Gardner, letter to Joseph Thompson Shaw, 4 Mar. 1927; Erle Stanley Gardner, letter to Joseph Thompson Shaw, 27 Oct. 1927 (both in Erle Stanley Gardner Papers, HRC).

43. Although Alfred Knopf published Dashiell Hammett, Raymond Chandler, and George Harmon Coxe in high-quality Borzoi mystery hardcovers, the vast majority of sales of hard-boiled detective novels were always cheap paperback reprint editions. Detective, mystery, and suspense fiction was the largest special category on general best-seller lists, but almost never appeared on hardcover lists before 1965. The bulk of initial hardcover runs were sold to lending libraries. Alice Payne Hackett, *70 Years of Best Sellers, 1895–1965* (New York: Bowker, 1967) includes figures for three Hammett and Chandler novels on the list of all-time best-sellers. Hammett's *The Thin Man* sold 1,398,445 copies between its initial publication in 1934 and 1965, of which 1,363,000 were paperbacks. *The Maltese Falcon* sold 1,098,001 copies total, of which 1,085,800 were paper. Figures for Chandler's *Farewell, My Lovely* are 1,388,220 total copies, of which 1,384,340 were paperback. For a discussion of the world of the hard-boiled paperbacks, see Geoffrey O'Brien, *Hardboiled America: The Lurid Years of Paperbacks* (New York: Reinhold, 1981).

44. John Tebbel, *Between Covers: The Rise and Transformation of Book Publishing in America* (New York: Oxford University Press, 1987), p. 296.

45. Kenneth C. Davis, *Two-Bit Culture: The Paperbacking of America* (Boston: Houghton, 1984), p. xii.

46. Ibid., p. xi.

47. Ibid, Chap. 5.

48. Pierre Bourdieu argues that the "quasi-miraculous correspondence" between the tastes of audiences and the products offered for sale is a result of homologies between the logic of the field of production and the logic of the field of consumption (232). Pulp-fiction writers were piecework prose producers; working-class readers were piecework goods producers.

49. See Helen Damon-Moore and Carl F. Kaestle, "Gender, Advertising, and Mass-Circulation Magazines," in Carl F. Kaestle, Helen Damon-Moore, Lawrence C. Stedman, Katherine Tinsley, and William Vance Trollinger, Jr., *Literacy in the United Stated: Readers and Reading Since 1880* (New Haven, CT: Yale University Press, 1991), pp. 245–71, for a more detailed examination of how the needs of advertisers determined the specific ways in which middlebrow magazines were gendered.

50. Gruber, *Pulp Jungle*, p. 150.

51. Raymond Chandler, letter to Hamish Hamilton, 10 Nov. 1950, in *Selected Letters of Raymond Chandler*, ed. Frank MacShane (New York: Columbia University Press, 1981), p. 236.

52. Hersey, *Pulpwood Editor*, p. 1.

53. Goulart, *Cheap Thrills*, p. 115.

54. "Street & Smith News Trade Bulletin, June 1930," Editorial Files, Box 41, Street & Smith Collection, Syracuse.

55. A. H. Bittner, letter to Erle Stanley Gardner, 6 July 1928, Erle Stanley Gardner Papers, HRC.

56. Server, *Danger*, pp. 69, 71. William Nolan's complete listing of crime-genre pulp magazines between 1920 and the early 1950s lists 178 titles, not all of which were in print simultaneously or survived more than a couple of issues (*"Black Mask" Boys*, 267).

57. The best publishing history of *Black Mask* is William F. Nolan's "History of a Pulp: The Life and Times of *Black Mask*" in ibid., pp. 19–34. My narrative here is informed by Nolan's account.

58. *Black Mask* VIII, No. 11 (Jan. 1926).

59. *Black Mask* XVI, No. 2 (Apr. 1933), p. 7.

60. *Black Mask* XIV, No. 12 (Feb. 1932), p. 120.

61. Nolan, *"Black Mask" Boys*, p. 20.

62. Gruber, *Pulp Jungle*, p. 98.

63. Nolan, *"Black Mask" Boys*, p. 30; Gruber, *Pulp Jungle*, p. 77.

64. On female hard-boiled writers in general, see Bill Pronzini and Jack Adrian, eds., *Hard-Boiled: An Anthology of American Crime Stories* (New York: Oxford University Press, 1995), pp. 163, 348. One extraordinary "Behind the Mask" column in 1942 identified the writer Alan Farley as Mrs. Lee Harrington of Kansas City (*Black Mask* XXV, No. 7 [Nov. 1942], p. 8).

65. See Editorial Records, Box 7, Street & Smith Collection, Syracuse.

66. *Black Mask* VI, No. 4 (15 May 1923), p. 127; No. 20 (15 Jan. 1924), p. 128. See also No. 8 (15 July 1923), p. 127.

67. *Black Mask* VI, No. 8 (15 July 1923), p. 127.

68. *Black Mask* VI, No. 20 (15 Jan. 1924), p. 128.

69. Joseph Thompson Shaw, letter to Robert Thomas Hardy, 23 Aug. 1926; Joseph Thompson Shaw, letter to Erle Stanley Gardner, 31 Aug. 1926; Erle Stanley Gardner, letter to Joseph Thompson Shaw, 27 Oct. 1927 (all in Erle Stanley Gardner Papers, HRC). Martin had a whole series running in Street & Smith's *Top-Notch*, told from the angle of the secretary who repeatedly saved her boss, a lawyer, from his screwups (see Erle Stanley Gardner, letter to Joseph Thompson Shaw, 24 Oct. 1932, Erle Stanley Gardner Papers, HRC). Theodore Tinsley, a *Black Mask* regular, wrote about his female private detective, Carrie Cashin, for Street & Smith's *Mystery* (see, for example, *Mystery* VII, No. 6 [Jan. 1942]).

70. Joseph Thompson Shaw, letter to Erle Stanley Gardner, 17 Apr. 1934; Joseph Thompson Shaw, letter to Erle Stanley Gardner, 1 May 1934 (both in Erle Stanley Gardner Papers, HRC).

71. Hersey, *Pulpwood Editor*, p. 85.

72. On "imagined communities" fostered by print capitalism and their role in constituting nationalism and other forms of community not characterized by face-to-face interactions, see Benedict Anderson, *Imagined Communities: Reflections on the Origin and Spread of Nationalism*, 2d. ed. (New York: Verso, 1991).

73. Paula Baker, "The Domestication of Politics: Women and American Political Society, 1780–1920," in *Unequal Sisters: A Multi-Cultural Reader in U.S. Women's History*, 2d ed., ed. Vicki L. Ruiz and Ellen Carol DuBois (New York: Routledge, 1994), pp. 85–110.

74. On women as wage-earners, see Joanne J. Meyerowitz, *Women Adrift: Independent Wage Earners in Chicago, 1880–1930* (Chicago: University of Chicago Press, 1988), esp. pp. xvii, 5.

75. Kathy Peiss, *Cheap Amusements: Leisure in Turn-of-the-Century New York* (Philadelphia: Temple University Press, 1986), Introduction.

76. Erle Stanley Gardner, letter to Joseph Thompson Shaw, 13 Oct. 1929; Erle Stanley Gardner, letter to Phil Cody, 31 Mar. 1930 (both in Erle Stanley Gardner Papers, HRC).

77. Duffield, "The Pulps," pp. 26–27.

78. *Black Mask* X, No. 7 (Sept. 1933), p. 5.

79. Quoted in Helen Damon-Moore and Carl F. Kaestle, "Surveying American Readers," in Kaestle et al., *Literacy in the United States*, pp. 199–200.

80. See, for example, Gray and Munroe: "Inquiries made of children and parents reveal the fact that a surprisingly large number of the cheap, sensational types of magazines are subscribed for regularly or purchased at the newsstand. The prominence of these magazines on the home library table suggests the urgent need of campaigns among adults to elevate their tastes and to stimulate interest in magazines of a better class" (*Reading Interests*, p. 266).

81. *Black Mask* XV, No. 4 (June 1932), p. 123.

82. *Black Mask* XVII, No. 1 (Mar. 1934), p. 9.

83. See, for example, *Black Mask* XIII, No. 4 (June 1930), pp. 119–20; No. 11 (Jan. 1931), p. 9; *Black Mask* XV, No. 6 (Aug. 1932), p. 126; *Black Mask* XVI, No. 1 (Mar. 1933), pp. 124–25; No. 7 (Sept. 1933), p. 126; *Black Mask* XIV, No. 7 (Sept. 1931), p. 7.

84. *Black Mask* XIV, No. 5 (July 1931), p. 5.

85. Erle Stanley Gardner, letter to Joseph Thompson Shaw, 23 Apr. 1934, Erle Stanley Gardner Papers, HRC.

86. Gardner's nonhierarchical categorization of different kinds of stories resonates with the editorial practices at the Book-of-the-Month Club, founded in 1926. See Janice A. Radway, "The Book-of-the-Month Club and the General Reader: The Uses of 'Serious' Fiction," in *Reading in America: Literature and Social History*, ed. Cathy N. Davidson (Baltimore: Johns Hopkins University Press, 1989), pp. 259–84.

87. Erle Stanley Gardner, letter to Phil Cody, 5 Apr. 1930; Erle Stanley Gardner, letter to A. H. Bittner, 9 Apr. 1930 (both in Erle Stanley Gardner Papers, HRC).

88. *Clues* XLI, No. 1 (Dec. 1938).

89. Most hardback books cost $2 to $2.50 during the Depression. On Knopf's reputation for producing high-quality books and the "literariness" of the Borzoi line specifically, see Tebbel, *Between Covers*, pp. 229–33.

90. Richard Layman, *Shadow Man: the Life of Dashiell Hammett* (New York: Harcourt, 1981), p. 107.

91. For a brilliant analysis of the way these writers' uneasy positioning in the publishing world appears in their writing as tensions between the criminal classes (the trashy world of pulps) and the authorities (highbrow literary gatekeepers), see Sean McCann, "'A Roughneck Reaching for Higher Things': The Vagaries of Pulp Populism," *Radical History Review* 61 (1995): 4–34.

92. Will Cuppy, rev. of *The Thin Man* by Dashiell Hammett, *New York Herald Tribune Books*, 7 Jan. 1934, p. 11. See also Walter R. Brooks, "Behind the Blurbs," rev. of *The Glass Key* by Dashiell Hammett, *Outlook and Independent* 157 (29 Apr. 1931): 601.

93. "Murder at the Old Stand," rev. of *The Little Sister* by Raymond Chandler, *Time* 54 (3 Oct. 1949), p. 82.

94. T. S. Matthews, "Mr. Hammett Goes Coasting," rev. of *The Thin Man* by Dashiell Hammett, *The New Republic* 77 (24 Jan. 1934), p. 316.

95. See, for example, Jon Thompson, *Fiction, Crime and Empire: Clues to Modernity and Postmodernism* (Chicago: University of Illinois Press, 1993), pp. 134–46.

96. Reprinted in Raymond Chandler, *The Simple Art of Murder* (1950; New York: Vintage, 1988). Subsequent page references are in the text. Considering Chandler as a spokesman for the *Black Mask* school of writers is a complicated move. Although career pulp writers generally lacked education and a vision of themselves as people whose lives were worth documenting, Chandler possessed both. He is useful to critics as a participant-observer in that he brings their tools (an elite British education, prolific letter-writing, a taste for theorizing and meta-commentary) to bear on the "trashy" world of the pulps. His commentary, therefore, is qualified by the knowledge that although he was not typical of the writers whose cause he took up, he did address himself to justifying, theorizing, and translating their project in a way that no one else did.

97. Dashiell Hammett reviewed mysteries for *The Saturday Review of Literature* and *The New York Evening Post*, where he engaged in some similar ridicule of clas-

sic country-house fiction. (See William Marling, *Dashiell Hammett* [Boston: Twayne, 1983], p. 100; Howard Haycraft, ed., *The Art of the Mystery Story: A Collection of Critical Essays* [New York: Simon, 1946], pp. 382–83).

98. See Panek, *An Introduction*, p. 90.

99. Claims of this nature are made by contemporary critics as well. Hard-boiled detective fiction is exceptional or not quite "pure" detective fiction. In *Adventure, Mystery, and Romance: Formula Stories as Art and Popular Culture* (Chicago: University of Chicago Press, 1976), John G. Cawelti argues that it is a hybrid—half mystery (the English prototype being the "pure" form) and half Western (p. 80). Cynthia Hamilton states that the hard-boiled detective is a cowboy who wandered off the frontier and into the city, and that hard-boiled novels have absolutely nothing to do with classical detective fiction. I argue here that classical detective fiction provided the conventions and the literary prototypes against which hard-boiled writers rebelled.

100. Chandler's adamant "Americanness" is particularly noteworthy. Although American-born, he was raised from a young age in England. See Frank MacShane, *The Life of Raymond Chandler* (New York: Dutton, 1976), Chap. 1.

101. Nina Baym, "Melodramas of Beset Manhood: How Theories of American Literature Exclude Women Authors," in *The New Feminist Criticism*, ed. Elaine Showalter (New York: Pantheon, 1985), pp. 63–80.

102. Hard-boiled writers' reaction against female British mystery writers was part of a larger ideology, what Ann Douglas calls "the dark legend of matricide" at the heart of the modernist impulse. Male and female modernists, Douglas argues, wrote matricidal texts, rebelling against the figure of the all-powerful Victorian mother god and the "feminization" of American culture she had wrought. See Ann Douglas, *Terrible Honesty: Mongrel Manhattan in the 1920s* (New York: Farrar, 1995), Chap. 6.

103. These rules were codified in the oath of the Detection Club, Ronald Knox's "A Detective Story Decalogue" (1929), and S. S. Van Dine's "Twenty Rules for Writing Detective Stories" (1928). All are reprinted in Haycraft. The members, nonetheless, broke these rules regularly. Agatha Christie's 1926 *Murder of Roger Ackroyd* has the narrator as murderer (a clear example of "cheating" the reader), and others included the love interest that S. S. Van Dine claimed was off-limits. Many indulged in lengthy descriptions and side plots that were supposed to be taboo.

104. Recall the female writers and editors using male pseudonyms or first initials in pulp publishing.

105. Judith Butler, *Gender Trouble: Feminism and the Subversion of Identity* (New York: Routledge, 1990) and *Bodies That Matter: On the Discursive Limits of "Sex"* (New York: Routledge, 1993).

106. John Dickson Carr, a member of the London Detection Club, characterizes Chandler's discussion of the English detective story as "a fit of screaming hysterics" ("With Colt and Luger," rev. of *The Simple Art of Murder, New York Times Book Review*, 24 Sept. 1950, p. 36). The comment is particularly suggestive in light of Stephen Heath's definition of hysteria as failed masquerade. See Stephen Heath, "Joan Riviere and the Masquerade," in *Formations of Fantasy*, ed. Victor Burgin, James Donald, and Cora Kaplan (New York: Routledge, 1989), p. 51.

107. Amy Kaplan, *The Social Construction of American Realism* (Chicago: University of Chicago Press, 1988), pp. 1, 8.

Chapter Two

Epigraph: Harold Hersey, *Pulpwood Editor: The Fabulous World of Thriller Magazines Revealed by a Veteran Editor and Publisher* (New York: Stokes, 1937), pp. 77, 83.
1. *Black Mask* VIII, No. 8 (Oct. 1925), p. iii.
2. Roland Marchand, *Advertising the American Dream: Making Way for Modernity, 1920–1940* (Berkeley: University of California Press, 1985), p. xviii.
3. On admen and the structure of advertising agencies in the early twentieth century, see ibid, Chaps. 1 and 2; Ellen Gruber Garvey, *The Adman in the Parlor: Magazines and the Gendering of Consumer Culture, 1880s to 1910s* (New York: Oxford University Press, 1996), Chap. 6; T. J. Jackson Lears, *Fables of Abundance: A Cultural History of Advertising in America* (New York: Basic, 1994), Chaps. 7 and 8; and Richard Ohmann, *Selling Culture: Magazines, Markets, and Class at the Turn of the Century* (New York: Verso, 1996), Chap. 6. I use the term "admen" because only about one-tenth of advertising workers were women during this period, and those were mostly in low-level positions (Marchand, *Advertising the American Dream*, p. 33).
4. Pulp magazines were unusual in that they continued to run mail-order ads into the 1950s. Slick-paper magazines, which relied more heavily on advertising to make a profit, had largely abandoned this kind of advertising by 1900 (Ohmann, *Selling Culture*, p. 186).
5. Hersey, *Pulpwood Editor*, p. 72. For a more general discussion of advertising in pulp magazines, see ibid., Chap. 5.
6. Marchand distinguishes between a "class" and a "mass" audience for advertisements in the 1920s and 1930s. The "class" ads targeted an elite audience composed of the wealthiest 5 percent or 6 percent of the population. Even the "mass" audience, however, excluded 30 percent to 65 percent of the inhabitants of the United States—laborers, immigrants, and blacks, to name a few (*Advertising the American Dream*, p. 64).
7. Ibid, p. xvii.
8. Hersey, *Pulpwood Editor*, pp. 68–69.
9. *Black Mask* XIV, No. 1 (Mar. 1931), p. viii; *Black Mask* II, No. 1 (Oct. 1920).
10. *Black Mask* VII, No. 8 (Oct. 1924), p. 7.
11. *Black Mask* II, No. 6 (Mar. 1921), p. 125.
12. *Black Mask* III, No. 3 (June 1921), p. 125.
13. On advertising history, see Marchand, *Advertising the American Dream*; Lears, *Fables of Abundance*; Ohmann, *Selling Culture*; Garvey, *The Adman in the Parlor*; also T. J. Jackson Lears, "From Salvation to Self-Realization: Advertising and the Therapeutic Roots of the Consumer Culture, 1880–1930" and Christopher Wilson, "The Rhetoric of Consumption: Mass-Market Magazines and the Demise of the Gentle Reader, 1880–1920," both in *The Culture of Consumption: Critical Essays in American History, 1890–1980*, ed. Richard Wightman Fox and T. J. Jackson Lears (New York: Pantheon, 1993), pp. 1–38 and 39–64; and Richard Ohmann, "Where Did Mass Culture Come From? The Case of Magazines" and "Advertising and the

New Discourse of Mass Culture," *Politics of Letters* (Middletown, CT: Wesleyan University Press, 1987), pp. 135–151, 152–170.

14. Ohmann, *Politics of Letters*, p. 147; Wilson, "Rhetoric of Consumption," p. 43.

15. Theodore Peterson, *Magazines in the Twentieth Century* (Urbana: University of Illinois Press, 1956), p. 18. The demands of advertisers led to standard page size in the slicks (so the same plates could be used to print ads in a variety of magazines), ads running side by side with editorial materials, and more use of color and illustration in editorial copy to match the standards set by ads (32).

16. Garvey, *The Adman in the Parlor*; Ohmann, *Selling Culture*.

17. The pulps are almost absent from histories of American magazines. Peterson devotes less than seven of 397 pages to pulp magazines. In *The Magazine in America, 1741–1990* (New York: Oxford University Press, 1991), John Tebbel and Mary Ellen Zuckerman spend nine pages out of 382 on the pulps.

18. Peterson, *Magazines*, p. 284; Tebbel and Zuckerman, *Magazine in America*, pp. 340–41.

19. Sean McCann, "'A Roughneck Reaching for Higher Things': The Vagaries of Pulp Populism," *Radical History Review* 61 (1995): 21.

20. Ibid., p. 20.

21. Hersey, *Pulpwood Editor*, pp. 84–85.

22. Tebbel and Zuckerman, *Magazine in America*, p. 141; Peterson, *Magazines*, p. 22.

23. Although scholarship on consumption is overwhelmingly focused on middle-class women as consumers, in "Consuming Brotherhood: Men's Culture, Style and Recreation as Consumer Culture, 1880–1930," *Journal of Social History* 31.4 (Summer 1998), Mark A. Swiencicki convincingly argues that between 1880 and 1930, men spent roughly 30 percent of a family's disposable income and consumed about twice as many recreational and leisure goods as women. This consumption has been overlooked because scholars followed the lead of late–nineteenth- and early–twentieth-century trade journals and women's magazines, which argued self-interestedly that the best way to sell products was to reach a feminine audience (20).

24. Peterson, *Magazines*, p. 64.

25. Editorial Records, Box 41, Street & Smith Collection, Syracuse.

26. Peterson, *Magazines*, p. 286.

27. In the 1930s, the net profit on 100,000 copies of a pulp magazine was $460 to $730. In order to stay in business, a publisher had to carry a great many different titles (ibid., p. 73).

28. For a sketch of "The Establishment" of pulp publishing as of July 1934, see Frank Gruber, *The Pulp Jungle* (Los Angeles: Sherbourne, 1967), pp. 20–22. See also Lee Server, *Danger Is My Business: An Illustrated History of the Fabulous Pulp Magazines* (San Francisco: Chronicle, 1993), p. 14.

29. Peterson, *Magazines*, p. 57. In the early 1920s, *Black Mask* carried ads for the "newsstand group," a string of ten pulp publications (including *Black Mask*) whose combined circulation was more than a million copies a month (*Black Mask* V, No. 5 [Dec. 1922]). By the mid-1920s, the ad pages had "Newsstand Group—men's list" printed across the bottom of each page.

30. Gruber, *Pulp Jungle*, p. 20.

31. Editorial Files, Box 41, Street & Smith Collection, Syracuse.

32. Richard Layman, *Shadow Man: the Life of Dashiell Hammett* (New York: Harcourt, 1981), p. 36; H. C. North, letter to Erle Stanley Gardner, 7 July 1924, Erle Stanley Gardner Papers, HRC.

33. Peterson, *Magazines*, p. 81.

34. Frederick Clayton, letter, *New York Times*, 4 Sept. 1935, quoted in Robert Lesser, *Pulp Art: Original Cover Paintings for the Great American Pulp Magazines* (New York: Gramercy, 1997), p. 15.

35. See especially Wilson, "Rhetoric of Consumption," p. 42. Editors of Western pulp magazines also regularly requested reader feedback on their stories (see Christine Bold, *Selling the Wild West: Popular Western Fiction, 1860–1960* [Bloomington: Indiana University Press, 1987], Chap. 1; and Tebbel and Zuckerman, *Magazine in America*, p. 198).

36. *Crime Busters* II, No. 2 (June 1938), p. 25.

37. *Crime Busters* II, No. 6 (Oct. 1938), pp. 115–16.

38. Erle Stanley Gardner, letter to Don Moore, 2 Feb. 1931, Erle Stanley Gardner Papers, HRC.

39. See, for example, Erle Stanley Gardner, letter to Joseph Thompson Shaw, 3 May 1929; Erle Stanley Gardner, letter to Joseph Thompson Shaw, 23 Dec. 1929; Erle Stanley Gardner, letter to Joseph Thompson Shaw, 1 Dec. 1929 (all in Erle Stanley Gardner Papers, HRC).

40. Erle Stanley Gardner, letter to Phil Cody, 1 May 1928, Erle Stanley Gardner Papers, HRC.

41. Gardner and Raymond Chandler were fascinated by the 1940 plan of the Brentano's bookstore to survey readers about how satisfactory they found the mystery books they bought (see Erle Stanley Gardner, letter to Raymond Chandler, 28 Nov. 1940, Erle Stanley Gardner Papers, HRC).

42. Erle Stanley Gardner, letter to Don Moore, 11 Feb. 1931, Erle Stanley Gardner Papers, HRC.

43. Erle Stanley Gardner, letter to Joseph Thompson Shaw, 1 Dec. 1929, Erle Stanley Gardner Papers, HRC.

44. *Black Mask* V, Nos. 6 and 7 (Oct. and Nov. 1922).

45. Hersey describes these reader columns as "providing the personal touch" and says that the "illusory companionship" that arose from them was crucial to the success of the magazine. He compares these departments to a hotel lobby, arguing that their size must be appropriate to make them seem filled with lively talk at all times (*Pulpwood Editor*, p. 87).

46. *Black Mask* V, No. 11 (Feb. 1923), p. 23.

47. Marchand, *Advertising the American Dream*, p. xxi.

48. *Black Mask* XII, No. 10 (Dec. 1929), p. iv.

49. Kathy Peiss, *Cheap Amusements: Leisure in Turn-of-the-Century New York* (Philadelphia: Temple University Press, 1986), p. 21.

50. *Black Mask* XIII, No. 3 (May 1930), p. 120.

51. See Marchand, *Advertising the American Dream*, p. 1; Garvey, *The Adman in the Parlor*, Chap. 6. The working assumption of advertisers at the time was that 85 percent of purchases were made by women. Women's magazines of the period

dubbed women the "purchasing agents" of American homes (Marchand, *Advertising the American Dream*, p. 66).

52. Bernarr Macfadden's extraordinarily successful pulp *True Story* offers the most extreme example of this strategy at work. *True Story* offered what were supposedly actual readers' accounts of their (mostly sexual) exploits. "Macfadden's great innovation," Ann Fabian writes, "was to offer his readers a hand in the production of the artifacts they so happily consumed, to urge them at every turn to become writers as well as readers, producers as well as consumers. Even if his invitations to write were largely fictitious, he made the production of mass culture seem accessible and offered the pages of his magazines as occasions for the sort of popular ratification that helped turn twentieth-century mass culture into a culture of the people" (52). See Ann Fabian, "Making a Commodity of Truth: Speculations on the Career of Bernarr Macfadden," *American Literary History* V (Spring 1993): 51–76.

53. *Black Mask* IX, No. 6 (Aug. 1926), p. 8.

54. *Black Mask* VII, No. 5 (July 1924), p. 4.

55. See, for example, *Black Mask* XIX, No. 6 (Aug. 1936).

56. *Black Mask* V, No. 6 (Sept. 1922).

57. On "editorial copy," see Marchand, *Advertising the American Dream*, p. 105.

58. *Black Mask* IX, No. 11 (Jan. 1927), p. 15.

59. *Black Mask* IX, No. 7 (Sept. 1926), p. 8.

60. On Hammett as a copywriter, see William Marling, *The American Roman Noir: Hammett, Cain and Chandler* (Athens: University of Georgia Press, 1995), pp. 93–106.

61. Marchand, *Advertising the American Dream*, p. 300.

62. Richard Ohmann argues that advertising permeated American culture by a process of diffusion that began with the emergent professional-managerial class around the turn of the century and didn't reach workers (whose smaller incomes made them a less profitable audience) until the 1920s (*Selling Culture*, p. 363).

63. Pulp magazines resemble the mail-order magazines that targeted poor and rural readers at the turn of the century in the types of products they promoted and the kinds of advertising appeals they made. See Garvey, *The Adman in the Parlor*, pp. 137–42.

64. *Black Mask* VI, No. 21 (1 Feb. 1924), p. 3; *Black Mask* VII, No. 2 (15 Apr. 1924), p. 8.

65. *Black Mask* V, No. 2 (May 1922); *Black Mask* VI, No. 10 (15 Aug. 1923), p. 2.

66. David M. Gordon, Richard Edwards, and Michael Reich, *Segmented Work, Divided Workers: The Historical Transformation of Labor in the United States* (New York: Cambridge University Press, 1982), p. 3.

67. *Black Mask* IX, No. 12 (Feb. 1927), p. vi.

68. *Black Mask* II, No. 3 (Dec. 1920); *Black Mask* XIII, No. 4 (June 1930), p. iii.

69. *Black Mask* IV, No. 3 (Dec. 1921).

70. David Montgomery, *Workers' Control in America: Studies in the History of Work, Technology, and Labor Struggles* (New York: Cambridge University Press, 1979), p. 13.

71. Accounts by social historians of the importance of physical strength for American working men include: Peter Stearns, *Be A Man! Males in Modern Society*

(New York: Holmes and Meier, 1979), pp. 59–78; Christine Stansell, *City of Women: Sex and Class in New York, 1789–1860* (New York: Knopf, 1986), pp. 77–78, 81, 95–96, 137–41; Sean Wilentz, *Chants Democratic: New York City and the Rise of the American Working Class, 1788–1850* (New York: Oxford University Press, 1984); Michael Denning, *Mechanic Accents: Dime Novels and Working-Class Culture in America* (New York: Verso, 1987), Chap. 9; and Montgomery, *Workers' Control in America*, pp. 13–14. Under capitalism, a powerful physique may have compensated for powerlessness at work. On changing definitions of masculinity in American history, see Michael Kimmel, *Manhood in America: A Cultural History* (New York: Free Press, 1996).

72. *Black Mask* V, No. 13 (1 Mar. 1923), p. 5.

73. *Black Mask* XIII, No. 1 (Mar. 1930), p. 11.

74. *Black Mask* V, No. 7 (Nov. 1922), p. 121.

75. *Black Mask* VI, No. 10 (15 Aug. 1923), p. 2; *Black Mask* V, No. 13 (1 Mar. 1923), p. 7.

76. *Black Mask* X, No. 7 (Sept. 1927), p. 2.

77. *Black Mask* IX, No. 10 (Dec. 1926), p. 23; *Black Mask* XI, No. 8 (Oct. 1928), p. vi.

78. *Black Mask* XIV, No. 8 (Oct. 1931), inside front cover.

79. On the "great parables" of advertising in the 1920s and 1930s, see Marchand, *Advertising the American Dream*, Chap. 7.

80. Warren I. Susman, "'Personality' and the Making of Twentieth-Century Culture," in *Culture as History: The Transformation of American Society in the Twentieth Century* (New York: Pantheon, 1984), pp. 271–86.

81. Ibid., pp. 273–77.

82. Susman's culture of personality bears some resemblance to Judith Butler's work on gender as performance or masquerade, which suggests that identities are citations or reiterations drawn from the raw materials of consumer culture. See also Mark Seltzer's distinction between liberal subjects and early–twentieth-century "disciplinary subjects" in *Bodies and Machines* (New York: Routledge, 1992).

83. Pierre Bourdieu, *Distinction: A Social Critique of the Judgment of Taste*, trans. Richard Nice (Cambridge, MA: Harvard University Press, 1984), p. 202.

84. *Black Mask* II, No. 3 (Dec. 1920).

85. Ohmann, *Selling Culture*, p. 199. Judith Williamson discusses these gaps in "hermeneutic ads" in Chap. 3 of *Decoding Advertisements: Ideology and Meaning in Advertising* (Boston: Boyars, 1978).

86. Garvey, *The Adman in the Parlor*, pp. 178–79.

87. See Williamson, *Decoding Advertisements*, Chap. 3.

88. See, for example, *Black Mask* XX, No. 8 (Oct. 1937), p. 3; *Black Mask* XX, No. 9 (Nov. 1937), p. 3.

89. *Black Mask* XIX, No. 12 (Feb. 1937), p. 3.

90. Peiss, *Cheap Amusements*, p. 63.

91. *Black Mask* XXIV, No. 2 (June 1941), inside back cover.

92. *Black Mask* XX, No. 9 (Nov. 1937), p. 3.

93. Jürgen Habermas argues that capitalist societies draw on the borrowed legitimacy of past cultural values and beliefs (the patriarchal family, religion, and the

like) to justify the current capitalist order, although capitalism itself contributes to the destruction of these institutions. In this case the rise of consumer culture—intimately linked to mass production and the de-skilling of artisanal work—is invoked as a way to further a skilled workman's interests. See Habermas, *The Legitimation Crisis* (Boston: Beacon, 1975), pp. 71–75.

94. *Black Mask* IX, No. 7 (Sept. 1926), p. 6; *Black Mask* XI, No. 5 (July 1928), p. 2; *Black Mask* XIV, No. 9 (Nov. 1931).

95. *Black Mask* IX, No. 7 (Sept. 1926), p. 6.

96. *Black Mask* XIV, No. 9 (Nov. 1931).

97. On the "vacuum of advice" created by proliferating consumer choices and increased mobility, urbanization, and generational discontinuities, see Marchand, *Advertising the American Dream*, p. 342.

98. Stuart Ewen believes that all advertising works this way (see *Captains of Consciousness: Advertising and the Social Roots of the Consumer Culture* [New York: McGraw, 1976], Part III). But as I've noted earlier, some of the pulp ads instead sought to graft commodity culture onto traditional ways of making sense of the world, appropriating the authority of traditional worldviews rather than seeking to discredit them. The advertising world of pulps, at least, was more complicated and contradictory than Ewen's argument implies.

99. *Black Mask* IX, No. 11 (Jan. 1927), p. iii; *Black Mask* X, No. 3 (May 1927), p. 1.

100. *Black Mask* X, No. 4 (June 1927), p. 11.

101. *Black Mask* IX, No. 11 (Jan. 1927), p. iii.

102. *Black Mask* II, No. 4 (Jan. 1921); *Black Mask* II, No. 6 (March 1921).

Part II

Epigraphs: Douglas Waples and Ralph W. Tyler, *What People Want to Read About: A Study of Group Interests and a Survey of Problems in Adult Reading* (Chicago: University of Chicago Press, 1931), p. xxvii; Douglas Waples, Bernard Berelson, and Franklyn R. Bradshaw, *What Reading Does to People: A Summary of Evidence on the Social Effects of Reading and a Statement of Problems for Research* (Chicago: University of Chicago Press, 1940), p. 83.

1. For an overview and analysis of this material, see Stephen Karetzky, *Reading Research and Librarianship: A History and Analysis* (Westport, CT: Greenwood Press, 1982).

2. Waples and Tyler, *What People Want to Read About*, pp. 53, 76.

3. See Lizabeth Cohen, *Making a New Deal: Industrial Workers in Chicago, 1919–1939* (New York: Cambridge University Press, 1990), Chap. 3, Conclusion.

Chapter Three

Epigraphs: Dashiell Hammett, letter to Harry Block, 8 March 1929, quoted in Richard Layman, *Shadow Man: the Life of Dashiell Hammett* (New York: Harcourt, 1981), p. 103; Ralph Partridge, "Detection and Thrills," rev. of *Playback* by Raymond Chandler, *New Statesman* 56 (30 Aug. 1958), p. 254.

1. Others have pointed out the similarities between proletarian fiction and hard-boiled detective stories. See Alfred Kazin, *On Native Grounds* (New York: Anchor, 1956). Also David Madden, Introduction (xxxii–xxxiii); Kingsley Widmer, "The Way Out: Some Life-Style Sources of the Literary Tough Guy and the Proletarian Hero" (3–12); and Benjamin Appel, "Labels" (13–17) in *Tough Guy Writers of the Thirties*, ed. David Madden (Carbondale: Southern Illinois University Press, 1968).

2. On the Pinkertons, see Marcus Klein, *Easterns, Westerns, and Private Eyes: American Matters, 1870–1900* (Madison: University of Wisconsin Press, 1994), pp. 174–77.

3. See Michael Denning, *The Cultural Front: The Laboring of American Culture in the Twentieth Century* (New York: Verso, 1996) on the influence of labor on American culture during this period.

4. See Raymond Williams, *Culture and Society, 1780–1950* (New York: Harper, 1966) on the fundamentally collective nature of working-class culture and the fundamentally individualistic nature of bourgeois culture (327). See also David Montgomery, *The Fall of the House of Labor: The Workplace, the State, and American Labor Activism, 1865–1925* (New York: Cambridge University Press, 1987). Montgomery claims that individualism was a luxury that only the prosperous and wellborn could afford (1–2).

5. See John Bodnar, *Workers' World: Kinship, Community, and Protest in an Industrial Society, 1900–1940* (Baltimore: Johns Hopkins University Press, 1982), Introduction and Part II.

6. The effect of work routines and work cultures of native-born and older immigrants on the second-wave immigrants from southern and eastern Europe is discussed in James R. Barrett, "Americanization from the Bottom Up: Immigration and the Remaking of the Working Class in the United States, 1880–1930," *Journal of American History* (Dec. 1992): 996–1020. See especially p. 999.

7. On interwar labor history, see David M. Gordon, Richard Edwards, and Michael Reich, *Segmented Work, Divided Workers: The Historical Transformation of Labor in the United States* (New York: Cambridge University Press, 1982); David Montgomery, *Workers' Control in America: Studies in the History of Work, Technology, and Labor Struggles* (New York: Cambridge University Press, 1979); James R. Green, *The World of the Worker: Labor in Twentieth-Century America* (New York: Hill & Wang, 1980); Herbert G. Gutman, *Work, Culture, and Society in Industrializing America: Essays in American Working-Class and Social History* (New York: Vintage, 1977); and Anson Rabinbach, *The Human Motor: Energy, Fatigue, and the Origins of Modernity* (New York: Basic, 1990).

8. Gordon, Edwards, and Reich, *Segmented Work*, p. 146.

9. In *Terrible Honesty: Mongrel Manhattan in the 1920s* (New York: Farrar, 1995), Ann Douglas writes that conventional plots, at least among self-consciously literary writers, were a casualty of World War I: "Nothing is clearer about the most important novelists of the post-Great War decades than that they abandoned plot as the indispensable framework, interest, and credential of the novel form" (203). See especially Chap. 5, "The Culture of Momentum."

10. Dorothy Gardiner and Kathrine Sorley Walker, eds., *Raymond Chandler Speaking* (Boston: Houghton, 1962), p. 221.

11. Raymond Chandler, *The Big Sleep* (1939; reprint, New York: Vintage, 1992).

12. *New York Times*, 24 Aug. 1946, Quoted in William Luhr, *Raymond Chandler and Film*, 2d ed. (Tallahassee: University of Florida Press, 1991), p. 123.

13. Rev. of *Farewell, My Lovely* by Raymond Chandler, *New York Times Book Review*, 17 November 1940, p. 29; "Running and Walking," rev. of *The Little Sister* by Raymond Chandler, *Times Literary Supplement* (London), 19 Aug. 1949, p. 533; Charles J. Rolo, rev. of *Playback* by Raymond Chandler, *Atlantic Monthly* 202 (Nov. 1958), pp. 176–77; "New Mystery Stories," rev. of *The Dain Curse* by Dashiell Hammett, *New York Times Book Review*, 18 Aug. 1929, p. 16; Harvey Breit, rev. of *The Little Sister* by Raymond Chandler, *Atlantic Monthly* 184 (Oct. 1949), pp. 81–82.

14. See Martha Banta, *Taylored Lives: Narrative Productions in the Age of Taylor, Veblen, and Ford* (Chicago: University of Chicago Press, 1993) for an examination of the ways in which the culture of management shaped the narratives of this period.

15. The complex and convoluted plots of hard-boiled fiction are particularly noteworthy given that it was "escape" literature—fiction read for distraction by people supposedly not paying a great deal of attention to what they read. Given that the laborers whom these stories targeted had worked ten- to twelve-hour days before even starting to read, the likelihood that they puzzled out the complexities of the plot with pleasure is slim indeed.

16. Tania Modleski, *Loving With a Vengeance: Mass-Produced Fantasies for Women* (Hamden, CT: Archon Books, 1982), Chap. 4.

17. Ibid., p. 100.

18. "Structures of feeling" is Raymond Williams's term. See especially *The Long Revolution* (Harmondsworth, UK: Penguin, 1965), pp. 63–65.

19. Irvin Faust, Afterword to *Fast One* by Paul Cain (Carbondale: Southern Illinois University Press, 1978), p. 309.

20. Lee Server, *Danger Is My Business: An Illustrated History of the Fabulous Pulp Magazines* (San Francisco: Chronicle, 1993), p. 11.

21. See, for example, Will Cuppy, rev. of *Farewell, My Lovely* by Raymond Chandler, *New York Herald Tribune Books*, 6 Oct. 1940, p. 25; "Criminal Record," rev. of *The Big Sleep* by Raymond Chandler, *The Saturday Review of Literature*, 11 Feb. 1939, p. 20; rev. of *Farewell, My Lovely* by Raymond Chandler, *New York Times Book Review*, 17 Nov. 1940, p. 29; Will Cuppy, rev. of *The Dain Curse* by Dashiell Hammett, *New York Herald Tribune Books*, 11 Aug. 1929, p. 1; Herbert Asbury, rev. of *Red Harvest* by Dashiell Hammett, *Bookman* 69 (March 1929), p. 92; John Dickson Carr, "With Colt and Luger," rev. of *The Simple Art of Murder, New York Times Book Review*, 24 Sept. 1950, p. 36.

22. On the theoretical implications of "time-space compression," see David Harvey, *The Condition of Postmodernity: An Enquiry into the Origins of Cultural Change* (Cambridge, MA: Blackwell, 1989). On business and economic history, see Alfred Chandler, *The Visible Hand: The Managerial Revolution in American Business* (Cambridge, MA: Harvard University Press, 1977); and James Beniger, *The Control Revolution: Technological and Economic Origins of the Information Society* (Cambridge, MA: Harvard University Press, 1986).

23. E. P. Thompson, "Time, Work-discipline, and Industrial Capitalism,"*Past & Present* 38 (Dec. 1967): 56–97.

24. Dashiell Hammett, *Red Harvest* (1929; reprint, New York: Vintage, 1992).

25. John Kasson, *Amusing the Million: Coney Island at the Turn of the Century* (New York: Hill & Wang, 1978), pp. 73–74, 108.

26. Glenn Most argues in "The Hippocratic Smile: John Le Carré and the Traditions of the Detective Novel" that the difference between classical and hard-boiled fiction is that classical fiction emphasizes the outcome of interpretation, its certainty and "truth," whereas hard-boiled fiction emphasizes the process of interpretation as a fiction-making activity whose outcome is much less certain (*The Poetics of Murder: Detective Fiction and Literary Theory*, ed. Glenn W. Most and William W. Stowe [New York: Harcourt, 1983], p. 350).

27. Agatha Christie, *Murder On the Orient Express* (1933, 1934; reprint, New York: Harper, 1991), p. 22. Subsequent page references are in the text.

28. Hanna Charney argues that readers of classical fiction—what she calls "detective novels of manners"—move with ease from Jane Austen and Henry James to Agatha Christie and Dorothy Sayers, but that the "tortured quests" of Sam Spade and other hard-boiled detectives offer little to appeal to these same middle-class readers. See Hanna Charney, *The Detective Novel of Manners: Hedonism, Morality and the Life of Reason* (Rutherford, NJ: Farleigh Dickinson University Press, 1981), p. xiv.

29. Frederick Nebel, *Sleepers East* (Boston: Little, 1933), pp. 5–8, 12. Subsequent page references are in the text.

30. On railroad workers as part of a labor aristocracy, see Ileen DeVault, *Sons and Daughters of Labor: Class and Clerical Work in Turn-of-the-Century Pittsburgh* (Ithaca, NY: Cornell University Press, 1990), p. 92.

31. "Labor aristocracy" is Eric Hobsbawm's term. See "The Labour Aristocracy in Nineteenth-Century Britain," *Labouring Men* (New York: Basic, 1965), pp. 272–315. DeVault applies the term to the American context (91–97).

32. See Chap. 2, note 73.

33. Michael Denning, *Mechanic Accents: Dime Novels and Working-Class Culture in America* (New York: Verso, 1987), p. 175.

34. There is some disagreement over the ratio of wage-related strikes to strikes over "control" issues in the 1910s and 1920s, but organizing drives of the 1930s focused as much on "technical control" (management regulation of the pace and manner of work) as they did on wages (Gordon, Edwards, and Reich, *Segmented Work*, pp. 178–79). This pattern of protest over the de-skilling and speed-up of work is particularly striking during the Depression and World War II, because it differs so markedly from postwar trends in which control over working conditions was more or less ceded to management in exchange for higher wages and better benefits (ibid., pp. 183–84).

35. Ibid., p. 163.

36. Rabinbach, *The Human Motor*, p. 4; Montgomery, *Workers' Control in America*, pp. 5–7.

37. Thompson, "Time, Work-discipline, and Industrial Capitalism," pp. 60–61.

38. Gutman, *Work, Culture, and Society*, pp. 14–18.

39. On attempts by Ford's sociology department to regulate workers' home lives, see Green, *The World of the Worker*, pp. 13–14.

40. Stephen Kern, *The Culture of Time and Space, 1880–1918* (Cambridge, MA: Harvard University Press, 1983), p. 12.

41. Rabinbach, *The Human Motor,* p. 239.

42. Dashiell Hammett, *The Maltese Falcon* (1929, 1930; reprint, New York: Vintage, 1992), p. 46.

43. On workers' reception of scientific management policies, see Rabinbach, *The Human Motor,* p. 241. For an intriguing analysis of how leisure-time pursuits mirror the work lives that they are designed to help people escape, see Kasson, pp. 73–74, 108. See also Lewis Erenberg, *Steppin' Out: New York Nightlife and the Transformation of American Culture, 1890–1930* (Westport, CT: Greenwood, 1981) for an analysis of how revues playing in New York cabarets in the 1910s and 1920s ("escape" for the business classes) replicated the logic and structures of industrial capitalism (212).

44. On the links between hard-boiled writing and the movies, see Edmund Wilson, "The Boys in the Back Room," in *Classics and Commercials: A Literary Chronicle of the Forties* (New York: Farrar, 1950), pp. 19–56; and James T. Farrell, "Cain's Movietone Realism," *Literature and Morality* (New York: Vanguard, 1947), pp. 79–89.

45. For a particularly vivid picture of one hard-boiled writer in Hollywood, see Luhr. See also Chandler's poison-pen letter to Hollywood (which liked him about as well as he liked it), "Writers in Hollywood," *Atlantic Monthly,* Nov. 1945, reprinted in Gardiner and Walker, *Raymond Chandler Speaking,* pp. 116–25.

46. *Black Mask* XIX, No. 9 (Nov. 1936), p. 15.

47. On the working-class, immigrant roots of the movies, see Robert Sklar, *Movie-Made America: A Cultural History of the American Movies* (New York: Vintage, 1994), Part I; and Steven J. Ross, *Working-Class Hollywood: Silent Film and the Shaping of Class in America* (Princeton, NJ: Princeton University Press, 1998).

48. Montgomery, *Workers' Control in America,* pp. 13–14.

49. George Harmon Coxe, "Murder Mixup," in *The Hard-Boiled Omnibus: Early Stories from "Black Mask,"* ed Joseph T. Shaw (New York: Simon, 1946), pp. 181–224. Subsequent page references are in the text.

50. Lois Banner writes that journalists in the early twentieth century had a great deal of autonomy and space for individual initiative on the job—work conditions that made their occupation seem exciting and glamorous to outsiders (see Lois Banner, *American Beauty* [New York: Knopf, 1983], p. 246). On the professionalization of reporting and increasing specialization of labor at newspapers early in the century, see Christopher P. Wilson, *The Labor of Words: Literary Professionalism in the Progressive Era* (Athens: University of Georgia Press, 1985), Chap. 1.

51. Montgomery, *Workers' Control in America,* p. 13.

52. Hammett, *Red Harvest,* pp. 42, 44.

53. Ibid., p. 151.

54. Ibid., p. 117.

55. For a historical case study of "men" and "boys" at work, see Ava Baron, "An 'Other' Side of Gender Antagonism at Work: Men, Boys, and the Remasculinization of Printers' Work, 1830–1920," in *Work Engendered: Toward a New History of American Labor,* ed Ava Baron (Ithaca, NY: Cornell University Press, 1991), pp. 47–69.

56. Montgomery, *Workers' Control in America*, pp. 12–13.

57. Thompson, "Time, Work-discipline, and Industrial Capitalism," p. 73.

58. Ibid., p. 74.

59. Kathy Peiss, *Cheap Amusements: Leisure in Turn-of-the-Century New York* (Philadelphia: Temple University Press, 1986), pp. 17–18.

60. Green, *The World of the Worker*, p. 92.

61. On early temperance activity, see Ruth Bordin, *Women and Temperance: The Quest for Power and Liberty, 1873–1900* (Philadelphia: Temple University Press, 1981).

62. Mary Ann Clawson, *Constructing Brotherhood: Class, Gender and Fraternalism* (Princeton, NJ: Princeton University Press, 1989), p. 167.

63. Roy Rosenzweig, *Eight Hours for What We Will: Workers and Leisure in an Industrial City, 1870–1920* (New York: Cambridge University Press, 1983), p. 37.

64. David R. Roediger and Philip S. Foner, *On Our Own Time: A History of American Labor and the Working Day* (New York: Greenwood, 1989), p. 17.

65. Lawrence Glickman, *A Living Wage: American Workers and the Making of Consumer Society* (Ithaca, NY: Cornell University Press, 1997), pp. 1, 14. See also Sean Wilentz, *Chants Democratic: New York City and the Rise of the American Working Class, 1788–1850* (New York: Oxford University Press, 1984), pp. 10–13.

66. Glickman, *A Living Wage*, p. 9.

67. John G. Cawelti, *Adventure, Mystery, and Romance: Formula Stories as Art and Popular Culture* (Chicago: University of Chicago Press, 1976), p. 144; Leslie Fiedler, *Love and Death in the American Novel* (1966; New York: Anchor, 1992), p. 498.

68. See, for example, Raymond Chandler, "The Man Who Liked Dogs," *Black Mask* (Mar. 1936), reprinted in Shaw, *Hard-Boiled Omnibus*, pp. 112–56.

69. Raoul Whitfield, "China Man," *Black Mask* (1932), reprinted in *The Hard-boiled Dicks: An Anthology and Study of Pulp Detective Fiction*, ed Ron Goulart (Los Angeles: Sherbourne, 1965), pp. 147–48.

70. Dashiell Hammett, "The Gutting of Couffignal," in *The Hard-Boiled Detective: Stories from "Black Mask" Magazine, 1920–1951*, ed. Herbert Ruhm (New York: Vintage, 1979), pp. 65–66.

71. On the differences between Taylorism and the European science of work, see Rabinbach, *The Human Motor*, pp. 233–82.

72. Robert Lynd and Helen Merrell Lynd, *Middletown: A Study in Modern American Culture* (New York: Harcourt, 1956), Chap. 8.

73. Green, *The World of the Worker*, pp. 111–12.

74. In the early 1940s, this translated into a number of wildcat strikes by workers unhappy with the decision of their unions to leave "control" issues exclusively in the hands of management. See Gordon, Edwards, and Reich, *Segmented Work*, pp. 183–84, 189.

75. See Susan Porter Benson, *Counter Cultures: Saleswomen, Managers, and Customers in American Department Stores, 1890–1940* (Urbana: University of Illinois Press, 1986), on gender, class, and shopping.

76. For a complete list of relevant variables used in studies of the period, see Douglas Waples and Ralph W. Tyler, *What People Want to Read About: A Study of Group Interests and a Survey of Problems in Adult Reading* (Chicago: University of

Chicago Press, 1931), p. 14; and Stephen Karetzky, *Reading Research and Librarianship: A History and Analysis* (Westport, CT: Greenwood Press, 1982), p. 98.

77. Waples and Tyler, *What People Want to Read About*, pp. 53, 76.

78. Douglas Waples, Bernard Berelson, and Franklyn R. Bradshaw, *What Reading Does to People: A Summary of Evidence on the Social Effects of Reading and a Statement of Problems for Research* (Chicago: University of Chicago Press, 1940), p. 94.

79. Ken Worpole, *Dockers and Detectives* (London: Verso, 1983), Chap. 2.

80. On the appropriative power of audiences, see Ien Ang, *Living Room Wars: Rethinking Media Audiences for a Postmodern World* (New York: Routledge, 1996), p. 8; and John Fiske, *Power Plays, Power Works* (New York: Verso, 1993).

Chapter Four

Epigraph: Margaret Atwood, *Good Bones and Simple Murders* (New York: Doubleday, 1994), pp. 88–89.

1. Merle Constiner, "The Turkey Buzzard Blues," reprinted in *The Hard-Boiled Detective: Stories from "Black Mask" Magazine, 1920–1951*, ed. Herbert Ruhm (New York: Vintage, 1977), p. 299.

2. My argument about hard-boiled fiction in this chapter is informed by my reading of Pierre Bourdieu's *Distinction: A Social Critique of the Judgment of Taste*, trans. Richard Nice (Cambridge: Harvard University Press, 1984). Although Bourdieu's analysis of taste as the means through which class hierarchies are produced and maintained is based on ethnographic work in 1970s France, I find his analysis useful as a model for thinking about class, taste, and the maintenance of social hierarchies in general. The specific tastes of Bourdieu's subjects have nothing to do with Depression-era America, but the class-specific worldviews he discusses, which emerge from material conditions of poverty or plenty, have wider currency.

3. Constiner, "Turkey Buzzard Blues," p. 315.

4. Fredric Jameson, "On Raymond Chandler," reprinted in *The Poetics of Murder: Detective Fiction and Literary Theory*, ed. Glenn W. Most and William W. Stowe (New York: Harcourt, 1983), pp. 127–28.

5. John Kasson, *Rudeness and Civility: Manners in Nineteenth-Century Urban America* (New York: Hill & Wang, 1990), pp. 72, 77.

6. On the struggles of 1880s and 1890s realist writers, see Amy Kaplan, *The Social Construction of American Realism* (Chicago: University of Chicago Press, 1988), pp. 10–12.

7. The 1920s economic expansion increased income inequality dramatically. The share of total income received by the richest 5 percent of the country went from one-quarter to one-third (David M. Gordon, Richard Edwards, and Michael Reich, *Segmented Work, Divided Workers: The Historical Transformation of Labor in the United States* [New York: Cambridge University Press, 1982], p. 105). Robert McElvaine notes in *The Great Depression: America, 1929–1941* (New York: Times Books, 1984) that in 1929 the combined income of the richest 0.1 percent of families equaled that of the bottom 42 percent (38).

8. Few scholars have commented on the omnipresence of descriptions of commodities and consumer goods in hard-boiled detective fiction. Fredric Jameson

argues that these descriptions are evidence of the writers' sophistication about consumer culture ("On Raymond Chandler"). Dennis Porter writes in *The Pursuit of
Crime: Art and Ideology in Detective Fiction* (New Haven, CT: Yale University Press,
1981) that the pleasure that readers experience has far less to do with the denouement, which restores cognitive and social order at the end of the detective story,
than with the tension (experienced by the reader as suspense) between the drive
toward a solution and the delaying sections of description, which slow the progress
toward that end. In *Mystery Fiction and Modern Life* (Jackson: University Press of
Mississippi, 1998), R. Gordon Kelly states that the skills and cognitive styles modeled by the detective are necessary skills for making one's way in modern life, skills
that include the ability to draw conclusions about the background and reliability of
experts from their self-presentations.

9. Raymond Chandler, *The Big Sleep* (1939; reprint, New York: Vintage, 1992),
p. 3.

10. Kathy Peiss, *Cheap Amusements: Leisure in Turn-of-the-Century New York*
(Philadelphia: Temple University Press, 1986), p. 65.

11. Raymond Chandler, *Farewell, My Lovely* (1940; reprint, New York: Vintage,
1992), p. 4.

12. Kasson, *Rudeness and Civility*, p. 169.

13. Peiss, *Cheap Amusements*, p. 63.

14. Chandler, *Farewell, My Lovely*, pp. 4, 3.

15. Bourdieu, *Distinction*, p. 241.

16. Ibid., p. 202.

17. Ibid., p. 66.

18. Warren I. Susman, "'Personality' and the Making of Twentieth-Century
Culture," in *Culture as History: The Transformation of American Society in the Twentieth Century* (New York: Pantheon, 1984), p. 280.

19. Raymond Chandler, *The High Window* (1942; reprint, New York: Vintage,
1992), pp. 260, 27.

20. Raymond Chandler, *The Little Sister* (1949; reprint, New York: Vintage,
1988), p. 248.

21. See especially Jean-Christophe Agnew, "A House of Fiction: Domestic Interiors and the Commodity Aesthetic" (135) and Karen Halttunen, "From Parlor to
Living Room: Domestic Space, Interior Decoration, and the Culture of Personality" in *Consuming Visions: Accumulation and Display of Goods in America, 1880–1920*,
ed. Simon J. Bronner (New York: Norton, 1989).

22. Agnew, "A House of Fiction," p. 136.

23. Raymond Chandler, *The Lady in the Lake* (1943; reprint, New York: Vintage,
1992), pp. 3–4. Subsequent page references are in the text.

24. My reading of this interior is particularly influenced by "Design" in William
Marling, *The American Roman Noir: Hammett, Cain and Chandler* (Athens: University of Georgia Press, 1995), pp. 72–92; Agnew "A House of Fiction"; and Halttunen, "From Parlor to Living Room." For a useful juxtaposition of this mod-
ernistic design motif and its classical complement in advertising of the 1920s and
1930s, see Roland Marchand, *Advertising the American Dream: Making Way for
Modernity, 1920–1940* (Berkeley: University of California Press, 1985), pp. 127–28.

25. Bourdieu, *Distinction*, p. 40.

26. On the history of the cosmetics industry, see Kathy Peiss, *Hope in a Jar: The Making of America's Beauty Culture* (New York: Holt, 1998) and "Making Faces: The Cosmetics Industry and the Cultural Construction of Gender, 1890–1930," in *Unequal Sisters: A Multi-Cultural Reader in U.S. Women's History*, 2d ed., ed. Vicki L. Ruiz and Ellen Carol DuBois (New York: Routledge, 1994), pp. 372–94.

27. Such epiphanies were common in hard-boiled fiction. See, for example, Dashiell Hammett's *The Glass Key* (1931; reprint, New York: Viking, 1989), where the solution to the murder of a senator's son hinges on the absence of a hat and cane at the murder scene.

28. Dashiell Hammett, "The Big Knockover" and "$106,000 Blood Money," reprinted in Dashiell Hammett, *The Big Knockover* (1966; New York: Vintage, 1989), pp. 349–405, 406–51. Subsequent page references are in the text.

29. Erving Goffman discusses the importance of social performance or "impression management" to highly mobile societies in *The Presentation of Self in Everyday Life* (New York: Doubleday, 1959).

30. *Black Mask* VI, No. 10 (15 Aug. 1923), pp. 113, 116.

31. *Black Mask* did do a special Ku Klux Klan issue (VI, No. 5, 1 June 1923) in which the editors were careful to remain neutral. They supported the NRA and a man's right to bear arms. See, for example, *Black Mask* XVII, Nos. 2–5 (Apr.–July 1934).

32. Dashiell Hammett, *The Maltese Falcon* (1929, 1930; reprint, New York: Vintage, 1992), p. 43.

33. George Chauncey, *Gay New York: Gender, Urban Culture, and the Making of the Gay Male World, 1890–1940* (New York: Basic, 1994), p. 52.

34. Ibid., p. 51.

35. For a theoretical examination of discourses about sexuality in which sexual identity arises from either gender identity or the sex of object choice, see Eve Kosofsky Sedgwick, *Epistemology of the Closet* (Berkeley: University of California Press, 1990), Introduction.

36. Chauncey, *Gay New York*, p. 48.

37. Chandler, *The Big Sleep*, p. 23.

38. Evidence that readers preferred that heterosexual attachments be less important than those between men comes from the universal condemnation of Chandler's final novel, *Playback* (1958; reprint, New York: Vintage, 1988), in which Marlowe agrees to marry Linda Loring, an old flame, at the end. See William Marling, *Raymond Chandler* (Boston: Twayne, 1986), pp. 150–51.

39. On the dynamics of male-male desire, see Eve Kosofsky Sedgwick, *Between Men: English Literature and Male Homosocial Desire* (New York: Columbia University Press, 1985).

40. See Gershon Legman, *Love and Death* (New York: Hacker Art Books, 1963), p. 70; Michael Mason, "Marlowe, Men and Women," in *The World of Raymond Chandler*, ed. Miriam Gross (New York: A & W, 1977), pp. 89–102.

41. Chandler, *Farewell, My Lovely*, pp. 245, 247. Subsequent page references are in the text.

42. Chandler, *The Little Sister*, p. 242.

43. Raymond Chandler, *The Long Goodbye* (1953; reprint, New York: Vintage, 1992).

44. Chandler, *The High Window*, pp. 4–5.

45. Erle Stanley Gardner, "Hell's Kettle," reprinted in William F. Nolan, *The "Black Mask" Boys: Masters in the Hard-Boiled School of Detective Fiction* (New York: Morrow, 1985), p. 104. Subsequent page references are in the text.

46. *Black Mask* XV, No. 6 (Aug. 1932), pp. 124–25.

47. *Clues* XLI, No. 2 (Jan. 1939), p. 6.

48. Dashiell Hammett, "Dead Yellow Women," reprinted in Hammett, *The Big Knockover*, p. 189. Subsequent page references are in the text.

49. Sean McCann, "Constructing Race Williams: The Klan and the Making of Hard-Boiled Crime Fiction," *American Quarterly* 49, No. 4 (December 1997): 677–717.

50. David Roediger, *Toward the Abolition of Whiteness: Essays on Race, Politics, and Working Class History* (New York: Verso, 1994), p. 66.

51. Raymond Williams, *Culture and Society, 1780–1950* (New York: Harper, 1966), p. 327.

Chapter Five

Epigraphs: Herbert Asbury, rev. of *Red Harvest* by Dashiell Hammett, *Bookman* 69 (March 1929), p. 92; Joseph Thompson Shaw, letter to Erle Stanley Gardner, 16 Feb. 1932, Erle Stanley Gardner Papers, HRC.

1. Dashiell Hammett, *Red Harvest* (1929; reprint, New York: Vintage, 1992), p. 3.

2. On the dictionary as "an exercise in cultural hegemony: an attempt to win over subordinate and marginalized groups to particular linguistic usages," see Morag Shiach, *Discourses on Popular Culture: Class, Gender & History in Cultural Analysis, 1730 to the Present* (Stanford, CA: Stanford University Press, 1989), pp. 20–21.

3. Will Cuppy, rev. of *Farewell, My Lovely* by Raymond Chandler, *New York Herald Tribune Books*, 6 Oct. 1940, p. 25.

4. Donald Douglas, "Not One Hoot for the Law," rev. of *The Maltese Falcon* by Dashiell Hammett, *The New Republic*, 9 April 1930, p. 226; rev. of *The Big Sleep* by Raymond Chandler, *Times Literary Supplement* (London) 11 March 1939, p. 152. See also John Dickson Carr, "With Colt and Luger," rev. of *The Simple Art of Murder*, *New York Times Book Review*, 24 Sept. 1950, p. 36. Carr admonishes Chandler that "you cannot create an American language merely by butchering the English language" (36).

5. Isaac Anderson, "New Mystery Stories," rev. of *The Thin Man* by Dashiell Hammett, *New York Times Book Review*, 7 Jan. 1934, p. 18. In *Terrible Honesty: Mongrel Manhattan in the 1920s* (New York: Farrar, 1995), Ann Douglas notes that the slang in American literature of the 1920s had everything to do with its rebellion against a vision of proper-speaking, white, middle-class women, a vision Douglas names "the Victorian mother god" (376).

6. Dennis Porter, *The Pursuit of Crime: Art and Ideology in Detective Fiction* (New Haven, CT: Yale University Press, 1981), p. 184.

7. Ibid., p. 142.

8. Ken Worpole, *Dockers and Detectives* (London: Verso, 1983), p. 47.

9. Frederick Nebel, *Sleepers East* (Boston: Little, 1933), p. 67. Subsequent page references are in the text.

10. This is not to say that bourgeois facility with words is inherently better than working-class forms of speech, which might be useful for different purposes. "Playing the dozens," a game at which young African-American men honed their name-calling and their ability to take abuse without visible distress, functions quite differently from the bourgeois rhetoric used in politics and business, for example.

11. William Vance Trollinger, Jr., and Carl F. Kaestle, "Highbrow and Middle-brow Magazines in 1920," in *Literacy in the United States: Readers and Reading Since 1880*, ed. Carl F. Kaestle, Helen Damon-Moore, Lawrence C. Stedman, Katherine Tinsley, and William Vance Trollinger, Jr., (New Haven, CT: Yale University Press, 1991), p. 205.

12. *Black Mask* X, No. 5 (July 1927), p. 128.

13. Lillian Hellman, "Introduction," in *The Big Knockover: Selected Short Stories and Short Novels of Dashiell Hammett*, by Dashiell Hammett (1966; reprint, New York: Vintage, 1989), pp. xvii–xviii.

14. *Black Mask* XV, No. 2 (Apr. 1932), p. 119. Daly's private eyes shared his disdain for spelling and grammar. Daly's 3-Gun Terry, who appeared in *Black Mask* in the early 1920s, was introduced by the editor as follows: "Pay no attention to the spelling or grammatical errors in this tale. It's in Terry's own language, and he can handle an automatic better than he can the mother tongue" (*Black Mask* VI, No. 4 (15 May 1923), p. 5). In *The "Black Mask" Boys: Masters in the Hard-Boiled School of Detective Fiction* (New York: Morrow, 1985), William F. Nolan calls Race Williams, Daly's better-known private eye, a "swaggering illiterate" (35).

15. *Black Mask* X, No. 5 (July 1927), p. 128.

16. Hellman, *The Big Knockover*, pp. xvii–xviii.

17. *Black Mask* VI, No. 24 (15 Mar. 1924), p. 14; *Black Mask* II, No. 3 (Dec. 1920). On the tenuous relevance of much that was taught in high school to the day-to-day lives of adults during this period, see Robert Lynd and Helen Merrell Lynd, *Middletown: A Study in Modern American Culture* (New York: Harcourt, 1956), Section III, "Training the Young," especially pp. 185 and 188. See also Wendy Luttrell, "Working Class Women's Ways of Knowing," in *Education and Gender Equality*, ed. Julia Wrigley (Washington, DC: Falmer Press, 1992), pp. 173–92.

18. *Black Mask* X, No. 5 (July 1927), p. 33; ibid., No. 12 (Feb. 1928), p. vi.

19. *Black Mask* V, No. 10 (Jan. 1923), p. 125.

20. *Black Mask* XIII, No. 5 (July 1930), p. 120.

21. *Black Mask* V, No. 11 (Feb. 1923), p. 97; *Black Mask* VI, No. 20 (15 Jan. 1924), p. 128.

22. *Black Mask* V, No. 13 (1 Mar. 1923), p. 127.

23. *Black Mask* I, No. 2 (May 1920), p. 127.

24. *Black Mask* V, No. 13 (1 Mar. 1923), p. 17.

25. William Brandon, "It's So Peaceful in the Country," in *The Hard-Boiled Detective: Stories from "Black Mask" Magazine, 1920–1951*, ed. Herbert Ruhm (New York: Vintage, 1977), pp. 356–68. Subsequent page references are in the text.

26. Chandler's "literariness" gives him a scholarly appeal lacking in most other hard-boiled writers. He gets the lion's share of critical attention given to hard-

boiled fiction—roughly 25 percent more entries in the past thirty years of the MLA index than Hammett, his closest competitor. To read Chandler in "literary" ways, however, is to ignore what his writing must have meant to working-class readers who encountered his work in the pulps.

27. Raymond Chandler, *Farewell, My Lovely* (1940; reprint, New York: Vintage, 1992), p. 162. See also Raymond Chandler, *The High Window* (1942; reprint, New York: Vintage, 1992), pp. 341–42, in which Marlowe deploys learned language and literary allusion against a minimally educated chauffeur.

28. See Sean McCann, "'This Grotesque Position': Hard-boiled Crime Fiction and American Literary Culture" (dissertation, City University of New York, 1994), pp. 40–41.

29. Contrast this reading—that hard-boiled detectives use language to dominate other people—with the position that hard-boiled detectives use language as a way to dominate the world, to define it in their own terms. See William W. Stowe, "From Semiotics to Hermeneutics: Modes of Detection in Doyle and Chandler," in *The Poetics of Murder: Detective Fiction and Literary Theory,* ed. Glenn W. Most and William W. Stowe (New York: Harcourt, 1983), pp. 366–83; and Scott Christianson, "Tough Talk and Wisecracks: Language as Power in American Detective Fiction," in *Gender, Language, and Myth: Essays on Popular Narrative,* ed. Glenwood Irons (Toronto, Ontario: University of Toronto Press, 1992), pp. 142–56.

30. In 1920, for example, only 32 percent of fourteen- to seventeen-year-olds were still in school; by 1950 more than 77 percent were (Carl F. Kaestle, "Standardization and Diversity in American Print Culture, 1880 to the Present," in Kaestle et al., *Literacy in the United States,* p. 283). Between 1920 and 1930, enrollment in secondary schools doubled, from 2.2 million to 4.4 million. The number of Americans enrolled in college more than doubled, from 341,000 to 754,000, and the number of college graduates went from half a million to more than a million between 1920 and 1930. See Alice G. Marquis, *Hopes and Ashes: The Birth of Modern Times, 1929–1939* (New York: Free Press, 1986), pp. 103, 109; and Joan Shelley Rubin, *The Making of Middlebrow Culture* (Chapel Hill: University of North Carolina Press, 1992), p. 31. See also Lynd and Lynd, *Middletown,* pp. 182–84.

31. Ibid., pp. 187, 219.

32. Ibid., pp. 185, 221.

33. Ibid., pp. 219–220.

34. Trollinger and Kaestle, "Highbrow and Middlebrow Magazines," p. 205.

35. Ibid., p. 205.

36. On the dramatic increase in magazine circulation between 1865 and 1945, especially after World War I, see John Tebbel and Mary Ellen Zuckerman, *The Magazine in America, 1741–1990* (New York: Oxford University Press, 1991), pp. 66–68; and Theodore Peterson, *Magazines in the Twentieth Century* (Urbana: University of Illinois Press, 1956), pp. 44, 59, 223–24, 260–61. On the expansion of book publishing after World War I, see John Tebbel, *Between Covers: The Rise and Transformation of Book Publishing in America* (New York: Oxford University Press, 1987), Part IV. See also Lynd and Lynd, *Middletown,* pp. 229–32.

37. Although the vast majority of Americans read newspapers in the early twentieth century and roughly half read magazines, only 20 percent to 25 percent were

regular book readers (Helen Damon-Moore and Carl F. Kaestle, "Surveying American Readers," in Kaestle et al., *Literacy in the United States*, p. 189). Robert and Helen Lynd found that fifty-four magazines that boasted 115 subscriptions from thirty-nine business-class families had not a single subscription from 122 workers' families. Forty-eight magazines with ninety-six subscriptions from working-class families had no business-class families as subscribers. Only a narrow group of twenty periodicals crossed class lines (*Middletown*, p. 240).

38. See William S. Gray and Bernice E. Leary, *What Makes a Book Readable* (Chicago: University of Chicago Press, 1935), p. v; and Stephen Karetzky, *Reading Research and Librarianship: A History and Analysis* (Westport, CT: Greenwood Press, 1982), p. 325.

39. Ibid., p. 326.

40. Trollinger and Kaestle, "Highbrow and Middlebrow Magazines," p. 207. This is not to say that these structural features were the most important variables related to readability, only the ones most easily measured and quantified. Other variables—level of reader interest, familiarity of topic, concreteness or abstractness of concepts, purpose for reading, and organization or format, for example—may have been equally or more important, but were too difficult to study systematically (see Gray and Leary, *What Makes a Book Readable*, pp. 6–9).

41. William Marling, *Dashiell Hammett* (Boston: Twayne, 1983), pp. 44–46.

42. Trollinger and Kaestle, "Highbrow and Middlebrow Magazines," p. 209.

43. Gray and Leary, *What Makes a Book Readable*, p. 176.

44. Ibid., pp. 291–92.

45. John Guillory, *Cultural Capital: The Problem of Literary Canon Formation* (Chicago: University of Chicago Press, 1993), p. 168.

46. Ibid., pp. xi–xii.

47. Louis Adamic, "What the Proletariat Reads: Conclusions Based on a Year's Study Among Hundreds of Workers Throughout the United States," *The Saturday Review of Literature* XI, No. 20 (1 Dec. 1934). Although Adamic is concerned with proletarian literature here, he limits his discussion to books that are experimental in form, a characteristic of modernist literature written from any number of political positions. His failure to discuss more "realistic" (and more accessible) works is surprising, since a substantial number of writers on the left (most notably Max Eastman) argued that proletarian writers must reject modernist bourgeois experiments with form and invent an authentically proletarian form based on reportage. For a good introduction to proletarian literature and the debates over its accessibility and aesthetics, see Part II, "Tradition on the Left," in Marcus Klein, *Foreigners: The Making of American Literature, 1900–1940* (Chicago: University of Chicago Press, 1981). My argument here is concerned with Adamic's findings regarding workers' reactions to formal experimentation rather than with this literature as specifically proletarian.

48. Adamic, "What the Proletariat Reads," p. 322.

49. Pierre Bourdieu, *Distinction: A Social Critique of the Judgment of Taste*, trans. Richard Nice (Cambridge, MA: Harvard University Press, 1984), p. 33.

50. Ibid., pp. 41–42.

51. Karetzky, *Reading Research*, p. 326.

52. Barbara Foley, *Radical Representations: Politics and Form in U.S. Proletarian Fiction, 1929–1941* (Durham, NC: Duke University Press, 1993), pp. 101–3.

53. Quoted in ibid., p. 55.

54. "The Pulps and Shinies," *Pen & Hammer Bulletin* 2 (5 Apr. 1934), pp. 117–18, reprinted in *Dictionary of Literary Biography Documentary Series*, Vol. 11, "American Proletarian Culture: The Twenties and the Thirties," ed. Jon Christian Suggs (Detroit: Gale, 1993), pp. 219–21.

55. *Black Mask* III, No. 4 (July 1921), p. 126; *Black Mask* IV, No. 2 (Nov. 1921), p. 126.

56. *Black Mask* V, No. 8 (Dec. 1922), p. 124.

57. See Janice A. Radway, "The Book-of-the-Month Club and the General Reader: The Uses of 'Serious' Fiction," in *Reading in America: Literature and Social History*, ed. Cathy N. Davidson (Baltimore: Johns Hopkins University Press, 1989).

58. Janice Radway, "On the Gender of the Middlebrow Consumer and the Threat of the Culturally Fraudulent Female," *South Atlantic Quarterly* 93.4 (Fall 1994): 871–93.

59. Janice A. Radway, *A Feeling for Books: The Book-of-the-Month Club, Literary Taste, and Middle-Class Desire* (Chapel Hill: University of North Carolina Press, 1997), pp. 17, 263.

60. Janice Radway, "The Scandal of the Middlebrow: The Book-of-the-Month Club, Class Fracture, and Cultural Authority," *South Atlantic Quarterly* 89.4 (Fall 1990): 708.

61. See Sean McCann, "'A Roughneck Reaching for Higher Things': The Vagaries of Pulp Populism," *Radical History Review* 61 (1995): 21–23, on the similarities between hard-boiled detective stories, which distinguished themselves from mass culture from below, and high modernist little magazines, which distinguished themselves from mass culture from above.

62. *Black Mask* V, No. 6 (Oct. 1922), p. 35.

63. Norbert Davis, "Red Goose," reprinted in *The Hard-Boiled Omnibus: Early Stories from "Black Mask,"* ed. Joseph T. Shaw (New York: Simon, 1946), pp. 157–80. Subsequent page references are in the text.

64. These differences resonate with Basil Bernstein's controversial distinction between the "restricted code" of working-class speech and the "elaborated code" of bourgeois speech. Bernstein claims that restricted-code users are more bound to the local, concrete situation, focusing on "substance" rather than on "process," on the "here and now" rather than on motives or intentions. The elaborated code of the middle class allows the communication of abstraction (including reflection on language itself), and more clearly delineates relationships of modification and subordination. This more sophisticated, less context-bound code uses more adjectives, adverbs, prepositions, complex verbs, passives, expressions of probability, questions, and so on. Richard Ohmann summarizes the societal outcome of these class-specific codes: "The class system sorts people into elaborated and restricted code users; the codes perpetuate the class system" (281). (See Basil Bernstein, *Class, Codes and Control*, 3 Vols. [London: Routledge, 1971–77]). For a summary and powerful critique of Bernstein's theories that emphasizes the context of the speech over the class background of the speaker, see Richard Ohmann, "Reflections on Class and Lan-

guage," *Politics of Letters* (Middletown, CT: Wesleyan University Press, 1987), pp. 275–94.

65. Scholars of critical and feminist pedagogy argue that less privileged students can perform better in school if they understand the different ways in which language is used at home and at school, and are encouraged to translate between the different class codes used in each context. See especially Shirley Brice Heath, *Ways With Words: Language, Life, and Work in Communities and Classrooms* (New York: Cambridge University Press, 1983); and bell hooks, *Teaching to Transgress: Education as the Practice of Freedom* (New York: Routledge, 1994).

66. Raoul Whitfield, *The Virgin Kills* (1932; Harpenden, UK: No Exit Press, 1988). Subsequent page references are in the text.

67. These scenes could undoubtedly be read in a number of ways. Part of the fun of the book for many readers, no doubt, was understanding the learned allusions and feeling superior as a consequence. Another avenue of satisfaction might have been sneering at the shallowness of all this learned posturing, an avenue that might or might not exclude the first.

68. On the distinction between "front regions," where one performs an idealized self for others, and "back regions," where social actors can relax from strict social control and prepare for the next performance, see Erving Goffman, *The Presentation of Self in Everyday Life* (New York: Doubleday, 1959), Chap. 3.

69. As it turns out, O'Rourke doesn't need to kill Vennel. Someone beats him to it.

70. Dashiell Hammett, "Dead Yellow Women," reprinted in Hammett, *The Big Knockover* (1966; reprint, New York: Vintage, 1989). Subsequent page references are in the text.

71. See, for example, Steven Marcus, "Introduction," *The Continental Op* by Dashiell Hammett (1974; reprint, New York: Vintage, 1992); Carl Freedman and Christopher Kendrick, "Forms of Labor in Dashiell Hammett's *Red Harvest*," *PMLA* 106.2 (Mar. 1991): 209–21; Gary Day, "Investigating the Investigator: Hammett's Continental Op," in *American Crime Fiction*, ed. Brian Docherty (London: Macmillan, 1988), pp. 39–54; and Glenn W. Most, "The Hippocratic Smile" and William W. Stowe, "From Semiotics to Hermeneutics," both in *The Poetics of Murder: Detective Fiction and Literary Theory*, ed. Glenn W. Most and William W. Stowe (New York: Harcourt, 1983).

72. Marcus, "Introduction," p. xix.

73. Stowe, "From Semiotics to Hermeneutics," pp. 374–82.

74. Dashiell Hammett, *The Thin Man* (1933, 1934; reprint, New York: Vintage, 1992), pp. 200–201.

75. Most, "The Hippocratic Smile," p. 350.

Chapter Six

Epigraph: Gertrude Stein, *Everybody's Autobiography* (New York: Random, 1937), p. 5.

1. Norbert Davis, "Red Goose," reprinted in *The Hard-Boiled Omnibus: Early Stories from "Black Mask,"* ed. Joseph T. Shaw (New York: Simon, 1946), p. 166.

2. Davis, "Red Goose," p. 165.

3. On the attractiveness of a man's secretary as a sign of power and prestige, see Sharon Hartman Strom, *Beyond the Typewriter: Gender, Class and the Origins of Modern American Office Work, 1900–1930* (Chicago: University of Illinois Press, 1992), p. 185; and Rosemary Pringle, *Secretaries Talk: Sexuality, Power, and Work* (New York: Verso, 1988), p. 14.

4. Bill Pronzini, "Where Have All the Secretaries Gone?" in *Murderess Ink: The Better Half of the Mystery,* ed. Dilys Winn (New York: Workman, 1979), p. 162.

5. On the history of clerical work, see Strom, *Beyond the Typewriter;* Pringle, *Secretaries Talk;* Ileen DeVault, *Sons and Daughters of Labor: Class and Clerical Work in Turn-of-the-Century Pittsburgh* (Ithaca, NY: Cornell University Press, 1990); Margery Davies, *Woman's Place Is at the Typewriter: Office Work and Office Workers, 1870–1930* (Philadelphia: Temple University Press, 1982); Angel Kwolek-Folland, *Engendering Business: Men and Women in the Corporate Office, 1870–1930* (Baltimore: Johns Hopkins University Press, 1994); and Lisa M. Fine, *The Souls of the Skyscraper: Female Clerical Workers in Chicago, 1870–1930* (Philadelphia: Temple University Press, 1990).

6. Davies, *Woman's Place,* p. 175.

7. DeVault, *Sons and Daughters of Labor,* p. 102.

8. Ibid., p. 44.

9. Ibid., 74–75.

10. Kwolek-Folland, *Engendering Business,* p. 187.

11. Judith Butler's theories about gender as a "corporeal style" are compelling for the historical period in question. (See *Gender Trouble: Feminism and the Subversion of Identity* [New York: Routledge, 1990] and *Bodies That Matter: On the Discursive Limits of "Sex"* [New York: Routledge, 1993]). Under the conditions of consumer culture peculiar to twentieth-century, Western capitalist countries, races, genders, and other identities are constructed in and through performance.

12. For a contemporaneous historical account of the battle over placing women in what used to be men's jobs, see Patricia Cooper, "The Faces of Gender: Sex Segregation and Work Relations at Philco, 1928–1938," in *Work Engendered: Toward a New History of American Labor,* ed. Ava Baron (Ithaca, NY: Cornell University Press, 1991), pp. 320–50.

13. Erle Stanley Gardner, "Leg Man," reprinted in *The Hard-Boiled Detective: Stories from "Black Mask" Magazine, 1920–1951,* ed Herbert Ruhm (New York: Vintage, 1977), pp. 201–43. Subsequent page references are in the text.

14. Strom, *Beyond the Typewriter,* p. 372.

15. Ibid., pp. 190–91.

16. Ibid,, p. 348.

17. On the distinction made between lower-class stenographers and typists and better-educated personal secretaries whose work was arguably more traditional, see ibid., pp. 318–19.

18. Dashiell Hammett, *The Maltese Falcon* (1929, 1930; reprint, New York: Vintage, 1992). Subsequent page references are in the text.

19. On the contrast between early–twentieth-century patriarchal office relationships and the companionate marriages with which they were contemporary, see Kwolek-Folland, *Engendering Business,* pp. 67–68.

20. Joanne J. Meyerowitz, *Women Adrift: Independent Wage Earners in Chicago, 1880–1930* (Chicago: University of Chicago Press, 1988), pp. 44, 125.

21. Raymond Chandler, *The High Window* (1942; reprint, New York: Vintage, 1992), p. 262.

22. Ibid.

23. Raymond Chandler, *Farewell, My Lovely* (1940; reprint, New York: Vintage, 1992), p. 91.

24. Ibid., p. 183.

25. Leslie Fiedler, *Love and Death in the American Novel* (1966; New York: Anchor, 1992), p. 498. On hard-boiled misogyny, see John G. Cawelti, *Adventure, Mystery, and Romance: Formula Stories as Art and Popular Culture* (Chicago: University of Chicago Press, 1976), pp. 153–54, 159; Geoffrey Hartmann, "Literature High and Low: The Case of the Mystery Story," *The Fate of Reading and Other Essays* (Chicago: University of Chicago Press, 1975), pp. 203–22; Michael Mason, "Marlowe, Men and Women," in *The World of Raymond Chandler*, ed. Miriam Gross (New York: A & W, 1977); Peter Wolfe, *Something More than Night: The Case of Raymond Chandler* (Bowling Green, OH: Bowling Green State University Popular Press, 1985), pp. 182–83; and Jon Thompson, *Fiction, Crime and Empire: Clues to Modernity and Postmodernism* (Chicago: University of Illinois Press, 1993), pp. 143–44. On the conservative gender politics of popular and proletarian fictions of the Depression more generally, see Laura Hapke, *Daughters of the Great Depression: Women, Work and Fiction in the American 1930s* (Athens: University of Georgia Press, 1995). Hapke argues that fiction of the 1930s effaced women's paid work to portray them either as earth mothers, supportive saints to the men on the picket line, or their monstrous, promiscuous opposites (who are never pictured on the job either). "Literature," Hapke concludes, "was enlisted in a widespread cultural campaign against changes in woman's traditional role.... The urgency to sustain the nation's morale resurrected a controlling myth of womanhood" (222–23).

26. See, for example, Cawelti, *Adventure, Mystery, and Romance*, p. 156.

27. On the "New Woman," see Carroll Smith-Rosenberg, "The New Woman as Androgyne: Social Disorder and Gender Crisis, 1870–1936," *Disorderly Conduct: Visions of Gender in Victorian America* (New York: Knopf, 1985), pp. 245–96.

28. Raymond Chandler, *The Lady in the Lake* (1943; reprint, New York: Vintage, 1992), p. 4. Subsequent page references are in the text.

29. The connections between the characters of Miss Fromsett and Mr. Kingsley are particularly noticeable in the 1947 MGM film *The Lady in the Lake*. Many lines that were his in the novel become hers in the film.

30. "Style of the flesh" is Judith Butler's phrase from *Gender Trouble*, p. 139. See Angel Kwolek-Folland, "Gender, Self, and Work in the Life Insurance Industry, 1880–1930" in Baron, *Work Engendered*, for an analysis of how women who wanted to move into positions of power and influence had to perform "masculine" behavior, "to become like a man" in order to achieve their goals (189).

31. See Kathy Peiss, *Cheap Amusements: Leisure in Turn-of-the-Century New York* (Philadelphia: Temple University Press, 1986) on gender-related differences in work and leisure patterns around the turn of the century (5).

32. Frederick Nebel, "Chains of Darkness," reprinted in *Tough Guys and Dangerous Dames*, ed. Robert E. Weinberg, Stefan Dziemianowicz, and Martin H. Greenberg (New York: Barnes & Noble, 1993), pp. 95–122.

33. Nebel, "Chains of Darkness," p. 114.

34. Angel Kwolek-Folland discusses the gendering of positions within an organization independent of the bodies that inhabited them: "People in the lower positions were associated with a wide array of feminine qualities, and those in the upper reaches with masculine qualities. A female manager was expected to adopt masculine business behaviors and beliefs; a male secretary, attributes increasingly defined as feminine" (*Engendering Business*, p. 169). The rationalization of office work, she writes, resulted in the interpellation of subjects whose ideal characteristics more closely resembled docile true women than autonomous men.

35. The lack of companionship of other working women, Jane Addams wrote in 1912, was a chief contributor to the "unwholesome" atmosphere of office work. Being the sole woman in an office of men, Addams insisted, constituted a "danger" to her virtue (*A New Conscience and an Ancient Evil* [New York: Macmillan, 1912], pp. 213–14 [quoted in Lisa M. Fine, p. 58]).

36. On Dinah Brand's sexual labor, see Carl Freedman and Christopher Kendrick, "Forms of Labor in Dashiell Hammett's *Red Harvest*," *PMLA* 106.2 (Mar. 1991).

37. Dashiell Hammett, *Red Harvest* (1929; reprint, New York: Vintage, 1992), p. 107. Subsequent page references are in the text.

38. In Angel Kwolek-Folland's view, corporate employers in the late nineteenth and early twentieth centuries held up such a life as an ideal for which employees should strive, an ideal that urged "the complete and seamless identification of the self with its institutional position" (*Engendering Business*, 53).

39. Peiss, *Cheap Amusements*, "Introduction."

40. See Chap. 2, note 73.

41. On the links between tuberculosis and ideals of beauty in the nineteenth century, see Lois Banner, *American Beauty* (New York: Knopf, 1983), pp. 51–52.

42. Eve Kosofsky Sedgwick's *Between Men: English Literature and Male Homosocial Desire* (New York: Columbia University Press, 1985) is the best discussion of how manhood is produced and performed for other men, with women's bodies serving as mediators of relations between men.

43. See Cora Kaplan, "'The Thorn Birds': Fiction, Fantasy, Feminism" in *Sea Changes: Essays on Culture and Feminism* (London: Verso, 1986), p. 143; Alison Light, "'Returning to Manderley'—Romance Fiction, Female Sexuality and Class," *Feminist Review* 16 (Summer 1984): 8; and Judith Fetterley, *The Resisting Reader: A Feminist Approach to American Fiction* (Bloomington: Indiana University Press, 1978). Also Judith Fetterley, "Reading about Reading: 'A Jury of Her Peers,' 'The Murders in the Rue Morgue,' and 'The Yellow Wallpaper'"; and Elizabeth Segel, "'As the Twig Is Bent ...': Gender and Childhood Reading," in *Gender and Reading: Essays on Readers, Texts, and Contexts*, ed. Elizabeth Flynn and Patrocinio Schweickart (Baltimore: Johns Hopkins University Press, 1986), pp. 147–66, 165–86.

44. Most, "The Hippocratic Smile," in *The Poetics of Murder: Detective Fiction and Literary Theory*, ed. Glenn W. Most and William W. Stowe, (New York: Harcourt, 1983), pp. 348–49.

45. Carol Clover's groundbreaking work on the cross-gender identification of adolescent male horror-film fans offers an analogous situation. Clover argues that the girl who remains alive at the close of these films—the so-called final girl—is profoundly androgynous. She is frequently an early adolescent, she is not involved in sexual relationships, and she has a decidedly masculine-sounding nickname. The adolescent boys who are the majority of horror-film fans, Clover argues, read this androgynous young woman as one of them, projecting their own liminal masculinity onto her embattled position with relative ease. See Carol J. Clover, "Her Body, Himself: Gender in the Slasher Film," *Representations* 20 (Fall 1987): 187–228; and *Men, Women and Chainsaws* (Princeton, NJ: Princeton University Press, 1992), Chap. 1.

46. Barbara Sicherman, "Reading and Ambition: M. Carey Thomas and Female Heroism," *American Quarterly* 45 (March 1993): 73–103.

Afterword

Epigraph: Quoted in Marilyn Stasio, "Lady Gumshoes: Boiled Less Hard," *New York Times Book Review*, 18 Apr. 1985, p. 39.

1. Chester Himes, *Cotton Comes to Harlem* (1965; reprint, New York: Vintage, 1988), p. 125.

2. Chester Himes, *Blind Man With a Pistol* (1969; reprint, New York: Vintage, 1989), pp. 7–14.

3. For a brief introduction to the 1980s and 1990s wave of women's detective fiction, see Kathleen Gregory Klein, Afterword to the Second Edition, *The Woman Detective: Gender & Genre*, 2d ed. (Chicago: University of Illinois Press, 1995); and Chap. 1, "The Private Eye and the Public: Professional Women Detectives and the Business of Publishing" in Priscilla L. Walton and Manina Jones, *Detective Agency: Women Rewriting the Hard-Boiled Tradition* (Berkeley: University of California Press, 1999). See also Sally R. Munt, *Murder by the Book? Feminism and the Crime Novel* (New York: Routledge, 1994).

4. Susan Morgan, "Female Dick," *Interview* 20 (May 1990), p. 2; Dick Lochte, "When the Dick Is a Dame," rev. of *"I" is for Innocent*, by Sue Grafton, *Los Angeles Times*, 10 May 1992, p. 2.

5. Sara Paretsky, *Indemnity Only* (New York: Dell, 1982), p. 28.

6. A good introduction to lesbian crime fiction is Munt, *Murder by the Book*, Chap. 3, "The Inverstigators." See also Kathleen Gregory Klein, "*Habeas Corpus*: Feminism and Detective Fiction"; Ann Wilson, "The Female Dick and the Crisis of Heterosexuality"; and Rebecca A. Pope, "'Friends Is a Weak Word for It': Female Friendship and the Spectre of Lesbianism in Sara Paretsky"(all in *Feminism in Women's Detective Fiction*, ed Glenwood Irons [Toronto, Ontario: University of Toronto Press. 1995]).

7. There is some evidence that in the minds of some publishers and readers, "hard-boiled fiction" necessarily involves a male detective. For example, the 1992 catalog of MysteryBooks: Dupont Circle, a mystery bookstore in Washington, DC, offers a section called "Mean Streets" featuring only male detectives, and one called "Crime on Her Mind" featuring female detectives, hard-boiled and otherwise.

8. Barbara Wilson, *Gaudí Afternoon* (Seattle: Seal, 1990).

9. Barbara Wilson, *Murder in the Collective* (Seattle: Seal, 1984), p. 127.

10. Wilson, *Gaudí Afternoon*, pp. 55, 59.

11. Dashiell Hammett, *The Maltese Falcon* (1929, 1930; reprint, New York: Vintage, 1992), p. 211.

12. Ibid., p. 214.

13. Mary Wings, *She Came Too Late* (Freedom, CA: Freedom Press, 1987), p. 195.

14. Carolyn Anthony, "Mystery Books: Crime Marches On," *Publishers Weekly*, 13 April 1990, p. 24.

15. Walton and Jones, *Detective Agency*, pp. 43, 278.

16. Klein, *The Woman Detective*, p. 8; Margaret Maron, "Women of Mystery," *Independent Weekly* XI, No. 128 (14 July 1993), p. 13; Robert A. Carter, "Scene of the Crime," *Publishers Weekly*, 29 March 1991, p. 21.

17. Erica Noonan, "Gay detectives seeking acceptance in mainstream mystery world," *Daily Herald* (Elk Grove Village, IL), 6 Aug. 1998, p. 1.

18. On lesbian writers' choice of publishers, see Walton and Jones, *Detective Agency*, pp. 105–8.

19. Quoted in Noonan, "Gay detectives seeking acceptance," p. 3.

20. John Morgan Wilson, *Simple Justice* (New York: Bantam, 1996).

21. See Linda Barnes, *A Trouble of Fools* (New York: Fawcett, 1987), *Coyote* (New York: Dell, 1990), and *Snapshot* (New York: Dell, 1994).

22. Michael Nava, *The Little Death* (1986; Los Angeles: Alyson Books, 1996).

Index

Adamic, Louis, 135–37
Advertising: and consumer culture, 11, 146; in mass-market magazines, 26, 37–38, 47–49, 50, 65; in pulp magazines, 9, 13, 16, 22–23, 44–47, 50, 52, 130, 149; as a way of reconstructing readers, 44–45. *See also Black Mask*, advertising in
Aesthetic disposition, 110, 140, 149. *See also* Bourdieu, Pierre
African-American detective fiction, 5, 14, 167
Agnew, Jean-Christophe, 108–09
Alcohol. *See* drinking
"Americanness" in literature, 39
Argosy, 19, 21, 27, 50, 51, 135
Artisan republic, ideal of, 98
Atwood, Margaret, 103
Authorship, models of, 4, 21–23, 179 n. 12

Babcock, Dwight W., 35
Ballard, W. T., 95
Barnes, Linda, 173
Baym, Nina, 39, 185 n. 101
Beadle & Adams, 19
Bernstein, Basil, 204 n. 64
"The Big Knockover," (Hammett), 114–16
The Big Sleep (Chandler), 81–82, 105, 118, 156
Black Mask, 2, 6, 18, 20, 21, 22, 31–32, 33, 36, 39, 43, 51, 54–55, 57, 71, 77, 80, 83, 90, 94, 95, 99, 103, 104, 114, 116, 120, 121, 126, 128, 130, 131, 139, 140, 144, 147, 150, 151, 153, 160, 167, 168; advertising in, 58–73, 130, 133, 143–44; history of, 27–32; women readers of, 29–30; women writers for, 29

Blind Man With a Pistol (Himes), 169
Book-of-the-Month Club, 138–39, 172, 184 n. 86
Bourdieu, Pierre, 23, 26, 64–65, 103, 106, 107, 110, 136, 138, 149, 176–77 n. 17, 182 n. 48, 197 n. 2. *See also* aesthetic disposition
Brandon, William, 35, 131; "It's So Peaceful in the Country," 131–32
Burke, Kenneth, 4
Butler, Judith, 41, 153, 206 n. 11

Cain, Paul, 2, 35, 83, 95; *Fast One*, 83
Cawelti, John G., 13, 99
Certeau, Michel de, 7, 15, 83, 165
"Chains of Darkness" (Nebel), 158–59
Chandler, Raymond, 2, 3, 26, 27, 35, 36, 40, 79, 81, 85, 99, 103, 105, 108, 109, 118, 119, 120, 132, 139, 151, 156, 170, 171; scholarly articles on, 202 n. 26; as spokesman for hard-boiled writers, 184 n. 96. Works: *The Big Sleep*, 81–82, 105, 118, 156; *Farewell, My Lovely*, 40, 105–06, 118–19, 132–33, 157; *The High Window*, 40, 108, 120, 156–57; *The Lady in the Lake*, 40, 109–14; *The Little Sister*, 108, 119; *The Long Goodbye*, 120; "The Simple Art of Murder," 36–42
Chartier, Roger, 7, 8, 176–77 n. 17
Chauncey, George, 117
Christie, Agatha, 3, 37, 39, 40, 41, 84, 88; *Murder on the Orient Express*, 37, 84–86, 87, 88
Classical detective fiction, 3, 13, 36, 39, 40, 41, 82, 84, 131, 143, 147

211